The
Wisdom
& Wit *of*
Rabbi Jesus

Also by William E. Phipps
published by Westminster/John Knox Press

Death: Confronting the Reality

WILLIAM E. PHIPPS

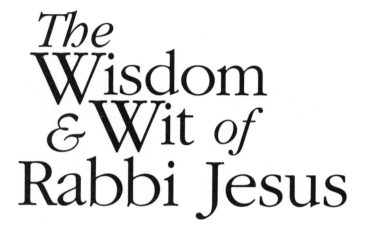

The
Wisdom
& Wit *of*
Rabbi Jesus

Westminster/John Knox Press
Louisville, Kentucky

Acknowledgments will be found on page ix.

Book design by Drew Stevens

Cover design by Drew Stevens

Cover illustration: Christ and the Woman of Samaria, *Rembrandt van Rijn.*
Courtesy of Superstock

First edition

Published by Westminster/John Knox Press
Louisville, Kentucky

This book is printed on acid-free paper that meets the
American National Standards Institute Z39.48 standard. ∞

PRINTED IN THE UNITED STATES OF AMERICA
2 4 6 8 9 7 5 3 1

Library of Congress Cataloging-in-Publication Data

Phipps, William E., 1930–
    The wisdom and wit of Rabbi Jesus / William E. Phipps. — 1st ed.
        p.   cm.
    Includes bibliographical references and index.
    ISBN 0–664–25232–X

    1. Jesus Christ—Teaching methods.   2. Jesus Christ—Teachings.
I. Title.
BT590.T5P48   1993
232.9'04—dc20   93–19528

To the students, faculty, staff, and trustees of
DAVIS AND ELKINS COLLEGE
who are devoted to its motto,
Pro Christo Perstare.

Long may those at that liberal arts institution,
where I have taught most of my life,
remain committed to the wisdom of Christ
while pursuing knowledge in various disciplines.

Contents

Acknowledgments

Copyright material from essays by the author is reprinted in revised form, and is used by permission of the publishers:

"Jesus, the Prophetic Pharisee," *Journal of Ecumenical Studies* 14:1 (Winter 1977)

"The Glittering Rule," *Theology Today* 39:2 (July 1982)

"Jesus on Marriage and the Afterlife," *The Christian Century* 102:11 (April 3, 1985)

Quotations from the Bible are usually the author's own translation, but indebtedness to a variety of versions can be found. Especially helpful has been this compilation of significant variations: Curtis Vaughan, ed., *The New Testament from 26 Translations* (Grand Rapids: Zondervan Publishing House, 1967).

.1.

Introduction

Both the title and the purpose of this book have been influenced by *The Wit and Wisdom of Alfred North Whitehead.* Editor Allison Johnson organized for the nonspecialist the luminous insights of that outstanding British-American philosopher. By way of introduction, she states: "Whitehead's writings are characterized by a subtle and somewhat ironic type of wit which both enlightens and amuses." If we substitute "Jesus' teachings" for "Whitehead's writings," this statement also provides an integrating theme for the forthcoming chapters.

In content as well as style, the sayings of Whitehead are similar to those of Jesus. Some of the quotations culled by Johnson resemble those attributed to Jesus. Although they may not provoke chuckles, they are both sagacious and witty. For instance, Jesus' warning about the easy road that leads to self-destruction (Matt. 7:13) no doubt influenced this Whitehead nugget: "In education as elsewhere, the broad primrose path leads to a nasty place." Without knowing that Whitehead wrote it, one might intelligently guess that Jesus spoke this pithy epigram: "The Law is the sepulchre of the Prophets." Both men muse over the bifurcation of principle and practice: "The love of humanity as such is mitigated by violent dislike of the next-door neighbor." To stress that diversity of opinions should be kept alive, Whitehead quotes Jesus: "This duty of tolerance has been summed up in the words, 'Let both grow together until the harvest' (Matt. 13:30)." Again, overtones of Jesus' perspective are reflected in this outlook: "The worship of God is not a rule of safety—it is an adventure of the spirit, a flight after the unattainable."[1]

With regard to witty wisdom, Jesus is also akin to the American literary genius who has attracted the most readers around the globe. The "Jesus Seminar," which has been engaged in recent years in a series of scholarly meetings on the Gospels, has called Jesus the Mark Twain of his day.[2] The theological commitment of Twain and Jesus motivated them to challenge popular piety. Before assuming his literary name, Samuel Clemens was reared a Presbyterian but attended a Sunday school of Methodism, another "religious *dis*order." As a safety precaution he even considered becoming a minister. Later he confessed his naïveté: "It never occurred to me that a preacher could be damned."[3] Twain's writings abound with biblical allusions, and his style shows the Bible to be the book that influenced him the most.

Although Twain was to revolt against the rigors of hellfire Christianity, he was a lifelong reformer. Even as Jesus displayed the self-critical spirit of a true prophet, Twain's barbs were often directed against his own religious group. Twain described the "pilgrims" touring the Holy Land with him as "the most malignant form of Presbyterianism—that sort which considers the saving [of] one's own paltry soul the first & supreme end & object of life."[4] While exposing portions of the Bible that he regarded as absurd and morally repulsive, Twain was ever a feisty Christian. He wrote: "All that is great and good in our particular civilization came straight from the hand of Jesus Christ."[5] Twain's empathy for the "man of sorrows" (Isa. 53:3) is revealed in his jottings on divine compassion:

> When I think of the suffering which I see around me, and how it wrings my heart; and then remember what a drop in the ocean this is, compared with the measureless Atlantics of misery which God has to see every day, my resentment is roused against those thoughtless people who are so glib to glorify God, yet never to have a word of pity for Him.[6]

Twain, like the founder of Christianity, did not regard holiness as an enemy of hilarity. He ranked humor as one of God's chief attributes.[7] Accordingly, as one made in the divine image,

2

Twain played the role of "God's fool."[8] He regarded laughter as the most effective way of dealing with the vanity, greed, and tyranny corrupting humans. While seriously trusting in God, he laughed at lesser commitments, to Bible and sect—and the world laughed with him.

Twain and Jesus illustrate what Harvard psychologist Gordon Allport posits: "A case might be made for the potentially superior humor of the religious person who has settled once and for all what things are of ultimate value, sacred and untouchable, for then nothing else in the world need be taken seriously."[9] Also relevant here is Nevin Vos's distinction "between healthy laughter which is born out of belief in a meaningful universe and the bitter, sardonic laughter which arises out of a meaningless void."[10] "Laugh, for *God's sake*," is an injunction that both Twain and Jesus heeded.

What Twain wrote about his fellow Protestants has much in common with what Jesus said. One of Jesus' best-known fictional vignettes is an attack on organized religion. Two Jewish clergy types are pictured as passing up a "half-dead" neighbor, probably fearful of becoming ritually unclean by touching a corpse (Luke 10:30–35; Lev. 21:11; Num. 19:16). They may have also been in a hurry to participate in a conference at Jerusalem on street crime. But a Samaritan from outside the presumed bounds of God's chosen people gives both immediate and long-term assistance. Jesus also inflamed the complacent "chief priests and the presbyters" by this broadside: "The tax collectors and the prostitutes go into the kingdom of God before you" (Matt. 21:23, 31).

With similar indignation, Twain denounced William Sabine, a leading New York clergyman who refused to permit the use of his Madison Avenue church for the funeral of George Holland, simply because the man had been an actor. Sabine referred Holland's friends to "a little church around the corner" that served as a sanctuary for the poor. Twain called Sabine a "slimy, sanctimonious, self-righteous reptile" for attacking the theater as immoral. While crediting pulpits such as that of "The Little Church Around the Corner"—as inadvertently permanently nicknamed by Sabine—with "disseminating the meat and marrow of the gospel of Christ," Twain found the theater "just as legitimate an instrument of

God." He then eulogized Holland, "whose theatrical ministry had for fifty years softened hard hearts, bred generosity in cold ones, kindled emotion in dead ones, uplifted base ones, broadened bigoted ones, and made many and many a stricken one glad and filled it brim full of gratitude." Twain was convinced that more Christian kindness is spread by actors, journalists, and novelists than by preachers with "cancerous piety" who intone "vapid platitudes from the pulpit."[11]

Unlike Whitehead and Twain, Jesus wrote nothing that is extant, so it is nearly impossible to ascertain exactly what he said. The reliability of the New Testament in recording his ideas needs to be addressed before probing for elements of his wisdom and wit. Modern scholars have wrestled with the complex historicity issues pertaining to Jesus. Albert Schweitzer concluded his epoch-making *Quest of the Historical Jesus* by informing people of our time that Jesus "comes to us as One unknown."[12]

Rudolf Bultmann, the famed "demythologizer" of the New Testament, was even more skeptical than Schweitzer. He wrote: "We can know almost nothing concerning the life and personality of Jesus."[13] In light of Bultmann's perspective on the historicity of the Gospel record, there is significance in this admission:

> It is at least clear that *Jesus actually lived as a Jewish rabbi.* As such he takes his place as a teacher in the synagogue. As such he gathers around him a circle of pupils. As such he disputes over questions of the Law with pupils and opponents or with people seeking knowledge who turn to him as the celebrated rabbi. He disputes along the same lines as Jewish rabbis, uses the same methods of argument, the same turns of speech; like them he coins proverbs and teaches in parables. Jesus' teaching shows in content also a close relationship with that of the rabbis.[14]

More recently, the best-selling *Jesus Through the Centuries* begins with a chapter entitled "The Rabbi." Jaroslav Pelikan, the Sterling Professor of History at Yale University, asserts, "It was as a rabbi that Jesus was known and addressed by his immediate followers and by others." Pelikan finds an

4

important authentic detail in Marc Chagall's treatment of Jesus. "The crucified figure in Chagall's painting wears not a nondescript loincloth, but the *tallith* of a devout and observant rabbi." The historian wistfully wonders if anti-Semitic pogroms would have arisen if the people who belong to Jesus had remembered the people to whom Jesus belonged. Pelikan hauntingly asks what might have resulted if every Christian home and church had focused some of its devotion on "*Rabbi Jeshua bar-Joseph*, Rabbi Jesus of Nazareth, the Son of David."[15]

On a personal note, my decision to be a teacher rather than a preacher has been influenced by my understanding of the role Jesus played. The first words attributed to him were uttered when he was at the intellectual center of Judaism, "sitting among the teachers, listening to them and asking them questions" (Luke 2:46). The great debaters Hillel and Shammai—or their disciples—were teaching in Jerusalem, and Jesus probably encountered them. At the threshold of adult life—in a rite of passage later to be called *bar mitzvah*—Jesus was engaged in a scholarly pursuit that was to continue throughout his life. Thus, he can best be imaged as a Jew discussing theology with inquirers, not as a clergyman delivering sermons to passive audiences. My teaching responsibilities in both religion and philosophy have convinced me that unquestioned faith is dead or dying, and that doubt without faith is empty.

Looking back on my own education, there are several influences that have especially contributed to my career and to my writing about biblical topics. I had several outstanding teachers who became challenging role models for me. While at Davidson College majoring in physics, I reluctantly enrolled in the required Bible courses. They were taught by James M. Robinson, Albert C. Winn, and Bernard H. Boyd, men who would later become widely recognized as distinguished teachers. They dispelled my suspicion that faith is believing what is not so, and they stimulated me to think critically more than had the faculty I encountered in the physical sciences.

Having been in some ways liberated by a liberal arts college from religious tunnel vision, I have devoted my career to teaching in such a college, in hopes of pointing provincial-minded youth toward broadening intellectual vistas. Teaching and writing predominantly for those who are unchurched has convinced me that much of traditional religious vocabulary is meaningless. Therefore, fresh expressions and analogies from contemporary culture must be introduced to convey religious ideas.

One key to comprehending Jesus that I found useful came from the eminent professor of Hebrew at Union Theological Seminary in Virginia. In what would subsequently be published as *The Kingdom of God*, John Bright gave me this insight:

> It is clear that Jesus did not intend to found a new religion. . . . He did not come to destroy Israel's faith and supersede it with another, but rather to bring it to its fulfillment. Nor did his disciples intend to found a new religion. . . . The two Testaments are organically linked to each other . . . and the bond that binds them together is the dynamic concept of the rule of God. There is indeed a "new thing" in the New Testament, but it lies precisely here. The Old Testament is illumined with the hope of the coming Kingdom . . . but in the New Testament we encounter a change: the tense is a resounding present indicative—the Kingdom is *here*![16]

Another key for opening the Gospels came from my doctoral studies. My work centered on the apostle Paul, who provides the earliest historical record of Jesus. Paul thought of "Christ" as the embodiment of the "wisdom of God," but acknowledged that many were looking for what they considered to be a more powerful expression of the divine (1 Cor. 1:20–24). The apostle refused to pander to those seeking for unnatural happenings, and consequently he never refers to Jesus as a miracle worker. In my *Paul Against Supernaturalism*[17] I argue that Christians—from the first century onward—err who think of Jesus as a crowd-mystifying magician. I do not regard as authentic the stories that suggest that Jesus displayed his power by violating the natural order. The adoring followers of Moses, Elijah, Jesus, and Muhammad are to blame for the bigger-than-life legends that inflate the status of their heroes. The wonderful qualities of Jesus as a teacher and healer are independent of such incredible stories as his levitating on water, causing a tree to wither, or raising a stinking corpse to life (Mark 6:46–52; 11:20–21; John 11:38–44).

After making a careful study of the Gospels, Thomas Jefferson concluded that miracle stories have been wrongly attributed to Jesus from shortly after his death onward and that they obfuscate his true mission and message. He claimed that the genuine teachings of Jesus are "as easily distinguishable as diamonds in a dunghill" from the Gospels in which they are embedded.[18] I am not as sanguine as Jefferson in thinking that one can easily separate out Jesus' pearls of wisdom from the surrounding environmental shell. Even so, I join with a host of scholars since the time of Jefferson who continue his search in the Gospels for "the most sublime morality which has ever fallen from the lips of man."[19] To make the quest intriguing, assurance is given in advance that Rabbi Jesus' wisdom is neither dour nor dull; rather, it dances with wit.

.2.

The Prophetic Pharisee

Resistance has been widespread to acknowledging with Julius Wellhausen that "Jesus was not a Christian."[1] Had Wellhausen convinced his fellow Germans that Jesus was a Semite, Adolf Hitler would probably not have become their ruler. John Holmes, writing at the time when that professing Catholic was elected to head the German government by alleged Christians, mused on the principal incongruity of our era: "If Christians were Christians, there would be no anti-Semitism. Jesus was a Jew. There is nothing that the ordinary Christian so dislikes to remember as this awkward historical fact."[2]

In this generation the gross misperception continues. As Markus Barth observes: "Many people today apparently find it possible to separate the memory of a *Jew* Jesus from the belief in Jesus Christ. To state that Jesus is a Jew is to insult, distress, annoy."[3] In defense of this statement, Barth illustrates how objectionable it is to the typical Christian, Jew, or Arab to have Jesus identified as a Jew. Leonard Swidler also describes the general contemporary mind-set:

> Both Christians and Jews automatically think of Jesus as the name of someone other than a Jew. This simple fact tends to cut Christians off from the taproot of their religion, the Hebrew-Jewish tradition. On the other side it also tends to cut Jews off from a very important son of their tradition, one who has become the most influential Jew of all history, surpassing in historical impact even such giants as Moses, David, Marx, Freud, and Einstein.[4]

Among scholars devoted to the historical origins of Christianity, the Jewishness of Jesus is no longer a matter of debate. Oxford exegete E. P. Sanders, in his thorough review of recent studies on Jesus, asserts that there is now "virtually unanimous consent" that Jesus lived as a Jew. He also argues that "we must read the New Testament as a source for first-century Judaism."[5]

James Charlesworth, who chairs the Department of Biblical Studies of Princeton Seminary, has edited an interfaith dialogue by distinguished Roman Catholic, Protestant, and Jewish scholars on the place of Jesus within early Judaism. The understandings they all share on the Jewishness of Jesus should aid in removing in the twenty-first century popular prejudices that Christians and Jews have held regarding Jesus. Disagreeing with Sanders and others who believe that Jesus principally saw himself as God's announcer of the present order's imminent end, Charlesworth is among those who cogently argue that Jesus "was *not* one of the apocalyptists."[6] Jesus did not promise a streets-paved-with-gold reversal for the poor and weak at the final judgment day. His ideas should not be confused with subsequent pie-in-the-sky-when-you-die preachments; his teachings were not intended to be an opiate for the disfranchised masses, enabling them to endure passively the social injustices of their day.

No scholarly consensus has been reached regarding the Jewish group of Jesus' day with which he had the most affinities. Hermann Reimarus, an early German New Testament critic, suggested that Jesus either belonged to or sympathized with the Zealots. That hypothesis has been painstakingly defended by a few Jewish and Christian scholars in our own time, but it has been thoroughly discounted.[7] Likewise there have been scholars who have claimed that Jesus was an Essene, but the implausibility of this has been demonstrated.[8]

Geza Vermes has argued that "Jesus did not belong among the Pharisees, Essenes, Zealots or Gnostics, but was one of the holy miracle-workers of Galilee."[9] Although many Christians from the first century onward have thought of Jesus as a supernatural performer, there is little evidence that Jesus thought of himself in that manner.[10]

9

Travers Herford portrayed Jesus as one of the *am ha-aretz*, or people of the land "outside the Pharisaic circle."[11] The fact that Jesus was apprenticed to his carpenter father (Matt. 13:55; Mark 6:3) has caused some to think that he received no formal education. However, Jewish fathers were expected to provide each boy with training in a craft even if he had the ability to become a scribe or rabbi in the Pharisaic leadership. Rabbi Gamaliel said: "Study combined with a secular occupation is a fine thing." A trade skill was of practical importance because rabbis were not compensated for their teaching.[12] Hillel combined Torah study with work as a manual laborer;[13] Saul of Tarsus became both a scholar and a tentmaker (Gal. 1:14; Acts 18:3).

Some eminent Jewish scholars have concluded that Jesus was a Pharisee. Over a century ago, Abraham Geiger called Jesus a Galilean Pharisee. The position of that German influenced Reform Judaism in America.[14] Early in the twentieth century Joseph Klausner, an Orthodox Jew, attempted to prove in his important book that "Jesus remained a true Pharisaic Jew."[15] Agreeing with Klausner on this Pharisaic connection, Martin Buber has stated: "Jesus, in so far as we are able to unravel his historical reality, occupied a position within this circle of belief."[16]

Some contemporary spokespersons for the Pharisaic tradition associate Jesus with the Pharisees. Hebrew Union College professor Ellis Rivkin, in an extended study, points to similarities between the doctrines of ancient Pharisaic literature and the New Testament.[17] In *Jesus the Pharisee*, Rabbi Harvey Falk defends the thesis that Jesus was devoted to the tradition practiced by Orthodox Jews throughout history.[18] Falk attributes his viewpoint to an overlooked letter of Jacob Emden, an eighteenth-century authority on the Talmud. Rabbi Emden stated: "The Nazarene brought about a double kindness in the world. . . . He strengthened the Torah of Moses majestically; . . . he did much good for the Gentiles."[19]

Most Christians have difficulty entertaining the idea that Jesus might have been a Pharisee. They recall that the Gospels represent Jesus as denouncing the Pharisees as hypocrites (e.g., Matt. 23:13; Mark 7:6). The word association that Jesus made has affected our language so much that Webster gives "hypocrisy" as a synonym for "pharisaism." Moreover, "self-righteous" and "sanctimonious" are given as synonyms of "pharisaical." Christians understandably abhor associating Jesus with hypocrisy—a sin their leader frequently exposed. Also, their rejection of self-righteousness as a virtue is largely due to their understanding of Jesus' teaching and life-style. Hence, Christians would generally regard "Jesus the Pharisee" as an oxymoron.

In recent decades some Christian scholars have suggested that Jesus belonged to the Pharisaic movement.[20] However, they have given little attention to detailing the particular points of comparison between Jesus and the Pharisees. I agree with those who insist that Jesus' message and mission cannot properly be comprehended without seeing him as a Pharisaic Jew. What evidence can be found to tie the Pharisaic party with the Jesus of the earliest Gospels? (Those Gospels—consisting of Matthew, Mark, and Luke—are called the Synoptics.) On the assumption that Pharisaic piety of the time when Jesus lived was for the most part faithfully transmitted in what was later recorded in the Mishnah and in the Talmud, my comparisons will make use of those authoritative writings of normative Judaism as well as documents that were written during or before the century when Jesus lived. The principal source will be the writings of the historian Josephus, who not only lived in the first century C.E.[21] but belonged to the Pharisaic party.

Jesus lived at the midpoint of the three centuries in which the Pharisees flourished, in the region called Palestina by the Romans. The stronghold of the party was at first in Judea, but later it was centered in Galilee. It emerged from the Hasidim ("Pious") who supported the Maccabean revolt against the Hellenistic paganism that was infiltrating Palestine. The name "Pharisee" was probably derived from *perush* ("separate"), and referred to those who struggled to set themselves apart from defiling religious practices. About the time when Jesus was born, some six thousand Pharisees risked their lives by refusing to pledge allegiance to Caesar and Herod. Among them were some who destroyed the golden eagle, a symbol of Rome, which King Herod erected over the entrance to the new Jerusalem Temple. They acted because they interpreted the eagle as idolatrous; in retaliation, Herod executed several of them.[22] The total number of Pharisees may well have been larger than six thousand, but even that many adult male Pharisees would suggest that at least twenty-five thousand people belonged to Pharisaic families. That would have been a sizable proportion of the total Jewish population of Palestine.

Josephus points out that the Pharisees had the masses on their side,[23] so the impact of the party went far beyond those who were recognized as members. Their popular appeal was due to several factors. They were admired for their quiet but determined refusal to compromise religious liberty when confronted by the alien Roman government. Also, the leaders of the Pharisees usually rose from the common people. In addition, the Pharisees devoted much of their efforts to supporting the synagogue, a place of assembly in most Palestinian towns.[24] The synagogue was a center for scribal work, religious education, and Sabbath worship, as well as for community decision making.

The Pharisees should not be thought of as sectarian in the sense that they were separate from the main body of Judaism. "Keep not aloof from the congregation," advised Hillel, their most outstanding leader.[25] They participated with their compatriots at the one Temple as well as in the many synagogues. Indeed, the Pharisees were so much a part of the mainstream of the Jewish community that, unlike the other ancient Jewish parties, they continued after the Jewish state was destroyed in 70 C.E. and formed the nucleus of subsequent Judaism.

Similarities to the Pharisees

Josephus presents two distinguishing doctrines of the Pharisaic party, both of which were championed by Jesus. First, the Pharisees advocated a view of divine providence that was consistent with human freedom. They rejected the extreme positions of the Essenes and the Sadducees. The former emphasized divine determinism, whereas the latter stressed human choice.[26] The Pharisees held this moderating position: "It has pleased God to make a temperament whereby what he wills is done, but so that human will can act virtuously or viciously."[27]

The Mishnah and the *Psalms of Solomon* contain views of the Pharisees in harmony with Josephus's summary statement on their doctrine of providence. Rabbi Akiba succinctly states: "All is foreseen, but freedom of choice is given."[28] One of the psalms of Solomon presents the paradox in this way: "Our works are subject to our own choice . . . but in your righteousness you [God] oversee human beings."[29] That poetry from the first century B.C.E. probably expresses "early Pharisaism."[30]

Jesus also championed both the almightiness of God and the freedom to assert one's own will, without attempting to resolve the logical dilemma. Such theology can be illustrated by one of his prayers: "Abba [Father], you can do anything; remove this cup from me; yet not what I will but what you will" (Mark 14:36).

The Pharisees favored picturing God as king. Among the most frequent prayers in the ancient synagogue was this: "Reign over us, O Lord, you alone, in loving kindness. . . . Blessed are you, O Lord, the King who loves righteousness and judgment."[31] Rabbi Johanan ben Zakkai even remarked that "a prayer in which there is no mention of the kingdom is no prayer."[32] To convey his theology, he told a parable of a king who invited his subjects to a banquet without indicating the precise time when it would be given. The prudent prepared for the party well in advance so that they would be ready whenever the palace gate opened. When the party began, the king was chagrined that some were caught by surprise and were improperly dressed. Those who lacked keen expectation were not permitted to join in the festivities.[33]

The sovereignty of God was also at the core of Jesus' teaching. Finding the kingship of God in his favorite psalms and prophetic books, he proclaimed that "the reign of God is near" (Mark 1:15). Also, in rabbinical fashion, Jesus used stories to describe the way in which joy and judgment would characterize the divinely initiated kingdom. Matthew joined together two such parables pertaining to a king who gave a marriage feast. When those who were first invited neglected to attend, the king became angry and filled the wedding hall with other guests. One fellow who was not in proper attire was cast out (Matt. 22:1–14). Rabbi Jesus and Rabbi Johanan taught that God's subjects were expected to exercise their freedom so that they would ever be ready to celebrate God's coming.

The second Pharisaic doctrine that Josephus mentions pertains to the hereafter. The Pharisees, unlike the Sadducees, believed that human life survives death.[34] Again, the Mishnah and the *Psalms of Solomon* convey this belief. Rabbi Jacob said: "This world is like a vestibule before the world to come: prepare yourself in the vestibule that you may enter into the banqueting hall."[35] The *Psalms of Solomon* describe the resurrection thus: "Those who fear the Lord shall rise up to eternal life, and their life shall be in the Lord's light." "The life of the righteous shall be forever; but the sinners shall be taken away to destruction."[36] In a later chapter Jesus' beliefs in life after death and in angels will be discussed. Those beliefs, as well as his method of defending them, were similar in some ways to what is found in the writings of the Pharisees.[37]

With regard to punitive matters, Josephus indicates that the Pharisees had the reputation for advocating less severe punishments than their rivals.[38] Whereas the Sadducees rigidly interpreted the "eye for an eye" standard of Moses, the Pharisees preferred compensatory payment in lieu of exact retribution.[39] The sympathetic outlook of their prominent spokesperson Hillel is well expressed in this maxim: "Judge not your neighbor until you have put yourself in his place."[40] Significantly, it was not the Pharisees and their scribes, but the Sadducees and their priests, who were mainly involved in the cruel events in Jerusalem that resulted in Jesus' death. Gamaliel may have typified the Pharisees when he counseled the Sanhedrin court to avoid capital vengeance with respect to the followers of Jesus (Acts 5:33–39).

The political moderation of the Pharisees was in stark contrast to the insurgents who struck out furtively against the Romans and the Herods who served as their puppets. The Pharisees supported the Romans' right to take a census in Palestine for the purpose of taxation, but this was anathema to the revolutionary guerrillas.[41] Their terrorist activities increased during the decade before the fall of Jerusalem, when they were known as the Zealot party.[42] Josephus regarded those firebrands as the cause of the destruction of the Jewish nation.

Rabbi Hillel and his prominent disciple, Johanan ben Zakkai, expressed the Pharisees' restraint with respect to killing. The former was known as a lover of peace and of all humanity.[43] On seeing evidence of death by violence, he observed that such conduct stimulates more of the same.[44] According to the Talmud, Rabbi Johanan also renounced the use of the sword, and thus opposed resisting Rome during the siege of Jerusalem.[45] Similarly, Jesus opposed the rebellion against Rome that was brewing (Luke 19:41–44), and he taught that civil obedience to a pagan ruler was not always inconsistent with serving the God of Israel (Mark 12:17).

The sources of ancient Judaism also attest to the nonmaterialistic orientation of most Pharisees. Josephus contrasts their simple life-style with that of the plutocratic Sadducees.[46] Hillel's detachment from possessions can be discerned in his saying: "The more meat, the more worms; the more property, the more anxiety."[47] Due perhaps to the poverty conditions from which he arose, he "made the poor and the broken a loving concern of his private life and represented the cause of the poor."[48] The Pharisees urged their people to replace the common morality that holds "What's mine is mine and what's yours is yours" with this unselfish principle: "What's mine is yours and what's yours is yours."[49] Jesus also taught his followers to live simply and to give to the poor (Mark 6:8–9; 10:21).

The Pharisees did not assume that assisting those in need necessarily implied the renunciation of pleasures for oneself. They favored the way of self-affirmation that avoided both extreme altruism and extreme egoism. As Hillel put it in his query, "If I am not for myself, who is for me? And when I am for myself only, what am I?"[50] Those questions reflect the "Love your neighbor as yourself" (Lev. 19:18) principle, which implies both self-love and concern for others. The Pharisees especially enjoyed eating and dancing, even though they occasionally devoted themselves to fasting. "Be sure to eat and drink," the Talmud advises, "for the world we leave is like a wedding feast."[51] The Pharisees, in contrast to the Sadducees, engaged in joyful dancing at the Tabernacle festival.[52]

Jesus compared his way of life to a wedding celebration (Mark 2:19), although he thought that the optimum life was inseparable from stern self-discipline (Mark 8:34). The moderate attitude toward pleasure by both Jesus and the Pharisees was in contrast to the "*No* thyself" theme of some Mediterranean cults.[53] Rudolf Bultmann rightly notes that Jesus was "far removed" from the asceticism that assumes "that the material world, the body, the senses, are evil."[54]

Indignation over sham righteousness is another point on which similarities between Jesus and the Pharisees can be discovered. One psalm of Solomon charges Jewish religious leaders with duplicity. They act virtuously when being watched, it is alleged, but they engage in illicit affairs "at night and in hiding." This harsh judgment is leveled: "Let ravens peck out the eyes of hypocrites, for they disgracefully empty many people's houses and greedily scatter them. . . . They defraud innocent people by pretense."[55] A Pharisee in Jesus' day wrote of some of his people who were deceitful robbers of the poor.[56] He also charged: "Their hands and hearts are all corrupt, and their mouths are full of boasting—and yet they complain: do not touch me lest you make me unclean!"[57] Rabbi Joshua included the "cunning knave" and "the plague of the Pharisees" among those things that were ruining the world.[58] In the Talmud the "knave" is identified as the scribe who applies the law to self in a way to lighten its requirements, but inflicts it in a more burdensome way on others.[59] Of the seven varieties of Pharisees that are described in the Talmud, only two are considered to be genuinely pious.[60]

Jesus heaped scorn on Pharisees who appeared morally immaculate but were inwardly defiled (Matt. 23:25–28). Ironically, Jesus showed his own Pharisaic spirit in those judgments.[61] For that party was, as has been shown, quite sensitive to and disgusted by the insincerity of some of its members. In a similar way the apostle Peter exposed the hypocrisy of a Christian couple (Acts 5:1–4). Another example is in the apostle Paul's letters, where the one use of the term "hypocrisy" is in reference to Peter. Paul heatedly accuses Peter of being untrue to the gospel when he separated himself from eating with Gentiles while conservative Jews were around (Gal. 2:11–14). Paul was not basically opposed to Peter, but was critical of his conduct in a particular situation. Elsewhere Paul singles Peter out as a leader of the apostles (1 Cor. 3:22; 15:5). No one goes to that polemical passage in Galatians to discover a general description of Peter. Honest internal criticism reveals more about the health of a group than about its sickness.

Unfortunately, memories of Jesus were becoming fixed in Palestine at the time when Christianity was being persecuted by Judaism. The Acts of the Apostles is filled with accounts of synagogue and Sanhedrin attacks on the infant church. Consequently, the compilers of the Gospels were disposed to emphasize the ways in which Jesus differed from the Pharisees and to omit, or play down, those episodes in which they were in substantial agreement. Jesus' criticisms of the Pharisees were probably made harsher during the years when his actual words were transmitted by word of mouth and translated into Greek. Given this start, plus the continued bitterness between the church and the synagogue throughout the Christian era, no wonder there has been little acknowledgment in the two communities of any strong positive bonds between Jesus and the Pharisees.

The caricature of the Pharisees by Christians is as absurd as that of Jesus by the Jews. In the talmudic collection of authoritative teachings of Judaism, he is alluded to as a bastard and a sorcerer.[62] In a parallel manner New Testament scholar Matthew Black, writing in a highly influential work, describes Pharisaism as "a sterile religion of codified tradition."[63] A religious tradition that sired medieval and modern Judaism can hardly be called impotent! Black's contemporary denigration of the Pharisees is relatively mild compared with the diatribes of past Christian scholarship. Alfred Edersheim, for instance, wrote a widely used tome that attempts to show "the infinite distance between Christ and the teaching of the synagogue."[64]

In spite of the acrimonious historical controversy between Jews and Christians, it is possible to detect in the Gospels that Jesus would have agreed with this succinct description by Josephus: "The Pharisees are a group of Jews who have the reputation of excelling the rest of their nation in religious observances."[65] Regarding the Pharisees, Jesus told his disciples: "Practice and observe whatever they tell you" (Matt. 23:3). He endorsed the Pharisaic belief that the Shema and the neighbor-love commandments were of central importance in the Torah.[66] Maurice Goguel rightly observes: "Jesus was not against the Pharisees root and branch; he saw in them the religious elite of Israel, and he would have liked to have gained their support."[67] Jesus had more sympathy for the Pharisees than for any other group in Judaism—the Sadducees, the Essenes, the Zealots, or the Herodians. In turn, it was primarily the Sadducees, not the Pharisees, who initiated actions leading to the capital trial for Jesus at Jerusalem. Indeed, it was Pharisees who gave Jesus this warning: "Get away from here, for Herod is out to kill you" (Luke 13:31).

Differences from the Pharisees

The main contrast between the general outlook of Jesus and the all-male party of Pharisees is in the way they treated outsiders—women, Gentiles, and the *am ha-aretz*. The haughtiness of the Pharisees in this regard is summed up in the prayer of Rabbi Judah: "Blessed be Thou for not having made me a Gentile, a woman, or an ignoramus."[68] The prayer is similar to one that has long been used in the liturgy of Orthodox Judaism.

During the century when the Pharisaic party originated, a Jerusalem scribe ridiculed women in a way that was to become typical of the Pharisees. Jesus ben Sirach charged: "Woman is the origin of sin, and it is through her that we all die. . . . Out of clothes comes the moth, and out of woman comes wickedness. A man's wickedness is better than a woman's goodness; it is woman who brings shame and disgrace."[69] Generally subscribing to Sirach's misogyny, Hillel

18

commented, "The more women, the more witchcrafts."[70] Pharisee Josephus stated that "woman is in all things inferior to man."[71]

Women were reminded of their lower status in various ways. A father could sell an unwanted daughter into slavery.[72] A recurring theme in the Mishnah is that only males should be educated. Teaching a daughter knowledge of the Torah was reckoned to be as bad as teaching her lechery. Women, along with slaves and children, were exempted from reciting the Shema creed, which was at the core of Jewish worship.[73] A Jewish menstruant was not accorded as much dignity as a Gentile male at the Jerusalem Temple. She was excluded from even the outermost of the four courts.[74]

The Torah declared a woman to be "impure" during her menstrual period and for a week afterward; during this time "whoever touches her shall be unclean until the evening." Moreover, a woman with a discharge beyond her regular period continued to be untouchable indefinitely (Lev. 15:19–30). In rabbinic tradition, the ordinary duration of ritual uncleanness for menstruants was increased to twelve days. In the division on cleanliness, the longest in the Mishnah, a whole tract is devoted to detecting the menstruant. There the taboo is expressed in this way: "The blood of a menstruant and the flesh of a corpse convey uncleanness."[75] Complete immersion in a ritual bath is required at the end of the taboo period.[76] Attitudes recorded in medieval Judaism display even more contempt: "The glance of a menstruous woman poisons the air. . . . She is like a viper who kills with her glance. . . . Men and women will distance themselves from her and she will sit alone and speak to no one. . . . The dust on which she walks is impure like the dust defiled by the bones of the dead."[77] According to the Talmud, menstruation originated as one of the ten curses given to rebellious Eve.[78] A menstruant threatened by a snake can cause it to retreat by simply announcing that she has the "curse"![79]

Wives accused of infidelity were subjected to a terrifying ordeal, but their sexual partners were not (Num. 5:11–28). To frighten a confession out of a woman accused of becoming pregnant by someone other than her husband, she was dressed in black and brought to the eastern gate of the Jerusalem Temple. There a priest humiliated her by untying her hair and tearing her dress so that her breast was publicly exposed.[80] Then he required her to drink a mixture of holy water, dust from the sanctuary, and ink from the scroll on which the accusation against her was written. Guilt was deemed certain if the potion caused a miscarriage and a change in her complexion.[81]

Jesus discarded the Pharisaic view of female inferiority as well as the Pharisaic double standard in sexuality morality (John 8:2–11). As Jewish scholar Claude Montefiore notes, "There can be little doubt that in Jesus' attitude toward women we have a highly original and significant feature of his life and teaching."[82] Christian scholar Marcus Borg maintains that one of the most remarkable aspects of the gospel is the way in which Jesus challenged the conventional wisdom of his time with respect to woman.[83] Jesus saw in the Garden of Eden story not that woman was the source of sin, but that she was half of holy matrimony.[84] Jesus was willing to teach women (Luke 10:39; John 4:21–24), and he included them in his traveling band (Mark 15:40–41; Luke 8:1–3).

A purification law of Leviticus was disregarded when Jesus accepted a woman with "a flow of blood" who touched him (Mark 5:25–34). He did not believe that religious defilement came from physical conditions. Giving personal encouragement to a stigmatized hemorrhaging woman was probably the main therapy he rendered. Also, according to Jewish oral tradition, Samaritan women were to be shunned as perpetual menstruants.[85] By contrast, Jesus conversed with one at Jacob's well and asked for a drink from her jar (John 4:5–30). His acceptance of women who had a marginal place in society had a positive impact on regulations during the early centuries of the church.[86]

The Pharisees commonly separated themselves from non-Jews, and some believed Gentiles would not be eligible to join faithful Jews in the life after death.[87] Norman Perrin points out that most Jews of that era presumed Gentiles to be "beyond the pale of God's mercy."[88] Even Jews in Gentile employment were defiling when they entered the house of another Jew. Fanatical hatred is expressed in this injunction:

"An Israelite midwife may not aid a Gentile woman in child-birth since she would be assisting to bring to birth a child for idolatry."[89]

A marble tablet recovered from ancient Jerusalem shows that ethnic segregation at the Herodian Temple was enforced by capital punishment. The tablet had been on the wall separating the outer from the inner precincts. Its inscription reveals intense Jewish animosity: "Let no foreigner enter within the screen and enclosure surrounding the sanctuary. Whoever is apprehended so doing will be responsible for his own death, which shall take place immediately."[90]

The Pharisees' contempt for the Gentiles is conveyed in a psalm they composed after General Pompey conquered Palestine. They longed for a Messianic king who would violently eliminate the Romans. They sang:

> O God, may the son of David reign over your servant Israel.
> Gird him with strength to shatter wicked rulers.
> May he purge Jerusalem from Gentiles
>   that trample and destroy it. . . .
> With an iron mace he will crush all their substance.
> He will blot out the lawless Gentiles
>   with a word of his mouth.[91]
>   (*Psalms of Solomon* 17:23–27)

Jesus thought the Temple should be cleansed, but not *from* the Gentiles, but *for* the Gentiles. He agreed with the inclusiveness that Isaiah, as God's spokesperson, proclaimed:

> As for the foreigners who give me their allegiance, who love and serve me, . . . I will bring them to my sacred hill and make them joyful in my house of prayer. Their sacrifices and offerings will be accepted on my altar; for my Temple shall be called a house of prayer for all peoples. (Isa. 56:6–7; Mark 11:17)

Jesus was raised in an environment in which Gentiles and women were depreciated. Yet, if we take seriously Luke's statement that the Nazarene grew religiously and socially (Luke 2:52), then it is likely that his development involved breaking out of the cultural narrowness in which he was reared. Jesus struggled to transcend intrinsic ethnocentricism and to internalize Isaiah's vision for Israel. That prophet urged his people to endure suffering as "the servant of the Lord" in order to bring justice to the nations (Isa. 42:1–4). As Jesus moved beyond a nationalistic mentality, he became "a light to the Gentiles" (Isa. 49:6; Matt. 12:15–21).

The episode regarding Jesus' confrontation with a Greek living in Phoenicia tells of a consciousness-raising experience (Mark 7:24–30; Matt. 15:21–28). Jesus is caught with his compassion down. His initial response to a woman in that foreign land shows both ethnic and gender prejudice. When the Phoenician begs for help, he first gives her the silent treatment—because Jewish men shunned talking with women in public.[92] Jesus comments to his disciples, "I was sent only to the lost sheep of the house of Israel." He then insults the Gentile woman by saying it is not proper to throw to Gentile "dogs" what belongs to Jewish "children." When she responds in a gracious but determined manner to Jesus' contemptuous remark, he comes to realize her depth of faith. He provides therapy for the Phoenician's deranged daughter after recognizing that females in a foreign land are as worthy of his concern as males in Israel.

The story of Jesus with the Phoenician woman provides the only example of anyone causing him to change his mind. That experience enlarged Jesus' sense of mission even as Peter's later confrontation with Cornelius gradually removed some of the apostle's cultural prejudices (Acts 10). A broadening of ethnic concern can be detected in the book of Matthew by comparing Jesus' outlook before and after the Phoenician episode. In the Gospel most oriented toward the Jews, Jesus charged his apostles to "go nowhere among the Gentiles" on an evangelistic mission, but he later commissioned them to "go . . . and make disciples of all nations" (10:5; 28:19).

Jesus' generous approval of Gentiles on other occasions is especially featured in Luke's Gospel. Astonished by a Roman centurion's love for Jews and concern for a sick servant, he admitted that he had not found such faith among his own people (7:1–10). Again, non-Jewish Samaritans are the heroes of a parable and an encounter during one of

Jesus' journeys (10:29–37; 17:11–19). He asserted repeatedly that Gentiles are generally more acceptable to God than Jews because the former, although less aware of the expectations of the one true God, have responded better to their partial knowledge (10:13–15; 11:29–32; 12:48). Luke, along with subsequent Gentile Christians, found the episode of the Phoenician woman counter to the international Jesus he admired, so he omitted the out-of-character story from what he obtained from the Gospel of Mark.

In addition to denigrating women and Gentiles, the Pharisees castigated other Jewish men who did not follow scrupulously the "tradition of the elders." Jacob Neusner, a leading contemporary authority on early Judaism, finds plausible the assertions in the Gospels that the Pharisees stressed eating the right foods with the right people.[93] They scorned those who did not perform fastidiously the rituals prescribed by rabbis. There is the story, for example, of Rabbi Yannai, who invited a stranger to dine in his home. The guest, when requested to say a blessing, confessed that he did not know any prayers. The rabbi then told him to repeat after him: "A dog has eaten the bread of Yannai."[94]

Jesus was notorious for accepting unrefined Jewish men and women who disregarded the oral traditions. He would not have approved of Hillel's judgment that "no *am ha-aretz* is religious"; nor would he have accepted the rule that "a Pharisee may not eat with an *am ha-aretz*."[95] Jesus was criticized by the Pharisees for eating with those whom they called "sinners" (Luke 5:29–30; 15:2); he did not accept their view that "the masses, who do not know the law, are accursed" (John 7:49).

The Prophet

The fact that Jesus had some significant disagreements with the general position of the Pharisees can best be understood by investigating his prophetic outlook. From the beginning to the end of his public ministry, Jesus thought of himself as a prophet. This biblical term does not primarily connote foretelling the future. Biblical prophets were interpreters of past divine-human covenants and, on the basis of historical patterns, discerners of present and future trends. The prophets who interested Jesus were principally spokespersons for God in their own generation.

John the Baptist was the living prophet who heavily influenced Jesus at the beginning of his ministry. John encountered people who thought they were insulated from God's judgment because they were descended from father Abraham. They presumed that there was a most-favored-nation status in the divine government. As God's alleged chosen they could contemplate their privileges rather than their responsibilities. In countering such smugness, John was convinced that Jews could not protect themselves by recalling the faith of their fathers, the merit of their mothers, or the fame of their families. He thundered:

> Do not fancy that you can get by with saying, "We have Abraham as our ancestor"; for I tell you, God is able to produce descendants for Abraham from these stones. The ax is ready to strike the trees at the root; every tree that fails to bear good fruit is cut down and thrown into the fire. (Matt. 3:9–10)

Important for John was changed life, not correct lineage. Jesus came to admire that prophet's emphasis on fruitfulness; a fig tree should be chopped down if it produces nothing after careful nurturing (Luke 13:6–9). Neither prophet believed that a people could live on the momentum of godly forebears, because faith cannot be inherited like possessions.

When Jesus was baptized in the Jordan River, a vision and voice were revealed to him that were similar to the momentous "call" experienced by some Israelite prophets (1 Kings 22:19–22; Isa. 6; Ezek. 1–2). "He saw the firmament open and the dovelike Spirit descending on him; and from heaven came this declaration, 'You are my chosen Son'" (Mark 1:10–11). After that dramatic inner experience, Jesus inaugurated his ministry at the Nazareth synagogue by making Isaiah's manifesto (61:1–2) his own. He announced his leading motif in this quotation:

The Spirit of the Lord is upon me,
  because he has anointed me
    to bring good news to the destitute.
He has sent me . . .
    to free the downtrodden,
    to proclaim the year of the Lord's favor.
                                    (Luke 4:18-19)

On that occasion, Jesus referred to himself as a prophet and
defended his acceptance of Gentiles by calling attention to a
neglected aspect of the work of two revered prophets who
lived nine centuries earlier. Jesus was impressed that both Elijah and Elisha concerned themselves with needy foreigners.
During a time of famine, Elijah traveled to the heathen homeland of Jezebel—his greatest enemy—and aided a widow.
What made that episode even more significant to Jesus was
that no mention is made of his helping people in Israel who
were also suffering from severe deprivation (1 Kings 16:31;
17:8–24). Likewise, Elisha assisted in restoring the health of a
Syrian army commander (2 Kings 5:1–14). Then, as in recent
decades, citizens of Israel considered Syria to be their main
enemy. Again, Jesus noted, the prophet could have expended
all his efforts on those of his own culture in similar need.
However, scripture does not tell of Elisha providing therapy
for any Israelites who had the same dreaded skin disease.

When the Nazarenes heard Jesus appeal to historical
episodes that they had conveniently overlooked, their earlier
admiration reversed (Luke 4:22–28). Had he only said that
he was at least as interested in non-Nazarenes as Nazarenes,
he would have generated no more than their disgust over his
loss of special affection for his native village. But to cite evidence from authoritative sources to prove that the Lord had
compassion on Israel's enemies was perceived as a threat to
the intensely nationalistic Galileans. Uncontrollable rage toward Jesus resulted, and the Nazareth worship service concluded with this attempted lynching:

When they heard this, all in the synagogue were infuriated. They sprang to their feet and put him out of town.
They led him to the brow of the hill on which their town

25

was built, intending to throw him off the cliff. But he walked through the mob and went away. (Luke 4:28–30)

Thus the religious establishment in Nazareth illustrated what Jesus had said to them: "Truly I tell you, no prophet is acceptable in his own community" (Luke 4:24; see Mark 6:4). He left the town where he had lived most of his life, never to return.

To argue that Jesus could not have been a Pharisee because of his polemics against the Pharisees is no more plausible than to maintain that Jeremiah could not have been a Jewish patriot because he was a caustic critic of the prevailing conduct of the Judean people. These two prophets regarded themselves as purifiers—as tearing down in order to rebuild the group from which they came. They were grieved when Jewish leaders thought of them as traitors and wanted them liquidated.

Toward the end of his ministry, Jesus announced, "It cannot be that a prophet should perish away from Jerusalem" (Luke 13:33). His self-consciousness of having a prophet's role corresponded with his public image. Some Galileans described Jesus as "a prophet like one of the old prophets" (Mark 6:15) and exclaimed, "A great prophet has arisen among us!" (Luke 7:16). Passover pilgrims at Jerusalem hailed Jesus as a prophet (Matt. 21:11, 46), and one of them referred to him as "a prophet mighty in deed and word before God and all the people" (Luke 24:19). In John's Gospel, as well as in the Synoptic Gospels, Jesus is frequently called a prophet (4:19; 6:14; 7:40; 9:17).

The biblical test for the true prophet is whether or not his or her prophecy comes to pass in accord with God's purposes (Deut. 13:1–5; 18:21–22; Jer. 28). Hence, the Gospel writers thought that the genuineness of Jesus was enhanced by the fulfillment of his predictions. They held that he forecast with accuracy the treachery of Judas, the failure of Peter, his own rejection by religious leaders, and the destruction of Jerusalem (Mark 8:31; 13:1–2; 14:17–21, 30).

That Jesus should be recognized as a prophet is quite significant, for most of his Jewish contemporaries assumed that the era of prophetic revelation had ended.[96] Montefiore points out that rabbis of Jesus' day "were not called prophets, and they could not properly have been called so. . . . Hillel was ever the servant of the Law, never its judge."[97] The cessation of prophecy is affirmed in the final prophetic books of the Hebrew Bible, but hope is also expressed there for its revival (Zech. 13:2–6; Joel 2:28–29; Mal. 4:5). That expectation continued in extrabiblical Jewish writings of the centuries immediately preceding the coming of Jesus.[98] Attention was focused on this forecast of Moses to the Israelites: "God will raise up for you a prophet like me from among you" (Deut. 18:15). At several places in the New Testament, Jesus is presumed to be the fulfillment of that scripture (Acts 3:22–23; 7:37; John 1:21, 25–27; 6:14; 7:40).

Tacit recognition of the revival of prophetic revelation is displayed in the comment by Galilean synagogue-goers, that Jesus taught "as one who had authority, and not as the scribes" (Mark 1:22). Similar to contemporary fundamentalists, the scribes accepted every sentence of their Bible as the inerrant word of God. The Talmud describes the interpretative stance that the scribe avoided: "The whole Torah is from God with the exception of this or that verse which not God but Moses spoke from his own mouth."[99]

Although Jesus frequently quoted scripture as authoritative, he also boldly stated views that were independent of, and even contradictory to, the written authority. We know of no other Pharisee who had the audacity to reject the Torah's "eye for an eye" principle. "But I say to you," a repeated phrase in the Sermon on the Mount, displays that Jesus occasionally substituted personal authority for biblical authority. The former is firsthand, whereas the latter is indirect, derived from the witnesses of earlier times.

Robert Grant, a noted biblical scholar, comments on the several "You have heard . . . but I say" antitheses that are clustered together in Matthew 5:21–48:

> The passage reproduces accurately the attitude of Jesus toward the legal portions of the Old Testament. He is a highly independent teacher. He might accurately be called a non-conformist. He does not set aside the Law, however; he deepens it, reinforces it, raises it all to its own highest level.[100]

The Gospels indicate that Jesus was selective in his rejection of the Pharisees' applications of the law of Moses. Luke reports that Jesus "went to the synagogue, as his custom was, on the sabbath day" and that there he read from scripture and commented on it (4:16–21). "The tradition of the elders" (Mark 7:5), not the law of Moses, gave sanction to such conduct.[101] Even so, he exercised independent judgment on which traditions to uphold. He approved of saying a blessing before meals (Mark 6:41; 14:22), as the Mishnah prescribes,[102] but he rejected the hand-washing ritual (Mark 7:1–5). Also, Jesus discarded the picayune regulations that prohibited Jews from helping someone in distress on the Sabbath because work was involved. Even to attend to a sprain or a fracture was not permitted, since the injured person would probably survive untreated until the holy day was over.[103] But Jesus believed that there was no time when assisting a person in need was not proper (Luke 6:6–10; 13:10–16). In contrast to the prevailing heavy "yoke of the Law,"[104] Jesus announced, "My yoke is easy, and my burden is light" (Matt. 11:30).

To explain why Jesus violated some Pharisaic traditions, Matthew twice (9:13; 12:7) records Jesus as appropriating Hosea's basic oracle: "I desire mercy, and not sacrifice" (Hos. 6:6). Prophets Hosea and Jesus criticized the corrupt religious establishment and focused on the obligation of love. Jesus prioritized the ethical over the ceremonial when he advised making peace with a neighbor before presenting a gift for the Temple altar (Matt. 5:23–24).

Jesus renewed the prophetic polemic against ritualism, believing that the Pharisees had been lax in fulfilling the stringent moral dimension of prophetic Judaism. He states: "Rightly did Isaiah describe you hypocrites in these words:

> 'These people honor me with their lips,
> but their hearts are far from me;
> Their worship is an empty show.'"
> (Mark 7:6–7; Isa. 29:13)

Apparently, many Israelite leaders over the centuries had been busy with pious performances to the neglect of steadfast love and social justice.

28

Jesus had both basic agreements and disagreements with some Pharisaic beliefs and attitudes. This can best be interpreted to mean that he was a Pharisee who engaged in intense interaction with other members of his party. Within its ranks considerable diversity was tolerated, for the opposition between Hillelites and Shammaites was quite wide on some issues. Jesus agreed with Shammai in rejecting easy divorce, and with Hillel in rejecting harsh punishment. Yet on other issues he championed fresh viewpoints independent from either party.

Vis-à-vis both the Pharisees and the Sadducees, Jesus' stance can best be discerned by examining the spectrum of attitudes toward social change. The Sadducees were understandably champions of the status quo, because they wanted to continue their position of power and wealth. The Pharisees were conservatives who were devoted to the Mosaic code but, unlike their reactionary rivals, they desired to interpret it to accommodate the environmental changes that had transpired over the millennium since Moses. While sharing the Pharisees' respect for scriptural tradition, Jesus pushed toward replacing calcified ceremonial law with more vital expressions of religious duty. Like John the Baptist, he was aware that the living faith of the dead easily becomes the dead faith of the living.

The interfacing of Jesus with his parent religion parallels his attitude toward his parents. There is a balance between indebtedness and independence. His values were similar to those attributed to Mary and Joseph in the infancy stories. Joseph is portrayed as both just and kind in his relations to Mary (Matt. 1:19). Mary's Song depicts God as against the arrogant and helpful to the poor (Luke 1:51–53). The adult Jesus shared the theology and ethics of his peasant parents. Yet the one canonical story of Jesus as a youth shows him with a mind of his own that exasperates his parents. After Mary scolds him for not traveling with them as they had expected, Jesus explains that his primary obligation is to God, not to his parents. Even so, he returned to Nazareth and expressed obedience to them in various ways (Luke 2:42–51).

There was this saying in Jesus' day: "There are four types among them that sit in the presence of the sages: the sponge, the funnel, the strainer, and the sifter." The "sponge" soaks up everything the instructor says and deposits it elsewhere unaltered, except that it is a bit adulterated. The "funnel" receives what is poured in one ear and slowly discharges it out the other ear. The "strainer" lets out the wine and keeps the worthless sediments. But the commendable student is the "sifter" who separates the coarse particles from the fine flour.[105] Jesus was a "sifter," discriminatingly refining religious traditions for contemporary use.

Jesus was like the resourceful scribe whom he commended because he "brings out of his treasure what is new and what is old" (Matt. 13:52). He thought of his gospel as "new wine" that would explode the hardened forms of ceremonial Judaism (Mark 2:22). Like his prophetic antecedents, Jesus carried on a lover's quarrel with some of the traditions of his people. However, he defended few novel ideas that had not been accepted by at least some of the Pharisees.

.3.

Interpreting Scripture

Countering Literalists

The comprehension of religious and poetic literature is perennially distorted by those who equate thinking seriously with thinking literally. To them, myths are necessarily false because they are fictions. Truth is equated with matter-of-fact prosaic data that can actually or potentially be sensed. The literalist is the ancestor of the mechanical computer; both process, store, and retrieve information but are incapable of responding to figurative nuances. The literal-minded person, whether she or he lives in a prescientific, ancient culture or in a technological modern culture, presumes that words make sense when they point to what is out there in the "real" world. Thus, devils and angels, paradise and hell, and the like have reality to the extent that they are objective and external. Teachers of "dead poets'" writings struggle continually with students who relegate imaginative thinking to the closet of outgrown childhood things.[1]

Throughout his earthly life, Jesus gave much attention to interpreting his scriptures. There is no evidence that he expected anything to be written down to supplement or to supplant those Hebrew scrolls. The synagogue instruction he probably received as a youth was completely focused on the scriptural anthology produced by his ancestors. Written by many authors over many centuries, it contained a variety of literary types: epic, saga, legal, historical, devotional, prophetic, and apocalyptic.

Jesus was aware of "scribes"—a term usually referring to interpreters rather than to copiers—who were more skilled in analyzing minutiae than in comprehending main themes. They had a centrifugal orientation, ever focusing on casuistry—that is, on applying the law of Moses to particular cases. Scribal treatment of the Sabbath is the best illustration of casuistry. The injunction to rest on the Sabbath—one of the Ten Commandments—was considered too broad for purposes of enforcement. Hence the Mishnah lists thirty-nine types of work prohibited on the holy day, one being tying a knot and another being loosening a knot. Arguments follow on how to define precisely when one is guilty of working at tying a knot. Rabbi Meir held that guilt is not incurred by any who manipulated knots with one hand. Rabbis Judah and Eliezer disagreed over whether it was sinful to tie a rope to a bucket for the purpose of drawing water from a well.[2]

In Jesus' opinion, Jewish legalism and literalism were overlooking the purpose of the Sabbath, to provide a rest that would be conducive to worship. Having a centripetal approach toward the law, Jesus wanted to reduce the number of trivial and hard-to-remember rules, so that religion could become a lift rather than a load. He followed Isaiah, who associated true religion with eagles' wings (Isa. 40:31) but false religion with a dead weight (46:1). According to Jesus, the law specialists of his culture were adding to obligations and were not assisting people in bearing the burden (Matt. 23:4). He called them "blind guides" (Matt. 23:24), because they could see the trees but not the forest.

Jesus was aware that his broad interpretation of the Torah would be unacceptable to the literalists who dominated Judaism. He compared their rejection of fresh viewpoints to wine drinkers: "Nobody who has been drinking old wine desires new wine. 'The old is better,' they say" (Luke 5:39). The scribal reactionaries held that the law would endure unchanged in its entirety even after the earth ends.[3] To goad those who were impervious to change, Jesus indulged in a bit of hyperbole. Luke records this remark: "It is easier for sky and earth to vanish than for an ornamental stroke of the law to drop out" (Luke 16:17). An equivalent zany exaggeration would be: It is easier to transplant a tree to an ocean than to alter a small point in the dogma of fundamentalists.

Jesus' expression of exasperation is followed by his criticism of the Deuteronomic divorce law.

The editor of the First Gospel found Jesus' irony on the Torah's immutability either too clever to grasp or unacceptable if correctly understood. "Matthew," as legend has named that editor, presumed that Jesus was endorsing the prevailing Jewish doctrine of the everlasting perpetuity of every detail of the Torah. Thus, he has Jesus say:

> Truly, I tell you: not until heaven and earth disappear will even the smallest letter or stroke of a letter be dropped from the law—until its purpose is accomplished. Therefore, whoever disregards even the least significant of these commands and teaches others to do the same, will have the lowest place in the kingdom of heaven. (Matt. 5:18–19)

Matthew's impossible interpretation is in the midst of a passage containing Jesus' radical modifications of some laws of the Torah!

How have leading New Testament interpreters dealt with this passage from the Sermon on the Mount? Rudolf Bultmann remarks: "In view of other sayings of Jesus and of his actual practice, [it] cannot possibly be genuine."[4] Similarly, Milo Connick states regarding these words that Matthew puts in Jesus' mouth:

> It is unlikely that Jesus ever uttered them. They teach that the Law is true and permanent in its minutest detail down to the last dotted "i" and crossed "t." They declare that seats in the kingdom are reserved only for those who teach and observe the entire Law. Such a standard would deny entrance to Jesus himself![5]

Bultmann and Connick do not realize that Matthew's problem is not the use of an inauthentic teaching of Jesus. Rather, Matthew places a humorless spin on a typical hyperbole of Jesus. An occupational hazard of any witty speaker is that hearers may suppose that what was said with tongue in cheek represents the humorist's viewpoint. Thomas Manson argues convincingly that Luke faithfully preserved the tone of Jesus' words about the decorative curl on certain Hebrew letters, while Matthew completely missed the meaning.[6]

Biblical words and phrases often have unintended meanings when interpreted literally. Consider, for instance, the child who asked if God works only with his left hand, on learning that God's Son "sitteth on the right hand of God the Father." Each word in that creedal phrase, derived from the New Testament, has a symbolic but not a literal meaning. The affirmation is not referring to an offspring procreated by an adult god who has sperm and hands. Jesus is no more literally the Son of God than some of Jesus' disciples were actually "sons of thunder" (Mark 3:17) or "the son of perdition" (John 17:12). The Semitic "son of . . ." idioms here refer to those whose personalities have explosive or destructive tendencies. Nor does the creed describe a physical realm where the weight of one person's body could hold down the arm of another. The composer of the metaphor did not intend to mean that Jesus, as the first astronaut, is sitting it out on a long, inactive vacation at the throne of God before reentry into the earth's gravity and atmosphere. Rather, it refers to the intimate bond between God and a human, which has resulted in a unique status of honor and power after an experience of humiliation.

A popular genre of childhood jokes is taking poetic words in a grossly literalistic manner. Consider, for example, this question: Why did the moron think someone was about to be born or had died when he looked under his bed? Answer: He had learned that we come from dust and will return to dust. Hearers who "get" the joke are those who understand that "dust" has a biblical meaning distinct from its common meaning.

The Gospel of John illustrates how ludicrous it can be to take theological metaphors literally. Jesus informs a Pharisee named Nicodemus: "No one can see the kingdom of God without being born anew." Nicodemus responds: "How can anyone already old be born? Is it possible to return to the mother's womb and be born again?" (John 3:3–4). The questions of that Pharisee may be sarcastic. However, they may show that Nicodemus naively thought Jesus was speaking biologically; if so, he totally misunderstood the regeneration doctrine. Many share his literalism in presuming that Jesus'

assurance in this episode of "eternal life" pertains to an un-
ending quasi-material realm in the sky. After they have
"slept" between burial and judgment day, the Spirit of God
will jump-start selected corpses and raise them to a sensuous
paradise.

The next chapter of John's Gospel contains the story of
Jesus' encounter with a Samaritan woman. He meets her at a
well and encourages her to drink from the "living water" he
can provide. Here Jesus is following earlier prophets' figurative
reference to God as "the fountain of living waters" (Jer. 2:13),
who can quench human thirst (Isa. 12:3; 55:1). The Samaritan,
unable to think poetically, asks: "Sir, you have no bucket, and
the well is deep; how do you get that living water?" For her,
"living water" is fresh spring water, not stagnant cistern water;
she is unaware of Jesus' theological use of "living water" as the
spiritual, life-giving qualities of his gospel. Jesus then attempts
this clarification: "Whoever drinks of the water I give will
never thirst again. The water I give will become an inner fountain, springing up for life eternal." Still thinking on a literal
level, the woman responds with scornful humor: "Give me that
water! Then I will not get thirsty and have to come here again
to draw water" (John 4:10–15).

In some cases, Jesus' metaphors were not misinterpreted
until long after the era of early Christianity. The most notorious example is the literal interpretation that has been given
to some words he spoke at the Last Supper, before his body
was torn by crucifiers. After breaking a loaf of bread, he said,
"This is my body" (Mark 14:22; 1 Cor. 11:24). There is no
more reason for assuming that the bread distributed to the
disciples at a house in Jerusalem was actually Jesus' body
than that he became transformed into a grapevine when he
said on that same occasion, "I am the vine" (John 15:5). However, in the medieval era there emerged a supernatural interpretation of Jesus' words that continues to be a major cause of
schism among Christians. It was presumed that the miracle of
transubstantiation followed his saying, "This is my body."
Moreover, it came to be thought that the miracle reoccurs
whenever his priestly representatives intone, "*Hoc est corpus
meum*" in Latin at the climax of the Mass. So interpreted, the
ceremony is similar to that of cannibals who commemorate

the death of a tribal elder by dividing a portion of his flesh and swallowing their leader.

Encouraged by the common medieval belief that the mere pronunciation of special words could change the nature of physical objects, magicians incorporated the Bible-based Latin formula in their deceptive ritual, and this is probably the source of the expression "hocus-pocus." "Hoax," a contraction of hocus-pocus, has come to mean tricking people into believing or accepting as genuine something false and often preposterous.

The alleged shroud of Jesus housed at Turin has been the medieval hoax with the longest hoodwinking record. Radiocarbon dating has now determined that it was made of organic material dating many centuries after Jesus' crucifixion, and the alleged bloodstains have been proved to be a pigment of the deceiver's paint. All that is actually known of the burial of Jesus are the Gospels' descriptions of typical Jewish funeral procedures. The way in which words of Rabbi Jesus and the Gospel accounts have been manhandled in Western history has the qualities of a sick joke.

Had Muhammad not interpreted literally the New Testament's use of symbolic language, Islam might not have arisen as a rival to Christianity. Muhammad presumed that Christians believe God physically sired a godling by having intercourse with goddess Mary. This seemed to the Arabian prophet to be another version of pagan polytheism. Over against the alleged Christian tritheism, he affirmed: "God is only one God: far be it from his glory that he should beget a son."[7] Muhammad, like many Christians, could not fathom the complex monotheism of the Nicene triunitarian formula which begins, "We believe in one God . . ." What Muhammad opposed has been championed by the Mormons, who believe that Jesus was born from a physical union of Mary with the Heavenly Father.[8]

The Temptations

Difficulties intrinsic to literal interpretation of scripture confronted Jesus as well as his later followers. Like the apostle Paul, he found that "the letter kills, but the Spirit gives life" (2 Cor. 3:6). The drama of Jesus' wilderness temptations, described as an encounter with the devil, is rife with hermeneutic problems. Many Christians have been so mesmerized by belief in an actual physical devil that they have missed the deep meaning of the Satan stories. They do not realize that the horned figure with scarlet leotards, forked tail, and pitchfork is not derived from the ancient Judeo-Christian tradition, but from later European folklore.

Jesus' temptations express, in a picturesque manner, ancient Jewish psychology. Each person has within, so it was thought, an evil and a good impulse (*yetzer*) which could be personified as a devil and an angel in battle.[9] The Jews did not interpret Satan or devils in a literal manner, with hell as their home address. They did not believe in an uncreated rival to God who existed from all eternity. One Jewish sage, Jesus ben Sirach, made this demythologizing clarification: "When a godless person curses Satan, he really curses himself."[10] Likewise, Jesus ben Joseph affirmed that evil does not come from outside an individual but "from within, out of the human heart" (Mark 7:21). The stories of Eve arguing with a serpent, and of Jacob wrestling with an angel, are examples of what Freudian psychology expresses more prosaically and secularly as the ego's confrontation with id and superego.

By the time of his baptism in the Jordan, Jesus was fully aware of being called to a special mission. After he withdrew to a solitary place to define his new role, several possibilities for the future appear to have crossed his mind. One was this: Should I aim at satisfying material needs? Another was: Should I choose any effective means for achieving control over others? The third was: Will showing off special personal power promote my cause?

Jesus may have thought of attempting to become a new Moses, delivering his people from latter-day pharaohs while providing physical sustenance. Through a weary wilderness similar to the one where he was meditating, Moses had led his people toward a land "flowing with milk and honey." The exodus story claims that water, manna, and quail miraculously appeared along the way for Israelite consumption. Is the role of a savior, Jesus pondered, inseparable from providing literal food for down-and-out people? He had with him the scroll of Deuteronomy—or had memorized verses from it—because his responses to this and other career possibilities come from that source. Jesus found a principle relevant to his situation in words attributed to Moses: "Bread is not the only human need" (Deut. 8:3; Luke 4:3).

In the second temptation—to follow the order in Luke's Gospel—Jesus is shown, in his mind's eye, all the world's kingdoms from a mountain. Authority over all humans is promised if devilish tactics are followed. In human history, before and after Jesus, conquest by war has been the most common means that leaders have used to gain international power. While Jesus desired to promote God's transcultural kingdom, he rejected the principle that a good goal justifies any evil means for diminishing nation-states. For Christian literalists who know that the earth is spherical, this temptation is especially absurd. If Jesus had infinite human vision, not even on Everest could he have seen all the "inhabited earth" (Greek, *oikoumene*, Luke 4:5).

Jesus' final wilderness temptation deserves a more thorough consideration, because it involves his rejecting not only literalism, but also the theology contained in scriptural passages. It appears that it occurred while he was meditating on a theme from the poetic anthology with which he was most familiar. Psalm 1 announces a motif that will occasionally be repeated in subsequent poems: that the pious prosper and the wicked wither. The most outspoken expression of that theme is in Psalm 91, where a poet claims that the person who trusts in God will remain unscathed by disaster:

> You will not fear the terrors of the night,
>   nor the dangers of the day;
> neither the plague that stalks in the dark,
>   nor the calamity that spreads havoc at midday.
> Though hundreds die at your side
>   and thousands close at hand,
>   the pestilence will not harm you.
> You will look about you
>   and see how sinners are punished.

Thus, the religious are promised safety during an epidemic. They can gaze with satisfaction at those who are dying all around them in recompense for their wickedness. A bold declaration is then made regarding the future:

> God has charged his angels
> to guard you wherever you go.
> They will carry you in their arms
> to keep you from hitting your foot against a stone.

Presuming that the divine Protector never allows bad things to happen to good persons, the psalmist concludes his encouragement to fearlessness by assuring those who are devoted to God that they will not only be rescued from trouble but will also be rewarded with longevity. That psalmist's concept of the role of angels is occasionally found elsewhere in biblical literature. Narrators claim that they preserve the life of the virtuous (Gen. 22:11–12; Acts 12:7–11) and kill the vicious (2 Kings 19:35; Acts 12:23).[11]

While apparently reflecting on the sentiments of a psalmist who believed religion could prevent pain and illness, an idea enters Jesus' imagination: could he, as one with strong religious convictions, jump off the highest building he had ever seen and be rescued in midair by guardian angels? Had not John the Baptist called him a mighty man (Luke 3:16)? The Temple in Jerusalem rose hundreds of feet above the ravine below. Josephus said that one could not look down from its pinnacle without becoming overcome with dizziness.[12] Although the psalmist promises the devout a kind of angelic parachute and long physical life, Jesus ponders the implications of special providence. Should a person expect God to counter dependable natural forces and save life and limb in a supernatural manner? Would a person who jumps from the Temple be a praiseworthy believer or a stupid exhibitionist?

Jesus and the writer of the prologue of the book of Job thought picturesquely as they worked through issues in the psychology of religion. The creator of Job pictures Satan testing his hypothesis that God has established a bribery scheme whereby immunity from personal tragedy is exchanged for worship. The fictional Job and the historical Jesus illustrate that there can be disinterested piety. Their trust in God was not dependent on being insulated from horrendous personal suffering. They rejected the simpleminded belief that the righteous can rest assured that their health will be miraculously preserved by divine intervention. Observant Jesus no doubt recognized, for example, that the depraved monarch who began the Herodian dynasty had wealth and longevity. Contrariwise, the devoutly religious person whose prayer is recorded as Psalm 22 was not saved by God from torture and premature death. Jesus did not endorse the Psalm 91 fantasy of God's agents hovering over the righteous to make emergency rescues that contravene the natural order.

Whereas Jesus found the wiles of Satan in Psalm 91, he discerned the will of God in a sermon attributed to Moses. In Deuteronomy, this declaration is made: "You shall not put God to the test as you did at Massah" (6:16). During the exodus from Egypt, some Israelites withheld their trust in God until receiving water at Massah in a spectacular manner (Ex. 17:2–7). While in another wilderness, Jesus decided that he should not attempt to test God as the Israelites had done. He appears to have associated the testimony in Psalm 91 with the evil inclination in humans that identifies fanatical foolhardiness with religious courage. There are other New Testament examples of the subtle confusion of devilish impulses with godly motivation (John 16:2; 2 Cor. 11:14).

In spite of Jesus' rejection of the outlook championed in Psalm 91, the devotional pap expressed there continues to be accepted by most who treasure the Bible. In a typical commentary, Artur Weiser remarks on the psalm: "Here faith reaches its ultimate soaring height."[13] Those inspired by that naive psalmist might be encouraged to enter situations of extreme danger without taking precautions. When warned of a bomb or an AIDS threat, they would presume that those "who dwell in the shadow of the Almighty" will be saved from the death that might destroy those around them.

Psalm 91 was a favorite song of the American troops during the 1991 war over oil rights in the Middle East. Consequently, verses from that psalm were sprinkled through a *Time* article about the bravado of those soldiers amid their threats.[14] The magical message conveyed is that God's angels hover over those on one side of the conflict. They are even more effective than American helicopters in guaranteeing protection and long life.

The evaluation of Psalm 91 by exegete Manson and theologian Reinhold Niebuhr follows that of Jesus. Manson offers this sound but unusual comment: "To thrust oneself into peril, merely to provide God with the occasion for a miracle, is not faith but presumption."[15] Niebuhr finds this psalm "a perfect illustration of all the illusions which may arise from an ultimate religious faith." The distinguished theologian explains:

It is easy to be tempted to the illusion that the child of God will be accorded special protection from the capricious forces of the natural world, or special immunity from the vindictive passions of angry men. Any such faith is bound to suffer disillusionment. Nor does it deserve moral respect. Stoic indifference toward the varying vicissitudes of mortal existence is preferable to lobbying, with whining entreaties, in the courts of the Almighty, hoping for special favours which are not granted to ordinary mortals or to godless men.[16]

Shakespeare discerned from Jesus' dialogue with the devil that biblical passages can be used as proof texts for sinister schemes. Thus his character Shylock cites a story from Genesis to justify an unscrupulous monetary venture. Antonio, the Venice merchant with whom he is dealing, responds: "The devil can cite Scripture for his purpose. An evil soul producing holy witness is like a villain with a smiling cheek, a goodly apple rotten at the heart." A friend of Antonio echoes that insight: "In religion, what damned error but some sober brow will bless it and approve it with a text, hiding the grossness with fair ornament?"[17]

Jesus must also have found sentiments expressed in other psalms to be contrary to acceptable praise to God. Devoted as he was to loving his enemies, he could not have approved of the passages that call for God's curse on persons whom the psalmist hated. For example, Jesus' religious orientation

stands in bold relief against the outlook expressed in the conclusion of Psalm 137. The blessing of God is there promised
to those who bash Babylonian babies against a rock.

The God of the Crucified One does not protect the faithful from death, but dwells within them in spite of death.
Psalm 23 conveys the faith that Jesus found genuine. That
best-known devotional poem in world literature tells of the
Shepherd who is present with those who walk through the
darkest valley. Although guardian angels were a common
motif in Jewish writings of Jesus' era,[18] they have little role
in his public ministry. This is understandable, because their
alleged function is incongruous with the story of Jesus. If angels really rescue the innocent from death, why were the
hands of the crucifiers not stayed? Why did an angel not save
him, as the Bible alleges happened for Isaac at a mountain
altar and for Peter in a Jerusalem prison?

Shema Binding

Jesus was aware of an appropriate and an inappropriate
use of some words attributed to Moses. Jesus joined with the
Pharisees in believing that Jewish theology and ethics are
summed up in this paragraph from Deuteronomy 6:

> Understand [*Shema*], O Israel: The Lord our God is Lord
> alone; and you shall love the Lord your God with all your
> heart, and with all your soul, and with all your might.
> Keep in your heart these words which I am commanding
> you this day. Teach them diligently to your children, and
> talk about them when you sit in your house and when you
> walk outside, when you lie down and when you rise. You
> shall bind them as a sign upon your hand, and they shall
> be as frontlets between your eyes. Write them on the
> doorposts of your house and on your gates.

The Pharisees had elevated this passage, which they called
the Shema, to "first" in importance among the hundreds of
Mosaic laws.[19] Jesus was thoroughly in accord with the succinct way in which it combined the unity of God's nature with

the singularity of loving devotion (Mark 12:29–30). He was critical of the way in which attention to some other laws of Moses had often resulted in neglecting "the love [*agape*] of God" (Luke 11:42).

While endorsing the Shema, Jesus disapproved of the way in which some Jews during the Roman era had used it in a literalistic and supernatural manner. Hebrew scholars point out that the "bind them as a sign" reference in the Shema was "originally intended only in a purely symbolic or figurative sense." Max Joseph, a Jerusalem rabbi, expresses the creedal meaning by this paraphrase: "Everything which you think, feel, and do ought to be hallowed by love of God."[20] After examining the Shema carefully, Archibald Kennedy likewise concludes that the injunction to "bind" was plainly a figure of speech.[21] It meant that Israelites should make love an absorbing concern by continually teaching it to children and by acting upon it in daily life. The Septuagint presumes that *tatafoth*, meaning "frontlets," is figurative; the phrase under consideration means that focus on the love of God "shall be unchanging (*asaleutos*) before your eyes." Thus as late as the Hellenistic era, when that Greek translation was made, the directives of the Shema were not taken literally. The Samaritans, who also regard the Torah as authoritative, have never interpreted literally this phrase from Deuteronomy.

Elsewhere in the Hebrew Bible there are similar metaphors pertaining to binding that obviously were not intended to be taken literally. Proverbs advises youth in picturesque ways to treasure religious teachings: "They are a fair garland for your head, and pendants for your neck" (1:9); "Bind them about your neck, write them on the tablet of your heart" (3:3); "Bind them on your heart continually; tie them around your neck" (6:21). Those are but various ways of conveying that the wisdom imparted by sages should be learned thoroughly and valued in daily living.

The popular practice of exorcism in the Roman era resulted in a manipulation of holy words for the purpose of expelling alleged evil spirits. The first book of church history tells of Jewish magicians who operated in various cities, and of apostles who denounced them (Acts 8:9–24; 13:6–11; 19:13–19).

In Ephesus the exorcists sold small parchments or papyri on which magical formulas were written. The writings were alleged to do wonders for the possessors who attached them to their bodies.[22] Lines of one magical papyrus assure demon removal to those who "write this phylactery [containing holy words] upon a little sheet of tin . . . and hang it round the sufferer."[23] One manual from the postbiblical era contains directions for making a Jewish amulet for curing fever. First, these words from Numbers 11:2 were to be written on parchment: "Moses prayed to God, and the fire abated." That sentence was then wrapped with leather to be worn around the neck of a feverish patient during sleep.[24]

The term "phylactery" comes from the Greek verb *phylatto*, meaning "to protect." The wearer of an amulet (*phylakterion*) on a headband, or on a neck chain, was presumed to be fortified against evil powers.[25] The Rosetta stone refers to golden *phylakteria* worn by Egyptian kings to safeguard them from malign influences.[26]

There is no evidence of phylactery use in Judaism before the Roman era. In Hebrew it was called *tefillin*. One Jewish writing from the beginning of the first century C.E. tells of a requirement to fasten on the hand a symbol of the laws.[27] Josephus, writing later in that century, alludes to two religious objects worn by devout Jews: "All show forth the power of God and his goodwill toward them by bearing a record thereof written on the head and on the arm. This demonstrates to people on every side the loving care of God which surrounds them."[28] In excavating Qumran in Judea, a phylactery dating from the first century was found, which has compartments containing sentences from the Torah on strips of parchment.[29] The alleged protective function of those objects is attested to in the Talmud: "Whoever has phylacteries on his body, fringe on his garment, and the mezuzah on his door may be presumed to be safe from committing sin."[30] Abraham Geiger, a Jewish leader in the nineteenth century, was right in maintaining that phylacteries were originally pagan amulets which the Jews adapted.

Although the Shema was intended to have an inward theological and ethical significance, it became a conspicuous personal decoration. A tiny piece of parchment containing the Shema and other laws was placed in a little cube, with a leather covering and straps to bind it to the body. One of the boxes was bound on the left arm above the elbow so that it would be "upon the heart" as commanded by Moses! Another box was strapped to the brow at the hairline; unseen by the wearer, it mainly reminded others of the wearer's religiosity. The emblem was also worn in hope of receiving future favors from God.

According to the Mishnah, the phylacteries worn on head and arm contained four passages of the Torah.[31] Except for holy days, male adults were expected to wear them all day.[32] On the Sabbath they could not wear either phylacteries or sandals with nails, because a weight of a few ounces would be a burden prohibited by the "Thou shalt not work" commandment.[33]

The one reference to phylacteries in the New Testament is in words attributed to Jesus. He criticized the Pharisees who wore them to show off their special status (Matt. 23:5). In a parallel manner, George F. Moore's only reference to phylacteries in *Judaism in the First Centuries of the Christian Era* is to hypocrisy. That classic study cites a source telling of a pious pretender who was "wrapped in his prayer shawl with his *tefillin* on his head."[34]

There is a parallel in church history to the pious practice of attaching phylacteries to the body. Christians can readily understand why Jesus considered it a travesty to use as magic the "greatest commandment," which is contained in the Shema. Yet they are often oblivious to the way in which a distinctive Gospel teaching has similarly produced a fetish object.

Jesus' cross-carrying command was a figurative way of urging disciples to dedicate themselves to his cause, even at the cost of martyrdom. The earliest Christians focused on the symbolism of the cross, but they did not wear small facsimiles to ward off demonic forces. In subsequent church history, however, Jesus' imperative pertaining to the cross has resulted in external observances as literal as those found in Orthodox Judaism. Julian, a fourth-century Roman emperor, informed Christians of a practice that he disliked: "You adore the wood of the cross and draw its likeness on your foreheads."[35] Beginning with Emperor Constantine, Christian rulers thought victory over "infidels" would be guaranteed if troops carried a cruciform banner with them into battle. From the fifth century onward, the cross has been widely worn as an amulet.[36] Many Christians continue to dangle polished miniatures of the cross over their hearts. Ironically, some treat the representation of an ancient torture device as a protecting charm. Starcrest of California advertises its "Good Luck Cross" in this way:

> Lead a charmed life with this pretty pendant! . . . You can trust it to begin attracting love, success, and financial reward the moment you put it on. And you can count on plenty of compliments, too! . . . Friends will surely admire its exquisite beauty—as well as your newly found fortune![37]

Undoubtedly, most Christians who have worn crosses have not trivialized a core teaching of Jesus about carrying one's cross. For them the symbol is not perceived as powerful magic or as a lovely decoration to impress others, but as a reminder, primarily to themselves, of their commitment to One who laid down his life in love for friends and enemies. Likwise, most Jews who have worn phylacteries have probably not thought of them as fetishes but as a reminder of their allegiance to the Lord.

Marriage and Divorce

Jesus also searched his scriptures to harmonize the conflicting principles espoused there on marriage. The resulting perspective is disclosed in his response to this question: "Is it lawful to divorce one's wife for any cause?" (Matt. 19:3). The point of this inquiry by some Pharisees is contained in the phrase "for any cause." The Jews disputed not whether divorce per se is right or wrong, but what ought to be the legitimate grounds for divorce. According to Deuteronomic law, a husband could write "a divorce certificate" if he found "something obnoxious" (Deut. 24:1, New Jewish Translation) about his wife. At issue in Jesus' era was what type of conduct made a woman offensive. Shammai contended that "a husband may not divorce his wife unless he has found unchastity in her." But Hillel affirmed that a husband had the right to divorce his wife for any cause—"even if she spoiled a dish for him."[38] Some other rabbis argued that divorce should be permitted if a wife scolds so loudly inside her house that the neighbors hear her voice, or if she goes out with her hair unbound.[39]

Divorce was exclusively a male prerogative in ancient Jewish culture; from Moses onward, chauvinism was taken for granted. The Mishnah states that a wife can be "put away with her consent or without it."[40] No hearing was required before a court of justice. Yet a wife could not divorce her husband even if he was cruel, lecherous, and otherwise irresponsible.

There is considerable evidence that Hillel's liberal interpretation of the divorce law was in line with past precedent. In the second century before the Christian era, divorce was advised on trivial grounds: "If your wife does not obey you at a signal or a glance, separate from her."[41] Philo, Jesus' contemporary, indicated that divorce was easy to procure.[42] Josephus spoke dispassionately of his many serial marriages and of divorcing those who "displeased him."[43] Rabbi Akiba believed that one should divorce and remarry "if he finds another woman more beautiful."[44]

Before Jesus began his ministry, Palestinian tetrarch Herod Antipas became enamored of his brother's wife, Herodias. She agreed to abandon her husband and marry Antipas if he would forsake a wife who was the daughter of the Nabatean king, Aretas.[45] When Antipas agreed to this scheme—irregular even by the tolerant mores of the time—criticism arose in his kingdom. John the Baptist was imprisoned and eventually beheaded because he condemned the scandal (Mark 6:17–29).

At a time when the sanctity of marriage was being denigrated by a widespread flippant attitude toward divorce, Jesus declared what he held to be the Creator's reason for making two human sexes. He thought that scrutinizing the Deuteronomic ordinance was myopic, because the divorce law should be subordinated to the creation principle. Rather than citing the grounds for divorce championed by Shammai, Hillel, or Moses, he directed his interlocutors to the view of marriage recorded in a Genesis story. Significantly, Jesus considered the last word on marriage to be the first word; he appealed to the Garden of Eden story, possibly composed by a woman,[46] which stresses companionship as the reason for marriage (Gen. 2:18). This distinguishes it from the later account, composed by the male priesthood, which focuses on procreation (Gen. 1:28). Jesus' quotation, "The two shall become one flesh," is the climax of an episode celebrating monogamous companionship.

Jesus' focus on spousal unity was not intended to be destructive to individuality. His advocacy of two-in-one matrimony can be compared to his prayer for his disciples in a Jerusalem upper room. When Jesus requested that they "be one" (John 17:21), he was not hoping that their personality differences would become extinguished. Likewise, the marital experience is one of mutual acceptance without absorption into the partner's ego. Each participant becomes aware of ways in which his or her distinctive role enhances the partnership.

After pointing to the ideal of a permanent two-in-one "cleaving," Jesus states that the Torah permitted divorce because of "hardheartedness" (Mark 10:2–9). He probably did not intend to rule out divorce, for he did not think of himself as a new lawgiver. For example, he once refused to adjudicate a legal matter brought to his attention, while pointing to a basic moral malady pertaining to the case (Luke 12:13–15). He diagnosed the marriage-destroying disease as cardiosclerosis (Greek, *sklerocardia*), or hardening of the heart. When this condition persists in one or both spouses, legal controls for divorce are needed. However, Jesus did not find the Mosaic law acceptable. He acknowledged the Roman practice that permitted either spouse to initiate a divorce (Mark 10:10–12). Following Jesus' teachings, Paul writes that a wife may initiate a separation from her husband (1 Cor. 7:10–11).

There is another Gospel teaching that relates to divorce as now practiced. Jesus asks: "Why do you not judge for yourselves what is right?" (Luke 12:57). Recognizing the legal costs and the possibility of judicial penalties for those who threaten lawsuits, out-of-court settlement is advised.

Regarding court cases, Jesus comments: "I tell you, you will never get out until you have paid the last cent" (12:59). Then, as now, the expense of litigation was a consideration not to be taken lightly.

John Riches perceptively treats the way in which Jesus criticized divorce in a nonlegalistic manner:

> His teaching on marriage and divorce should be seen not as introducing harsh regulations to torment the unfortunate, but as emphasizing the potential of the marriage relationship for allowing people to develop deep trust and mutuality. . . . What he was objecting to was the right of a man to dispose of his wife if she offended him.[47]

Forgiveness to the repentant was unflaggingly emphasized by Jesus in all areas of human life. This had been a frequent theme in the Jewish tradition, but it was conveniently associated more with divine acceptance than with the restoration of fellowship among humans. Pleading for God's mercy while sacrificing an animal is less demanding than working patiently to overcome domestic alienation. Jesus was chagrined to find that forgiveness was little considered by the dominating husband for either petty or major domestic offenses. Following Hosea, Jesus believed that even a spouse's infidelity should prompt the desire for reconciliation, not divorce.

Shakespeare's exquisite ode to "the marriage of true minds" contains overtones of Jesus' counsel regarding marital impediments:

> Love is not love
> Which alters when it alteration finds,
> Or bends with the remover to remove:
> O no! It is an ever-fixed mark
> That looks on tempests and is never shaken.
> . . . .
> Love's not Time's fool, though rosy lips and cheeks
> Within his bending sickle's compass come;
> Love alters not with his brief hours and weeks,
> But bears it out even to the edge of doom.[48]

Jesus appealed to what Moore calls the "utopian element" of Jewish ethical teaching.[49] In this and other situations he viewed the conduct of life not in terms of legal requirements, but in terms of fulfilling the categorical moral imperative of love. For those who see the meaning of life from that vantage point, questions about grounds for divorce become trivial. "What God has joined" (Mark 10:9) was Jesus' way of referring to his marital idealism. "Marriages are made in heaven" is a proverb that Jesus and some other rabbis endorsed.[50] In Jewish tradition that providential claim is based on the statement in Genesis 24:50 concerning Isaac's marriage: "The thing proceeds from the Lord."

The discrepancy between Genesis ideals and the law of Moses in Jesus' community parallels the American experience. The laws of the land are occasionally revised, giving fresh applications of the true intent of the broader moral law that stands behind them. If a grievance arises over human rights, statutory law and even interpretations of relevant clauses in the U.S. Constitution may be found to be inadequate. In such a case a person may appeal to a statement of American political morality made before our federal government was begun, and thus to accepted ideals that are not explicitly part of the Constitution. The Declaration of Independence's key sentence affirms that all people are created equal and then declares that a government cannot remove certain rights. The moral priority of the Declaration in the minds of Americans has resulted in broader interpretations of the Constitution and in amendments to it. Likewise, most Christians attempt to follow their founder in reinterpreting Mosaic legislation and doctrine, basing their positions on principles gleaned from the Creation stories of Genesis.[51]

Jesus wanted to go back to the root of legislative codes. Like Thomas Jefferson, he was a radical (from *radix*, root) who aimed at cultivating from early principles a new growth that would be more humanizing. By stating, "All men are created equal," Jefferson was anchoring a theory of natural rights in the Genesis image-of-God doctrine. In the prelegal order of creation, Jesus likewise found the highest standard of sex and marriage. The tacit assumption here is that marriage should not be considered principally a legal contract involving dowry payments, priestly pronouncements, and registered certificates. Rather, the original and final norm for all humans, Jew and Gentile alike, is that marriage is an unconditional, interpersonal covenant witnessed by God (see Mal. 2:14). Jesus did not consider the remedy for a frivolous attitude toward divorce to be new legislation. He was convinced that self-righteous vindictiveness that scorns and abandons is a travesty of divine-human love.

For Jesus, the ethical went far beyond the legal. Scorn, envy, gluttony, miserliness, and ingratitude are among the evils not penalized by law codes. As James Whitcomb Riley's couplet put it: "The meanest man I ever saw / Allus kep' inside o' the law."[52] Jesus recognized that if persons aim no higher than conducting themselves so as not to run afoul of the law, they may never rise above some major vices.

The Afterlife

Jesus' most insightful teaching on life after death was given in response to a *reductio ad absurdum* question pertaining to Torah interpretation. Included in the record of Jesus' last week in Jerusalem is this episode:

> Some Sadducees—who deny that there is a resurrection—came to him and asked this question: "Teacher, Moses prescribed for us that if there are brothers, and one dies leaving a wife but no child, the next must take the widow to have children for his brother's sake. Now there were seven brothers; the first took a wife and died childless. The second took the widow, and he too died childless; it was the same for all seven. Finally the woman died. At the resurrection, when the dead rise to life, whose wife will she be?" (Mark 12:18–23)

Those Sadducees were enraged by Jesus' denunciation of the commercialization of the Temple, which was their source of wealth. Rather than seeking information, they wanted to trap him into advocating publicly an absurd idea. To ridicule the notion that corpses revive and carry on what formerly had been their customary life, the Sadducees added their question to an old Jewish tale. Tobit had told a story of seven husbands dying in succession shortly after marrying the same bride.[53]

The Sadducees recognized that Moses had sanctioned polygyny but not polyandry. A husband could have multiple spouses concurrently, and remarriage of a childless widow to her deceased husband's brother was required (Deut. 25:5). Being strict constructionists with respect to the Law of Moses, the Sadducees found there no basis for an afterlife doctrine. According to Josephus, they believed "the soul perishes with the body and they disregarded the observation of anything except what the Law enjoins."[54]

Jesus' interlocutors presumed that those accepting a resurrection doctrine thought in a literalistic way. The term that is translated "resurrection" in this passage—and elsewhere in the New Testament—is a compound Greek word meaning "up" (*ana*) plus "stand" (*stasis*). Thus, "resurrection of the dead" literally meant the standing up of corpses that had been recumbent. Belief in a reanimation of relics on the day of God's final judgment was popular in apocalyptic Judaism. For example, one apocalypse states: "The earth shall then assuredly restore the dead, which it now receives, in order to preserve them, making no change in their form."[55] This view was probably influenced by the Egyptians, who believed in a physical afterlife in which wives and lands would bear abundantly.[56] Some rabbis assumed that marriage and procreation would continue unchanged in the life after death,[57] but this was denied by others.[58]

Jesus' view of the afterlife differed from the prevailing views of his time. In contrast to the Sadducees, Jesus held that after death there is life, which is based on the nature of God as revealed in the Torah. To those adversaries, Jesus charges: "You know neither the scriptures nor the power of God" (Mark 12:24). He twits them by asking if they have read the "passage about the bush" from a scroll they accepted as the word of God. Jesus then quotes from the burning bush story about God's call to the shepherd Moses: "I am . . . the God of Abraham, the God of Isaac, and the God of Jacob" (Ex. 3:6).

Regarding that verse, Jesus comments: "[God] is not God of the dead, but of the living; you are quite wrong" (Mark 12:27). In these enigmatic and enlightening words, Jesus claims that God, being faithful and powerful, does not permit the covenant he has established to be severed by the physical death of "those who are judged worthy" (Luke 20:35). Hence the present tense—"I *am*" (emphasis added)—was used to prove that the Hebrew patriarchs, who had physically died centuries before the time of Moses, continued to be in a personal relationship with God. To be dead to humans does not necessarily mean to be dead to God, and to be alive to humans does not necessarily mean to be alive to God. In stressing the undying presence of God, Jesus followed the verbal emphasis of an Exodus writer. Moses inquired about God's name and received this disclosure: "Say to the Israelites, 'I AM has sent me . . . the God of Abraham'" (Ex. 3:14–15). Jesus chides the priestly party for lacking a contextual understanding of their scriptures. The Sadducees did not comprehend the way in which the character of the eternal God they professed implied a doctrine of human life continuance.

Contrary to the outlook of the Sadducees' opponents, Jesus believed that the postmortem status is not a revival and extension of physical life. As Colleen McDannell and Bernhard Lang demonstrate: "He challenged both the Sadducean rejection of the afterlife and the apocalyptic expectation of a long life on earth."[59] Jesus affirmed: "When they rise from the dead, men and women do not marry; they are like angels in heaven" (Mark 12:25). One purpose of marriage is removed because "they cannot die any more" (Luke 20:36). Reproduction is needed only in a mortal society, which must replace the perpetually dying in order to avert species extinction.

If all persons are on a par in the afterlife, then the levirate custom of patriarchy that the Sadducees described would be discontinued. Their case denigrated the woman by presuming that she was an object that brother after brother could "take" without her say. Much as a master might give a slave to a relative in a last will, the childless widow was passed on as so much property. She was probably unable to conceive, but each successive male treated her as a pot for planting his "seed." Although the idea was incomprehensible to the Sadducees, Jesus suggested that women were ultimately not possessions subject to transfer by someone else.

Partners enjoy sharing in each other's company quite apart from procreation. Jesus suggested that personal interaction in the afterlife would have a quality similar to that of divine messengers. Angels communicate as spirits in ways mortals find difficult to imagine. The intense communion now widely experienced in marriage could be a distant simulation of the relationships in the transformed heavenly community.

Jesus envisaged an ultimate family that transcends biological and marital ties. He displayed his outlook when his Nazareth family, concerned about his sanity and safety, attempted to take him home. On that occasion Jesus announced that his strongest ties were not with his physical family. He showed fondness for the friends traveling with him in Galilee by saying: "Here are my mother and my brothers! Whoever does the will of God is my brother, and sister, and mother" (Mark 3:21, 31–35). Although "loved ones" are often defined in secular society as spouse, children, parents, siblings, and other kin, Jesus did not think of eternal life companions here or hereafter as primarily one's relatives. He valued those who serve God faithfully more than those bonded solely by blood relationship or marital covenant.

Recent interpreters have discussed the theological significance of Jesus' nonliteral references to his family. According to Evelyn and Frank Stagg, the way Jesus identified his family carries this implication: "Natural ties of flesh, ethnic identity, sexual identity, cultic distinction, etc., are purely secondary and not the basis or criterion for the true family. Personhood and faith/obedience to God are primary and sufficient."[60] Also, Susanne Heine states:

> Jesus continually stresses that the "true" family is represented by those bound together in common conviction and not physical relationship. . . . Inclusiveness and not exclusiveness is the criterion: following Jesus separates one from kinsfolk who do not understand what it is all about. But to be related to someone does not exclude following

Jesus, in so far as these kinsfolk are bound together in common conviction over and above family ties. So among the disciples of Jesus there are the two sons of Zebedee, i.e. brothers.[61]

Temporal as well as spatial considerations are irrelevant in the eternal community. Even as the Hebrew patriarchs are alive to God while long dead to earthlings, so Abraham and his children are in living fellowship with other mortals who lived in a different age. To convey this idea, Jesus pictured a beggar, recently deceased, who is leaning on the "bosom" of Abraham at the heavenly banquet (Luke 16:20–22). Jesus also taught that "many will come from east and west and feast with Abraham, Isaac, and Jacob in the kingdom of heaven" (Matt. 8:11). By extrapolation, the nonbiblical Abrahams and Elizabeths—such as Abraham Lincoln and Elizabeth Cady Stanton—along with the Gandhis of India and the Kings of Georgia, may be among "those who are judged worthy of a place in the other realm" (Luke 20:35). Individuals who once were spread across centuries and continents are together in the timeless celestial community. Fidelity to the will of the divine Host is the glue binding them together.

Two other extrapolations are relevant to Jesus' argument with the Sadducees. Philosopher Geddes Macgregor integrates this teaching on immortality with the progress of earthly love:

Even in this life the relationship of happily married couples does pass eventually from one in which sexual intercourse seems its essence and chief joy to one in which, much later in life, its importance diminishes, and husband and wife are bound together with closer bonds and in an even deeper and surer love than they could have known in their more tempestuous youth.[62]

Carrying on this thought of transmutation of human relationships, Sidney Callahan speculates:

In this life married people can experience through sexuality multidimensioned joy in knowing and loving another; perhaps this exclusive relationship prepares man for an

inclusive love and joy of all in the new life. . . . The ec-
stasy of male-female coupling could be expanded to all
human relationships.[63]

The exchange between Jesus and the Sadducees on the
"resurrection" illustrates the way in which earthbound imaginations pale at intuiting what is outside the realm of experience. Astronomer Carl Sagan has observed the mundane way
in which scientists rely on forms already known as they try to
imagine extraterrestrial life.[64] In a parallel manner, we are
often no more able to envisage what is beyond space and
time than fetuses, living in fluid with closed eyelids, are able
to imagine what it is like to smell stimulating aromas, see
colorful sights, and savor tasty foods. Imagining intelligent
life in another galaxy, or conceiving of fleshless selves
among whom there is personal communication, requires a
radically different mode of thinking. Jesus declares that the
nature of life after death, like the nature of God, transcends
all our conceptions. He suggests to the Sadducees that it is
not less than the happiest life of communal caring and sharing that we can now experience or conceive.[65]

.4.

Jesus as Teacher

His Primary Role

In spite of wide scholarly agreement that "rabbi" is one of the more adequate ways of designating Jesus' historical role,[1] Christians are generally unaccustomed to associating the title rabbi with Jesus. The reason for this is due partly to the New Testament writers and partly to later translators and interpreters. As Jaroslav Pelikan points out, a "de-Judaization" of the gospel set in even before the New Testament was complete.[2]

In Mark, the earliest Gospel, both friend and foe address Jesus as *rabbi* (literally, "my teacher"), an Aramaic word that is untranslated in the original Greek scroll (9:5; 10:51; 11:21; 14:45). *Rabbi* is used twice in Matthew (26:25, 49) and eight times in John (1:38, 49; 3:2; 4:31; 6:25; 9:2; 11:8; 20:16). The title was just being introduced in Judaism, and it did not imply some official ordination.[3] "Rabbi" did express the spontaneous respect given to one who was especially knowledgeable of the Jewish religion and exemplary in its practice. Indeed, the honor of being entitled rabbi was such that Jesus warned his disciples that those so designated could easily become corrupted by haughtiness (Matt. 23:5–12).

Luke describes his Gospel as what Jesus "began both to do and to teach" (Acts 1:1). Yet, in using Mark's writing, he substitutes the term Lord (*kyrios*) or Master (*epistates*) for Rabbi (9:33; 18:41). *Kyrios* means sovereign or boss, and Luke also uses it in reference to Caesar and to the God of Israel (Acts 25:26; Luke 1:6, 9, and elsewhere). *Epistates* refers to a commanding officer in the Septuagint (2 Chron. 31:12;

Jer. 52:25) and only Luke uses it in the New Testament. Neither of those terms conveys the same meaning as *rabbi*, namely, teacher or professor.

All the Gospel writers frequently refer to Jesus by *didaskalos,* the Greek term for teacher. For most of its forty-five usages, Jesus is addressed by others, but several are self-designations. Philo, writing at the time of Jesus, claims that synagogues were essentially schools (*didaskaleia*), so Jesus may occasionally have taught youth there during the weekday in addition to engaging in activity there on the Sabbath.[4]

John's Gospel explains for Gentile readers that *didaskalos* is a proper translation of *rabbi* or *rabboni* (1:38; 20:16). However, what ancient Gentiles would associate with *didaskalos* would be different from scribal dialogue in synagogues. In the Greco-Roman culture, "the most common method of instruction seems to have been the lecture, to which the students listened passively while they took down notes."[5]

Western culture has been heavily influenced by the educational methods and goals of classical times. Becoming an effective speaker was a main aim of education, so rhetoric was emphasized. Through most of the history of Christianity little effort has been made to understand Jewish pedagogy or other distinctive aspects of that culture. With one or two notable exceptions, the church fathers could not even read Hebrew. In medieval times, it was a rare scholastic who had access to rabbinic literature even if he had interest in learning about it.

Translators have often attempted to disguise both the Jewishness of Jesus and his role as teacher. Consequently, few Christians would recognize the founder of their religion by the designation "Rabbi Yeshua." "Jesus" is a European transliteration of the Aramaic *Yeshua,* which, like Joshua, is a shortened form of the Hebrew name *Yehoshua.* The name means one whose salvation is Yahweh, the God of Israel. In the King James Version, both *rabbi* and *didaskalos* are usually translated as "master," a term primarily associated with a schoolmaster in Elizabethan England. But in modern times, especially in the United States, few would associate "master" with either a teacher or a Jewish synagogue instructor. Current American dictionaries show the word "master" as referring to chieftain, slaveowner, or controller—inappropriate designations for Jesus. The Revised Standard Version retained "master" in dealing with Mark's use of *rabbi*, while properly translating *didaskalos* as "teacher." The Jerusalem Bible and the New Revised Standard Version have, at last, returned to the original Aramaic word, so Jesus is addressed as rabbi.

Christians frequently overlook the fact that Jesus was most commonly known as a teacher and so emphasize other titles. William Barclay wrote a book containing forty-two chapters, each dealing with one New Testament title for Jesus, but none was devoted to Jesus as rabbi/teacher.[6] In Christian history, "Savior" has been one of the most common titles for designating Jesus. Although it is used once in the Christmas story (Luke 2:11) and once in the account of Jesus and the Samaritan woman (John 4:42), Jesus is never directly addressed as "Savior" in the Gospels. "Redeemer" is also a frequent designation for Jesus in churches, even though this appellation for God in the Hebrew Bible is not used at all in the New Testament. "Christ" is so often used for Jesus that most presume it was his proper name (or his last name!), rather than a title meaning "Messiah." Actually, Jesus may never have used the designation himself.

Christians often think of Jesus as a preacher or as an evangelist, who specialized in sermonic monologue. However, he is never addressed in the Gospels as preacher (*keryx*) or as evangelist (*euaggelistes*), even though he proclaimed the gospel. When announcing the gospel, Jesus used an Aramaic term similar to the Greek *metanoeite* (Matt. 4:17; Luke 13:5). That imperative means "change [*meta*] your mind [*nous*]," a characteristic interest in teachers. Plato, one of the most outstanding teachers in history, had emphasized that education should be a kind of conversion experience that redirects students' minds. After turning from identifying reality with the flow of sensations, Plato hoped they would grasp ideas that transcend sense experience which would improve their moral actions.[7]

A good illustration of what Jesus meant by mental change that impacts moral decision making is found in his story of the prodigal son. After the boy goes to the dogs and lives with the hogs he thinks of another way to live. Recognizing his self-destructive behavior, he resolves to pursue a more mature course of action. Asking for forgiveness for past conduct is secondary to reflecting on his situation and setting out to change his life (Luke 15:11–21).

Metanoeite is generally poorly translated in the stories of both Jesus and John the Baptist as "repent" or, in the traditional Roman Catholic version, by the cognate expression, "do penance." To do penance is to undergo punishment imposed by the clergy. The English verb "repent" comes from the Latin *re*, "again," and *paenitens*, "sorry." "Repentance" means feeling regretful for past conduct, which is not the same as changing one's life for the better. The term is often given not only a negative meaning but also a heavily emotional connotation by contemporary evangelists who insist that sinners repent. Assuaging guilt was viewed by Jesus and by John the Baptist as secondary to setting out on a different road. The Latin and English versions for the past sixteen centuries have obscured the fact that Jesus hoped for a fundamental transformation of the mind, which he regarded as the seat of the personality.

Jesus' main role is not disclosed in most standard reference works. One would be unable to guess that he was a rabbi from the lengthy encyclopedia articles entitled "Jesus" by Jesuit Gerald O'Collins or by Jewish scholar David Flusser.[8] When interpreters do recognize Jesus' teaching role, they rarely indicate that it may be the best handle for understanding who he was. Clarifying exceptions include New Testament scholars Leander Keck and Thomas Manson. Keck begins his "Jesus" article with this lead: "Palestinian preacher and rabbi, regarded by many Jews as a great teacher. . . ."[9] Manson states accurately and succinctly: "The two most certain facts in the gospel tradition are that Jesus taught and that he was crucified."[10]

His Methods

In his classic *Art of Teaching*, Gilbert Highet discusses three essentials of a good teacher: comprehension of the subject matter, eagerness to impart it, and love of the students. In this regard, Highet singles out Jesus as one of the most exemplary as well as "the most famous teacher of the Western world."[11] At a number of places in the following discussion the second and third "essential" are illustrated. With respect to the first, Jesus displayed a thorough knowledge of the authoritative writings of his culture. His precocity as a youth amazed scholars in Jerusalem (Luke 2:46–47). When he came to Capernaum, the synagogue-goers were struck by the power of his teaching (Mark 1:21–22). Whereas the scribes tended to quote previous rabbinical interpretations of the Mosaic law, Jesus spoke with the freshness of an original thinker. He had a vital firsthand awareness not only of the Hebrew scriptures but also of the central Person described therein. Knowing in depth who and what he was talking about, he commanded more attention than the usual Sabbath interpreter.

Another test of a good teacher is to take unexceptional youth and enable them to think and act on their own. Jesus' disciples were a challenge to a teacher's mettle, because they were a mediocre lot. None were selected because of outstanding aptitude, and all were slow in catching on to his new ideas. Luke reports repeatedly these words of Jesus to his disciples: "Let these words sink into your ears: the Son of man is going to be handed over to powerful people" (9:44–45; 18:31–34). Those among "the Twelve" who later became most noteworthy were unrefined fishermen before joining his band. Two of them, James and John, Jesus jestingly nicknamed "thunderboys" (Mark 3:17). Demonstrating their explosive bigotry, these brothers once wanted lightning to strike some inhospitable Samaritans (Luke 9:51–55). There was also Matthew the tax collector, probably an unpatriotic Jew, and Simon the Zealot, probably a fanatical nationalist (Luke 6:15). According to early Christian tradition, these and most of the other disciples became prominent leaders.

What instructional techniques did Jesus use with his men and women followers? Unlike many instructors in modern educational institutions, where there is little informal contact with students, Jesus lived with his disciples. They camped with him in places less commodious than animal stalls (Matt. 8:20). He sailed with them through storm and calm; they walked together up hills and down valleys; and they worshiped together outdoors and in synagogues. In those various settings they were able to learn from Jesus' example as well as from his word. They could daily test his genuineness by seeing whether he "practiced what he preached" (Matt. 23:3), to borrow his expression. Jesus' warning about accumulating treasures (Luke 12:33–34) was appreciated when disciples realized that he never collected an offering for himself. His injunction to "bless those who curse you, pray for those who abuse you" (Luke 6:28) was no doubt more honored after he prayed from the cross for forgiveness of his cruel and dishonest persecutors (Luke 23:34).

The Gospel teachings were given in many places: on a journey, a boat, or a hillside; in a home, a synagogue, or the Temple. Whenever and wherever an interested crowd gathered, however small or large, Jesus' instruction was prompted by the situation. One example of this is when Jesus, while walking beside the Sea of Galilee, noticed Simon and Andrew catching fish. The Gospel of Mark states: "Jesus said to them, 'Come with me and I will teach you to fish for people'" (1:17). Those fishermen may have come to associate patience and inconspicuousness as qualities needed for effectiveness in either endeavor. Again, while Jesus was commenting on another subject, "a woman in the crowd shouted, 'Blessed is the mother who bore you and nursed you!' He replied, 'Blessed rather are those who hear the word of God and obey it!'" (Luke 11:27–28). Thus, Jesus brushed aside sentimental Madonna adoration and brought his listeners back to an awareness of more difficult duties.

Jesus did not think of truth as an injection from the outside, but as a discovery arising from within. This is well displayed in an episode pertaining to John the Baptist. On seeing Jesus at the Jordan, John exclaimed, "Behold, the Lamb of God, who takes away the sin of the world!" (John 1:29). John thought Jesus would be a combative person, quickly separating out and burning the worthless "chaff" (Luke 3:16–17). Later, from his prison cell, John wonders if he had been too hasty in his earlier judgment (Luke 7:18–23). He may have reflected: If Jesus is a ruler like David, why doesn't he overthrow King Herod, who unjustly incarcerated me? Therefore, John sends two of his disciples to Jesus with this question: "Are you the one who is to come, or should we expect someone else?" Rather than answer the question directly, Jesus invites the messengers from John to observe aspects of his ministry. Jesus was rehabilitating the marginalized, recovering for them a place in society. He realizes that an inference about his mission by skeptical inquirers that is based on observed data is more convincing than a dogmatic personal assertion.

Jesus hopes that after those disciples have reported back on their findings, John will conclude that his activities show him to be fulfilling Isaiah's prophecy (Isa. 35:5–6; 61:1–2), as he claimed in his announcement at the beginning of his ministry (Luke 4:18). Jesus was also probably attempting to convey that he, unlike John, was emphasizing the mercy rather than the wrath of God. Moreover, evil was to be overcome in a gradual manner, rather than the sudden manner of John's preconceptions.

After the deputation from John has left, Jesus uses bantering questions to get a crowd to think about John's significance. He asks: "What did you go out into the wilderness to behold? A reed waving in the wind?" The people respond in the negative, knowing that John would not be in prison if he had been easily swayed, bending with every political pressure. Jesus then asks if they had been attracted to the Judean wasteland by a royal dude parading in gorgeous and stylish clothing. Again, the amused people know that the ascetic preacher wore a rough camel-hide garment and that his diet was locusts and wild honey, not wine and fatted calf (Mark 1:6; Luke 7:33). While satirizing the spineless and luxurious Herodian royalty who were punishing John, the Galilean teacher leads the crowd in eliminating options. Jesus reinforces the crowd's picture of John as a rugged prophet with an important mission (Luke 7:24–28).

Jesus characteristically raised questions to stimulate decision making. For example, when contrasting insolence but obedience with courtesy and disobedience in a family situation, he skillfully used an introductory and concluding question:

> What do you think about this? A man had two sons. He went to the first and said, "Son, go and work in the vineyard today." He replied, "I will not"; but later he changed

his mind and went. Meanwhile, the father went to the other son and made the same request. He replied, "Certainly, sir," but did not go. Which son did as his father wished? (Matt. 21:28–31)

Jesus' concluding question was to elicit a personal decision to emphasize the performance of duty rather than the profession of devotion. From teachings elsewhere, it is obvious that Jesus hoped his disciples would discern that actions speak louder than words in human relationships. Saying "Lord, Lord," however respectfully, is worthless if there is no corresponding action in accordance with the Father's will (Matt. 7:21). Conversely, a person with a liturgy of raw profanity may live a life of loving service.

The persistence of inquiry as a mode of instruction in rabbinical history has given rise to this story: "Rabbi, why do you always answer my question with a question?" "What's wrong with asking questions?" responds the rabbi, always eager to get the student to think independently. The vigorous debate often precipitated by this approach is conveyed by the saying, "When two rabbis argue, there will be three opinions." Out of the opposing positions of the interlocutors, a more creative solution may emerge. Arthur Green, a rabbinical college president, told me of a way for distinguishing Judaism from some other form of religiosity. First, he noted a bumper sticker popular with Christian fundamentalists: "God said it, I believe it, that settles it." Rabbi Green commented that his tradition could accept this slogan if "now, let's discuss it" replaced the last clause. Scriptural texts are revered in Judaism but students are encouraged to explore multiple meanings through dialogue with a mentor.

Even as Jesus learned as a boy through combining questioning with listening, so he encouraged the same among the curious who came out to observe him. Accordingly, he told them a story about different kinds of soils, symbolizing types of people. The sower's seed, representing sound teaching, was wasted on the hard, the shallow, and the crowded soil. The sower's effort was made worthwhile, however, by a fourth type of soil: "The seed that fell in good soil stands for those who hear the message and retain it in an honest and generous mind and, with patience, become productive." While telling this story, Jesus urged: "You have ears, so listen! . . . Take care how you hear" (Luke 8:4–18). Jesus seemed to realize that only a small fraction of the crowds that often surrounded him would attain any depth of understanding of his mission. He believed that his effort was made worthwhile, however, by the few who would listen to his teaching and act accordingly.

The neglect throughout history of developing listening sensitivity is probably the reason sages have transmitted this ancient proverb: "We have two ears and one tongue because listening is twice as needed as speaking." There is no record of Jesus telling his disciples of the importance of speaking persuasively, but he did emphasize the need for auditory openness. Although Jesus was known as an accomplished speaker (John 7:46), he knew that the effectiveness of communication depended more on the receptivity of the audience than on the eloquence of the speaker. Jesus realized, as is now generally recognized, that the impact of words is mainly determined by the degree to which the art of listening has been cultivated. In the Hebrew tradition, attentive listening for the divine was considered a means for obtaining a revelation (e.g., Prov. 8:34; Jer. 13:15–17).

Jesus exemplified his teachings in concrete form by the use of material objects. In this regard, a saying of Confucius has been associated with Jesus. Highet observes:

> Like all great teachers he knew that a picture is worth a thousand words and that people learn most quickly by doing something or seeing something done. . . . The last lesson he taught his pupils before his arrest was the ritual of sharing a meal of bread and wine, to which he gave a deep and deathless meaning.[12]

The fleshy tone of bread and the bloody color of wine were not the only memory devices Jesus used at the Last Supper. At that table fellowship he also illustrated in a dramatic manner his central vocation, hoping to end the dispute among his disciples over who should be regarded as the greatest. He had earlier declared: "The Son of man did not come to be waited on, but to wait on others" (Mark 10:45).

There in a Jerusalem upstairs room he asserted: "Let the senior among you become like the junior, and the leader like one who serves. Who is more important, the diner or the waiter? Is it not the one who reclines at dinner? Yet here am I among you as one who serves" (Luke 22:26–27). To show in a simple manner that self-giving should replace self-seeking, Jesus engaged in a splendid bit of symbolism. He wrapped a towel around his waist, poured water into a basin, and washed his disciples' feet (John 13:3–5).

On an earlier occasion Jesus also used a simple but unforgettable demonstration to make the same point. When he realized that his dense disciples were arguing among themselves over which one was the most important, he used a visual aid that seared their memories. "He put a child in the midst of them" and said, "Whoever wants to be first must be last of all" (Mark 9:33–36). No wonder the apostles later emphasized that Jesus was a lowly servant (Acts 3:13, 26; 4:27; Phil. 2:7).

Another dramatic use of a visual aid was in Jesus' response to a touchy question by Pharisees about tax payment. Ever since Jesus was a boy, when there was an insurrection over the issue, the Jewish people had been polarized over submission to Roman assessments. Jesus asked those who had set up this entrapment to produce a coin and then to describe the inscription on it. By admitting that Caesar's image was there, they came to see the coinage as evidence of the Romans' legitimate involvement in the government and the economy of Judea. Jesus thought the Romans deserved some compensation for services rendered, so taxes could be paid without compromising one's ultimate devotion to God (Mark 12:13–17).

Word pictures were also used by Jesus to concretize his ideas. Here are some figures of speech from common life: "You are the salt of the earth" (Matt. 5:13). That metaphor would have been even more meaningful before the advent of refrigeration and canning, for salt was necessary to preserve meat. The disciples, though few in number, could visualize themselves as an ingredient for keeping society from rotting, even as a little salt can preserve fish. Some of the disciples also remembered that Jesus pictured them as "lambs amid wolves" (Luke 10:3). For a shepherd people this warning could be related to numerous dangerous situations. Or consider another striking figure in the Gospels. Jesus described a typical baking scene when a woman put a bit of yeast in the bread dough. Like God's reign, the yeast works silently to transform what it permeates (Luke 13:20–21).

Out of the complexity of the human situation, and to fix images in the memory, Jesus sometimes suggested connections between ideas that the mind classifies as logical opposites. He talked about a merry fellow who had been dead, about the dead who do physical labor, and about the famous who are infamous (Luke 6:26; 9:60; 15:32). The last of these paradoxes is well rendered in modern English by Phillips's translation: "Everyone who sets himself up as somebody will become a nobody, and the man who makes himself nobody will become somebody" (Luke 18:14). By pointing to truth in apparent contradictions, Jesus made his students aware that neatly defined words often do not fit real-life situations.

Jesus' most profound paradox was about losers who are winners and successful people who have lost themselves. He asserted: "Those who play it safe will be lost, but those who lose their life for me and the gospel will save it. What will they gain by winning the whole world at the cost of their true self? What can they offer in exchange for their life?" (Mark 8:35–37). The greatest discovery ever made may be contained in those words about commitment. Albert Schweitzer tells of being haunted by this teaching while enjoying the stimulus of Victorian Europe. A brilliant scholar, Schweitzer decided to absorb himself in a worthwhile task unrelated to climbing the usual success ladder. He sacrificed a genteel life to become a physician in equatorial Africa. He found that "direct service of humanity" gave him more "inward happiness."[13] Jewish psychiatrist Viktor Frankl paraphrases Jesus' wisdom when he writes that a person "finds himself only to the extent to which he loses himself in the first place, be it for the sake of a cause of a fellowman, or 'for God's sake.'" While in Nazi imprisonment, Frankl came to realize that individuals achieve psychic freedom by risking themselves in expressing love toward others.[14]

Learning by doing was another principle of Jesus' teaching. The twelve disciples were sent out on a training expedition "two by two," to provide mutual support. While spreading the gospel and assisting in healing, they were to travel light and stay wherever welcomed (Mark 6:7–13). Seventy other disciples, who may have been married couples, were sent out in pairs for the same purpose (Luke 10:1–9).

After the twelve disciples returned exhausted from their practice ministry in the Galilean villages, Jesus departed with them to a restful place (Mark 6:30–31). Combining leisure with work was part of his rhythm of life. Retreating with the disciples to the highlands, Jesus tested them informally on what they had learned about him and his mission. In response to his question about how people evaluated him, the disciples reported that some of his crowd of followers thought of him as a prophet like Elijah or John the Baptist. Jesus then asks the more penetrating question, regarding the disciples' understanding. Peter innovatively responds by calling Jesus the long-awaiting Messiah (Mark 8:27–29).

Jesus' intimate association with his students enabled him to discern potentiality and inspire confidence. With bifocal vision, he saw not only present weaknesses but also distant possibilities. In this regard, Walter Brueggemann—in his study of Hebrew wisdom literature entitled *In Man We Trust*—detects a similarity between Jesus and some of the Israelite sages. "He had high expectations toward those with whom he had to deal," Brueggemann observes. "Indeed, the whole notion of the depravity of man seems to be informed by a cultural situation much different from that of Jesus."[15]

An example of Jesus' faith in a particular disciple is provided in the New Testament. Confident that Simon, who had a temperament as shifting as sand, could become firm, Jesus renamed him Cephas—meaning "rock." His belief in Simon supplied the cement to accomplish this sand-to-concrete transformation. Jesus' encouragement enabled him to replace an inadequate self-image with a more productive one. Episodes about Cephas (or "Peter," as transliterated from Greek) confirm that this vascillating person, who made rash promises but easily caved in under pressure (Matt. 16:16–23; 26:35, 69–75), became sturdy in conviction and courageous in life-threatening situations (Acts 4:13–21; 5:27–42).

Duplicity was the personal weakness Jesus deplored the most, especially in potential teachers. Those who do not integrate thought and action are unable to inspire others for long. He noted much masquerading in real life. Some might be said to be sheep in wolves' clothing, pretending to be more devilish than they really were. Perhaps because of peer pressure, they were afraid to expose the "light" of God within. Jesus likened this disposition to hiding a flaming lamp under a bowl and thereby destroying its purpose. He thought that those with spiritual awareness should authentically display it in the dark world. This light should not glare, calling attention to itself and making it harder for others to see. Rather, Jesus taught, the illumination from those who are "the light of the world" should cause those helped by it to give God the glory (Matt. 5:14–16).

There are also those who disguise themselves "in sheep's clothing but inwardly are ravenous wolves" (Matt. 7:15). If we can judge by the amount of attention Jesus gave to such duplicity, he must have thought it was more pervasive than sheep masquerading as wolves. He warned:

> Beware of the scriptural interpreters, who like to walk about in long robes and be greeted respectfully in public. They like the best seats in the synagogues and the places of honor at banquets. They conceal their devouring of widows' property by offering lengthy prayers! (Mark 12:38–40)

Rabbi Gamaliel held that every day the Eighteen Benedictions should be prayed.[16] This main prayer of the synagogue is over one thousand words in English, and devout men prayed it three times a day. For some, Jesus observed, profuse solemn noises mask unethical behavior.

Largely because of Jesus, the word hypocrite has come to refer to a two-faced character. In classical Greece the term described stage actors who wore masks as they made different impersonations. The Greeks, who invented the European theater, admired skilled pretenders and gave prizes to good *hypokrites*. Among the Hellenistic Jews, the term developed a negative connotation, meaning a deceitful person.[17] For Jesus, a hypocrite was a person who playacts, consciously or unconsciously. In real-life drama the person's external religious garb cloaks greed and grudges. Jesus indicts frauds in a colorful manner:

Woe to you, scribes and Pharisees, hypocrites! You wash
the outside of cup and bowl, and leave the inside full of
violence and selfishness. . . . You are like whitewashed
tombs, which outwardly appear beautiful, but within are
full of bones of the dead and every kind of corruption.
(Matt. 23:25, 27)

Disgust is mingled with amusement as Jesus tells of religious leaders who carefully scrub and polish their exteriors
in order to enhance their public image while overlooking
their contaminated inner sanctums. Jesus asks: "Did not the
one who made the outside make the inside also?" (Luke
11:40).

Regarding group activity, Jesus observed that communities construct lavish memorials to individuals they would despise if they were still living (Matt. 23:29–31). Fyodor
Dostoevsky paraphrases Jesus' irony: "Men reject their
prophets and slay them, but they love their martyrs and
honor those whom they have slain."[18] For example, civic
officials may dedicate public constructions and establish a
national holiday to commemorate Martin Luther King, Jr.,
while failing to apply the principles of social justice for
which he died.

His Parables

Regarding the way Jesus taught, two Gospels state: "He
did not speak to the crowds without a parable" (Mark 4:34;
Matt. 13:34). Although this general statement may be an exaggeration, it does emphasize his most characteristic way of
instructing. Jesus used parables to get down to earth—to re-
late theology to everyday affairs. His parables have been
long defined as "earthly stories with heavenly meanings."
That old definition is incomplete, because parables provide
profound insight into human nature as well as divine nature.

Some of the dozens of parables in the Synoptic Gospels
are merely one-sentence similes that compare religious concerns with common Palestinian experiences. The saying,
"The kingdom of God is like the mustard seed," is the core

of a parable (Mark 4:30–32), and its meaning is that important enterprises grow from small beginnings. More intriguing are some of the brief narrative parables. The wisdom and wit of Jesus can be well illustrated by looking at a representative sampling of these stories.

In one parable Jesus exposes the self-centeredness of a praying person (Luke 18:9–14). The moral is stated at the outset: "He told this parable to [*pros*] some who trusted in themselves because they were righteous and despised others." Jesus first tells of a Pharisee who went up to the Jerusalem Temple and "prayed to [*pros*] himself." The hearer of the parable is informed that the Pharisee was unaware that he was actually indulging in self-congratulation. A prayer, unlike a soliloquy, should be addressed to another being who is recognized as superior. Even though the Pharisee may have thought he was magnifying the name of God, he was really patting himself on the back and boasting to others in the Temple who might hear him. According to Jesus, he "exalted himself," thereby substituting an idolatrous creature object for proper worship. By contrast, the tax collector, who went at the same time to the Temple to pray, humbly asked God to have mercy on his sinful self. His body language conveyed his attitude: in an inconspicuous place he lowered his eyes and beat on his chest.

Richard Crashaw, the celebrated English poet, has sharpened the comic contrast:

> Two went to pray? Oh, rather say
> One went to brag, the other to pray.
> One stands up close and treads on high
> Where the other dares not send his eye.
> One nearer to God's altar trod,
> The other to the altar's God.[19]

Most translators fail to convey the dramatic irony. The preposition *pros* means "directed toward," as illustrated in the introduction to the parable. But some translators prefer to be unfaithful to the original rather than have Jesus state an absurdity. Even though the parable informs us that the Pharisee had gathered with others for group worship, *Today's*

English Version and the New Revised Standard Version have him privately praying "by himself." The *New American Bible* has him praying silently "within himself." However, Luke uses different pronouns to express "by himself" or "within himself" (e. g., Acts 28:16; Luke 18:4).

The Pharisee confesses his virtues: "God, I thank you that I am not like everyone else: greedy, dishonest, or adulterous—or like this tax collector. I fast twice a week and I tithe on everything I get." He makes a point of his supererogation, knowing that fasting was required only on the annual Day of Atonement and that tithing was limited to farm products (Lev. 23:26; 27:30–33). The pronoun "I" is the key word of this "prayer," but the Pharisee is unaware of his "I" problem. As it is repeated five times, it is apparent who is most in the Pharisee's consciousness. By contrast, in the Lord's Prayer—which Jesus offered as a model—the pronouns are plural: "our" and "us" (Matt. 6:9–13). From his stance as a perfect being, the Pharisee arrogates to himself the right to judge whoever is nearby.

Jesus' sketch of the Pharisee is not altogether derisory. As a skilled humorist, Jesus presents generally admired qualities to establish a reluctant identification among his listeners. Presumably the Pharisee was not insincere when he claimed to live by standards set down in the Ten Commandments. Moreover, to attend a place of public worship and to give generously of one's income are considered commendable in any culture. What minister would not be pleased to have members who give one tenth of their income to religious causes!

The moral achievements of the Pharisee resulted in contentment toward himself and contempt toward others. He has a "holier than thou" outlook—to use an expression from the King James Version (Isa. 65:5). He smugly recalls how much better he is than a nearby tax collector, and for his superiority he "thanks" God. Having no awareness of personal faults, he does not ask for forgiveness or for improvement.

E. P. Sanders rightly warns against taking Jesus' anecdotes about Pharisees as a general factual description.[20] Surely he did not think the *typical* Pharisee despised others, was unaware of his sins, and "prayed" to himself any more than he thought that the typical tax collector was a man of sincere prayer and humility. The prayer of the tax collector, "God, be merciful to me, a sinner," could be found on the lips of many honest Pharisees. Warning against arrogance and censoriousness, they generally evaluated behavior the way Jesus does at the conclusion of this parable.[21] They, like Jesus, were influenced by the scriptural advice against seeking prominence (Prov. 25:6–7; Luke 14:7–11). The Mishnah countered spiritual pride by advising, "Trust not in yourself."[22] The Talmud states: "The school of Hillel teaches you that he who humbles himself the Lord raises up, and he who exalts himself the Lord humbles; greatness flees him who seeks greatness; greatness may follow him who flees from greatness." However, the Talmud approves of this egocentric prayer:

> I thank you, O Lord, my God, that you have set my lot with those who sit in the house of learning, and not with those who sit at the streetcorners. I and they rise early—I to the words of the Torah, but they to things of no account. I and they labor, but I labor and receive a reward while they labor and receive no reward. I and they run—I to the life of the world to come, but they to the pit of destruction.[23]

Jesus' parable of a Pharisee at prayer is similar to a poem by Robert Burns. "Holy Willie's Prayer" caricatures the leadership of Scotland's dominant church. Highet considers it an expansion of the prayer parody in Luke 18.[24] Willie briefs God on the uprightness of the pray-er and expresses contempt toward Gavin Hamilton. That Presbyterian elder is convinced that he is one of God's chosen and that Hamilton—a friend of Burns—has committed unpunished sins. Burns's estimation of Willie is transparent in this prayer excerpt:

> O Thou, wha in the Heavens dost dwell, . . .
> Sends one to heaven and ten to hell . . .
> I bless and praise thy matchless might, . . .
> That I am here afore thy sight, . . .
> A burnin' an' a shinin' light to a' this place.

O Lord, thou kens what zeal I bear,
When drinkers drink, and swearers swear. . . .
Lord, mind Gaw'n Hamilton's deserts;
He drinks, an' swears, an' plays at cartes. . . .

But, Lord, remember me and mine
Wi' mercies temp'ral and divine, . . .
And a' the glory shall be thine, Amen, Amen!

Humorless Willie, oozing with contempt, might have been among that 90 percent bound for hell! C. S. Lewis, the consummate English writer, describes hell as "a state where everyone is perpetually concerned about his own dignity and advancement, where everyone has a grievance, and where everyone lives the deadly serious passions of envy, self-importance and resentment."[25]

Jesus introduced the idea that truly good people have such humility that, unlike the Willies of all times, they are unaware of doing good. In a reinforcing parable he commends those who are unself-conscious with regard to their goodness when they perform acts of mercy for the hungry, thirsty, strangers, naked, sick, and imprisoned (Matt. 25:37–40).

In discussing prayer, Jesus told twin parables containing whimsical wit to illustrate the effectiveness of persistence in various undertakings of life. In one of them he asks if any have had the embarrassing experience of going to a friend's house in the middle of the night to borrow food to feed a late-arriving, hungry guest. Even though the whole neighboring family has retired, the father grumpily responds, not for friendship's sake but just to stop the banging on his door (Luke 11:5–8).

The second parable is about a town magistrate who is unfit for his office. A widow, too poor to provide a bribe, keeps pleading with him for protection from a man who is trying to ruin her. As Jesus puts it: "For a while the judge refused; but afterward he said to himself, 'Though I care nothing for God or man, yet because this widow pesters me, I will uphold her rights. Otherwise she may come and beat me up!'" (Luke 18:4–5). The badgered judge probably savored this sexist Hebrew proverb: "A continual dripping on a rainy day and a contentious woman are alike; to restrain her is to restrain the wind" (Prov. 27:15–16).

Jesus hoped his disciples would discern both a similarity and a contrast in those two parables, between making requests of God and making requests of humans. The similarity is contained in his concluding word of encouragement to the first parable: "Keep knocking and the door will be opened" (Luke 11:10). The heavenly Father answers prayer like a good earthly parent, Jesus believed. He asks: "Is there anyone among you who, if your child asks for a fish, will give a snake instead? Or if a child asks for an egg, will give a scorpion?" (vs. 11–12).

What is the contrast in the parables between petitioning God and petitioning humans? God is neither like a sleepy household head who does not want to be bothered nor like a corrupt judge who has no interest in ethical decision making. Regarding the latter story, Jesus said: "Will not God grant justice to his people who appeal to him day and night? Will he delay long his help? I tell you, he will vindicate them quickly" (Luke 18:7–8).

Neil Fisher uses the unjust judge story to illustrate the way in which parables are like jokes. He comments: "One function of a good joke is to present life's discontinuities, its dislocations and indignities, in such a manner that the tension caused by them is relieved. To 'get' the joke is to enter into the situation and experience the relief of laughter."[26]

Nearly half of Jesus' parables pertain to the use and abuse of riches. He has more to say about the psychology of wealth than about prayer or faith, probably because he recognized how closely monetary considerations are woven into the everyday living of most people. Human foibles are nakedly revealed in attitudes held toward possessions. Humor is the homage that Jesus pays to those who are addicted to piling up perishables. Dudley Zuver observes: "The attitude of Jesus toward the rich was never that of envy, never condemnation, but rather that mild sort of rebuke which follows close upon the heels of amusement."[27]

Jesus was aware of the charm of success stories. For example, among the beloved Hebrew patriarchs immigrant Abraham became "very rich" and Joseph rose from a penniless prisoner to a position of power and affluence (Gen. 13:2; 40–41). However, Jesus surprises his listeners by describing one successful person and then calling him a fool. In three sentences he graphically paints the values of an agribusinessman:

> The land of a rich man produced bountifully; so he thought to himself, "What shall I do, for I have nowhere to store my crops? I know what I will do: I will tear down my barns and build bigger ones, where I can store my grain and all my other goods. Then I can say to myself, Man, you have great wealth laid up for years to come; relax, eat, drink, and be merry!" (Luke 12:16–19)

Jesus told that story to illustrate that "an abundance of things does not give a person true life" (Luke 12:15). The hoarder thought he possessed things, but in actuality things possessed him. Jesus viewed a person who was controlled by the "tyranny of things"—to use an expression of Thoreau— as literally ridiculous (from the Latin verb, *ridere*, to laugh). As with the Pharisee in the Temple, the profuse repetitions of "I" and "my" pronouns display an adult who has retained infantile self-centeredness. If the rich fool prayed, it was "Give *me* this day *my* daily bread." He was unappreciative of Moses' judgment that "one does not live by bread alone" (Deut. 8:3), and he did not respond to Isaiah's advice: "Share your bread with the hungry" (Isa. 58:7). In his obsession, he had come to believe that a person lives by grain and the security that surplus grain can provide.

In Western culture, "Eat, drink, and be merry," has long been celebrated by hedonists as the end-all of life. The expression originated in the book of Ecclesiastes of the Hebrew Bible. There a philosopher, searching for meaning in human experience, finds no abiding satisfaction in increasing knowledge, or in dissipated affluence, or in religious enthusiasm (1:17–18; 2:1–9; 5:1–2). However, several things are repeatedly commended: "There is nothing better for people under the sun than to eat, drink, and be merry" (8:15; cf. 2:24; 3:13; 5:18). Although Jesus was not a hedonist, he approved of finding simple enjoyment in life, and he frequently referred positively to feasting. His tacit criticism in the rich-fool parable pertained to putting first things first. As regards the ancient Jewish philosopher with epicurean tendencies, Jesus recognized the loss to human potential when the proximate good of eating food and having fun are erected as ultimate goals.

Jesus' story of the rich fool concludes with the observation that those who pile up perishables tend to forget that they will soon leave it all behind at death. By means of a negative example, Jesus is expressing profound wisdom that eludes those who are driven by economic values. His conclusion is in sync with a reflection of philosopher George Santayana: "To see life, and to value it, from the point of view of death is to see and value it truly. . . . It is far better to live in the light of the tragic fact, rather than to forget or deny it, and build everything on a fundamental lie."[28]

Luke follows the parable of the rich fool with Jesus' teaching on the peril of equating the good life with having things. Being absorbed in one's possessions, far from increasing the span of one life, increases stress and hastens death. In contrast to the squirrel-like rich fool, the wise person is like the ravens: "they neither sow nor reap, they have neither storehouse nor barn, and yet God feeds them" (12:24). Birds are not an example of idleness, for few animals work harder for the necessities of life. They neither wait in their nests for food to be tossed in nor seem to worry about the supply of food running out.

Estate building is self-deceptive, Jesus believed, because it tends to increase anxieties rather than security. A person who is obsessed over possessions comes to identify core values with them. Natural deterioration or thieves or other creatures may destroy what is stored. The cure for being consumed with personal property is immersing oneself in causes associated with the rule of God. Psychic wellness can come through sublimation; excessive tensions can be released by participation in more significant activities. Investing surplus wealth in altruistic endeavors is recommended, "for your heart is where your treasure is" (Luke 12:29–34).

Luke 16 focuses on other parables pertaining to wealth. First there is a story of a business manager who is given a discharge notice because of wastefulness. Having no muscles for manual labor and being too proud to beg, he comes up with a scheme for providing himself with income after his employment ends. He decides to take advantage of the days remaining on the job to make those indebted to his firm grateful to him. He shrewdly falsifies the records so that promissory notes in particular accounts are greatly reduced. The manager presumes the clients are also unethical and will provide him a kickback for rigging the books. The story ends with a reversal of expectations. When the boss finds out what that swindler has done, he commends him for his resourcefulness in using present opportunities for his future welfare.

Jesus' listeners must have wondered why he would tell such a story. Surely it was not to encourage embezzlement and engaging in scams. Jesus chose this story as a way to intrigue the people into hearing well his exhortation for planning ahead. Prudence was the one admirable quality in the crooked manager. Those lacking this virtue, Jesus once pointed out, do such foolish things as laying the foundation for a building they cannot afford to complete (Luke 14:28–30).

By contrast, Jesus lamented, otherworldly "children of light" are shortsighted in the pursuit of good goals. The ethical issue raised in the parable can be put in contemporary terms: Why are the pious often reluctant to take long-range practical steps to deal with issues affecting the future of humanity, such as the grave effect of environmental pollution? "Good people" are often naive and without forethought that is crucial to their own future, thinking that God will make everything turn out well, even without their cooperation. The false dichotomy between being moral and being prudent is conveyed in a line of poetry expressive of Victorian Christianity: "Be good, sweet maid, and let who will be clever."[29] But Jesus combines the two qualities in saying: "Be shrewd as snakes but harmless as doves" (Matt. 10:16).

The parable of the dishonest manager is followed by an evaluation of *mammon*, the Aramaic word for money personified as a deity. Money-theism—to coin a term—is the idolatry that concerned Jesus. He said: "No one can belong to two masters: a servant will either despise the one and love the other. . . . You cannot serve both God and Money" (Luke 16:13). Money-grubbers sneered at Jesus' analysis of their neurosis (v. 14). The best picture of the impossibility of giving absolute loyalty to two different powers is found in a scroll uncovered in Egypt in 1945. The *Gospel of Thomas* contains what may be an authentic saying of Jesus: "It is as impossible to serve two masters as to ride two horses at once."[30]

Adapting Jesus' barbed wit, Washington Irving and Mark Twain attacked the unrestrained capitalists of their day. America is not a godless society, Irving sardonically mused, because "the almighty dollar" is worshiped with enthusiasm! He contributed to Americanisms in this comment: "The almighty dollar, that great object of universal devotion throughout our land."[31]

Twain suggested that, in the interest of honesty, the answers to two catechism questions he had encountered as a child be revised in this manner: "'What is the chief end of man?' 'To get rich.' 'Who is God?' 'Money is the one and only true God.'" In American history, Twain found more evidence for the pursuit of money than for "the pursuit of pleasure." He was amused by the "In God we trust" motto, which Americans decided in 1864 to print on money. He thought members of the Gilded Age—the era he named—might better dispense with the propaganda and honestly confess that Money was the trusted deity. In 1905, in a letter to his close friend the Reverend Joseph Twichell, Twain wrote: "All Europe and all America are feverishly scrambling for money. . . . Money-lust has always existed, but not in the history of the world was it ever a craze, a madness, until your time and mine."[32] Late in life Twain published a parable of greed entitled "The Man That Corrupted Hadleyburg." Twain followed Jesus in describing the vulgarity of ostentatious Solomons who lack a concern for those on whose backs their opulence was constructed.

Even though some of the experiences on which Jesus' parables are based have died out—such as storing wine in leather containers or weighing out monetary talents—the stories continue to have a vital impact on literary figures and on common people. For example, everyone talks about individual "talents," but few realize that the imagery originated in a parable of Jesus. He was a teacher with an unmatched historical influence, and his use of parables stands out as the most effective of his varied methods for conveying humor-coated wisdom.

.5.

Wry Humor

"Wry" pertains to clever and often ironical humor that produces a smile, if not a laugh. Consider, for instance, this Yiddish proverb: "If the rich could hire other people to die for them, the poor could make a wonderful living." *Jewish Wry* is the title of a book devoted to wit characteristic of Woody Allen and his fellow ethnics.[1] Here is a wry Allen sample: "I'm not afraid to die. I just don't want to be there when it happens."

The question of a humorous Jesus can be approached deductively and inductively. By deduction, the logic is that all mature humans have a sense of humor; Jesus was fully human; therefore, Jesus had a sense of humor. For inductive reasoning, a consideration needs to be made of particular episodes in the life and teachings of Jesus to see if the conclusion can be drawn that Jesus was humorous. First, what is the truth content of the deductive syllogism?

The Deductive Approach

There is wide agreement that humor is a hallmark of humanity. In the ancient Greek culture, "a human" (*anthropos*) was defined as "a laughing animal" (*zoion gelastikon*). Lucian of Samosata wryly claimed that laughter is what distinguishes humans from asses.[2] Our species is the only joker in nature: there is no bird that chuckles; there is no other mammal that laughs.[3] Even the uproarious "koo-huh-huh" of the kookaburra only *sounds* like laughter, for that Australian bird is not at all tickled. Likewise, the "wha-ha-ha-ha" howl of

80

the African "laughing" hyena is only coincidentally similar to human laughter. By contrast, humans in all cultures laugh frequently, and Americans average fifteen laughs a day.

In a delightful manner, Conrad Hyers illustrates the way in which humor differentiates us from our pets:

> If one has ever ventured to tell a joke, even the simplest of jokes, to one's dog or cat one senses the importance of the distinction. Animals take everything literally. They have no notion of double meaning, plays upon words, overstatement or understatement, incongruity or absurdity, irony or tongue in cheek.[4]

Aristotle, a preeminent ethicist, held that a person with ready wit has commendable virtue. He argued that virtue is a mean between the vices of excess and deficiency. Wittiness, the virtue of entertaining conversation, is the midpoint between buffoonery and gravity. The person who has no tact and is never serious has the vice of excess while the person who cannot crack a joke or take good-natured ribbing has the vice of deficiency.[5]

Our unique gift of humor comes from our ability to reflect on the disparity between the ideal and the actual. William Hazlitt began his classic analysis of comedy with this profound observation: "Man is the only animal that laughs and weeps; for he is the only animal that is struck with the difference between what things are, and what they ought to be."[6] Thus, humor comes from our awareness of the gap between pompous pretensions and pathetic performances.

Humor is a moral necessity because it exposes pettiness and punctures pride. Theological ethicist Reinhold Niebuhr writes:

> Humor is a proof of the capacity of the self to gain a vantage point from which it is able to look at itself. The sense of humor is thus a by-product of self-transcendence. People with a sense of humor do not take themselves too seriously. They are able to "stand off" from themselves, see themselves in perspective and recognize the ludicrous and absurd aspects of their pretensions.[7]

Psychologist Gordon Allport discerns a difference between the laughter of the immature and that of the mature.[8] Young children often laugh, but usually at the misfortunes of others. They tend to scorn authority figures and laugh at those who are different. Children's mirth is provoked by someone who dares to overcome inhibitions pertaining to inappropriate behavior—such as peeing on a lawn. Preschoolers have not attained the cognitive development stage which enables them to understand the world from a perspective other than their own. Without what Allport calls "self-objectification," they cannot see themselves as others see them. But mature adults have the potential to view themselves in a balanced perspective and laugh at their own idiosyncrasies. There is some truth in the saying, "You grow up when you have your first laugh at yourself."

Humor may be an attribute of both deities and humans. Several of the psalms feature the Lord as laughing (2:4; 37:13; 59:8). Depicted in Israel's main source of devotional poetry is a Deity who is as jovial as the Greco-Roman Jove. According to Homer, "Inextinguishable laughter arose among the immortal gods."[9] Psalm 2 portrays the Almighty as being highly amused at strutting and scheming politicians. They wheel and deal as though they control human destiny, not seeing who holds the trump cards. The myopia of those secular rulers is like that of the swellheaded senator who maintained that the nation that controls the spacecraft encircling our planet will become "the master of infinity."

One psalmist believed that humans imitate God's laughter at godless tyrants when they gain enough detachment to glimpse life from a divine perspective (Ps. 52:6). Another one reflected on God's great works and exclaimed: "Our mouth was filled with laughter, and our tongue with shouts of joy!" (126:2). William Kethe, a Scottish poet living in Geneva at the time of the Protestant Reformation, wrote a paraphrase of Psalm 100 ("All People That on Earth Do Dwell") that conveys the spirit of the Psalter: "Sing to the Lord with cheerful voice; / Him serve with mirth." Kethe was influenced by John Calvin, who wrote: "We are nowhere [in the Bible] forbidden to laugh, or to be filled with food, or to add new possessions to old ones, or to be delighted with music, or to drink wine."[10] Calvinists echo the psalmists' conviction when they affirm that "man's chief end is to glorify God, and to enjoy him forever."[11]

Believing that humans share their Creator's likeness, the Hebrews thought that those made in the divine image should be both mirthful and merciful, both jubilant and just. Playwright Christopher Fry alludes to the Creation story of God breathing into clay: "Laughter may seem to be only like an exhalation of air, but out of that air we came; in the beginning we inhaled it."[12] Dudley Zuver makes this tongue-in-cheek comment:

Whatever else may have happened in the Garden of Eden, there is no doubt that laughter was born there. This we know, for man's animal ancestors never laughed before, and he himself has been laughing ever since. Man, indeed, was born with the birth of his comic spirit.[13]

Hyers has tellingly criticized Christian culture for failing to emphasize the relationship between the humorous and the human differentia:

Theologians and moralists have had much to say about man's responsibility to work, but little about his responsibility to play; many words about seriousness and sobriety, few about nonsense and laughter. Still it is really as much in play as in work, in the game as in serious activity, and especially in the play and game of humor, that man is differentiated from the rest of the animal kingdom. Christian theologians in particular have expended copious efforts on the subject of the "image of God" in man; yet for all these laborious and occasionally heated deliberations precious little has ever been said about humor as an aspect of the *imago dei*, let alone as a dimension of the religious situation before the divine. The impression is given that laughter is the creation of the devil or a fumbling demiurge, or that it is a pale substitute left to man after his expulsion from the more holy joys of paradise.[14]

Thus, a variety of scholars agree on the truth of the major

premise: all mature humans have a sense of humor. Consider now the minor premise: Jesus was fully human. For most Christians and for some non-Christians this proposition is complicated by the creedal affirmation that Jesus was "complete both in deity and in human-ness."[15] Consider, for example, a comment by Charles Baudelaire, a noted French essayist: "The Word Incarnate never laughed. In the eyes of the One who knows everything and is capable of everything, there is nothing comic."[16] Baudelaire presumed that laughter is satanic, so the divine Jesus could not have indulged. Philosopher John Morreall has expressed a similar judgment about Jesus:

> His divinity . . . would make him a completely serious person, for the Christian God could have no sense of humor. He knows fully every thing and every event in the past, present, and future, and so nothing that happened could surprise him. . . . Because he is a changeless being, nothing that happened could amuse God; he could not experience the psychological shift that is behind laughter.[17]

Both Baudelaire and Morreall assume that the Christian God is emotionally changeless. They follow Origen, who looked at Christianity through the lens of pagan Greek philosophy. Origen stated: "The divine nature is far removed from every feeling of emotion and alteration; it always remains motionless and unperturbed on the summit of blessedness."[18] Many Christians adopted the view that passionless reason came from an Unmoved Mover, but—as we have seen illustrated in the passages from the Psalter—it was not rooted in biblical theology.

Baudelaire and Morreall also posit that omniscience is antithetical to humor. That presumption is arguable but irrelevant, because the New Testament acknowledges that Jesus was not omniscient. When asked about the timetable for the outcome of history, he admitted his lack of knowledge pertaining to the future (Mark 13:32; Acts 1:7).

Could there have been no place for humor in Jesus' life? Does mirth come from Satan and dullness from God? Many orthodox (literally, correct-thinking) Christians have thought of Jesus as showing his divinity *through* his manhood, not in spite of it. Thus, his experience of God deepened rather than diminished his humanity. The Jesus of the early Christians was not a quasi-human demigod; rather, he was as much of a full-fledged fellow as his followers. The New Testament affirms that Jesus, as God's "Son," participated in human emotions (Heb. 5:1–10). He maintained his relationship to God while involving himself in human comedy as well as tragedy.

Paul, the first and foremost Christian theologian, helps in understanding Jesus vis-à-vis authentic human nature. The apostle saw a brilliant reflection of the image of God in the person of Jesus. By bringing human potentialities to perfection, Christ has become the measure for evaluating maturity (2 Cor. 4:6; Eph. 4:13; Col. 1:15). Paul writes of the relationship between the human and the divine in this way:

> Have the same mind that Christ Jesus had. He possessed the image of God, yet he did not regard equality with God as something to be exploited. No, he stripped himself of privileges, taking a servant's role. Having the status of a common person, he revealed himself in human nature. He humbled himself, becoming obedient unto death— and a death by crucifixion at that! (Phil. 2:5–8)

Kenneth Foreman, Sr., made this perceptive comment on Paul's doctrine: "Jesus is the truly *normal*—that is to say, standard—human being. To become like him, to belong to his family rather than to that of Adam the First, is not to become freakish and abnormal; it is to discover what being human really is."[19] As one modern creed declares: "In Jesus of Nazareth true humanity was realized once for all. Jesus, a Palestinian Jew, lived among his own people and shared their needs, temptations, joys, and sorrows."[20] Christians have usually found Jesus' divinity at the apex of his humanity.

The Inductive Approach

As with all humans, Jesus was affected by his cultural environment. His Jewish ancestors were noted for their humor, especially the first couple to be called Hebrews. The Genesis saga tells of Abraham having a fit of laughter; he doubles over and falls on the ground when God informs him that his old wife is going to bear him a child (17:17). The ludicrous situation also prompts Sarah to laugh (18:12). The Genesis narrator joins in the comedy by telling of a king being attracted to postmenopausal Sarah and by calling Abraham a centenarian at the time of their son's birth (18:11; 20:2; 21:5). The unexpected child is appropriately named Isaac, meaning "laughter" (21:3–6).

Abraham and Sarah were treated as role models of faithfulness in the New Testament era (Rom. 4; Heb. 11:8–12); hence, glee was viewed as a companion of faith. In Judaism at that time, Philo of Alexandria commented on the naming of Isaac: "Laughter is the outward and bodily sign of the unseen joy in the mind. Joy is the most excellent and the most beautiful of the higher emotions. By it the soul is entirely filled with cheerfulness, rejoicing in the Father and Maker of all."[21]

Puns frequently can be found in the original languages of the Bible. In the Qur'an, the Jews are criticized for their bad puns (2:104; 4:46). Punsters accept the charge that puns are the lowest form of humor, knowing that wordplays are the foundation on which humorous high-rises are built! Although they are usually untranslatable, some Hebrew puns can be reproduced in English. One of the Creation stories tells of God forming the human (*ha adam*) from humus (*adamah*). A story later in Genesis about a Mesopotamian tower gives this explanation: "It was called Babel [*babhel*] because there the Lord made a babble [*balal*] of the language of all the earth" (11:9).

The book of Judges contains this couplet by Samson, the Hebrew Hercules: "With the jawbone of an ass [*hamor*] I have piled them in a mass [*hamar*]" (15:16). The prophet Isaiah contrasts the Lord's expectations with what was found in Israel: "He looked for morality [*mishpat*], but behold, a massacre [*mispah*]! For right [*sedaqah*], but behold, a riot [*seaqah*]!" (5:7). Doctoral dissertations have been written on the hundreds of wordplays in the Old and New Testaments.[22]

A good example of Jewish wry wit is found in an account of the conquests of Alexander the Great. His army had halted to await the judgment of a soothsayer, who was observing the movements of a particular bird. A Jewish archer named Meshullam, disgusted by what he recognized as superstitious fatalism, shot and killed the bird. When cursed by the pagans for interfering with their religion, he pointed out that if the bird had been gifted with divination it would not have come close to him for fear of being hit by his arrow.[23]

Given Jesus' Hebrew heritage, it is not surprising to find that he often spoke with a dry and restrained wit and enjoyed plays on words. Indeed, his first recorded words contain a double entendre on "father." When Mary tells Jesus that she and his father Joseph have been searching for him, he responds: "Why were you searching for me? Did you not know that I must be in my Father's house?" (Luke 2:49). His parents, unable to grasp Jesus' dawning awareness of being a son of two fathers, did not understand his dual interpretation. For a reader of Luke's Gospel, the puzzlement of Jesus' mother is ironic. That Gospel alleges that the angel Gabriel revealed to Mary, a virgin, that she should not worry over how she would conceive because the Son of God would be produced in her by the overshadowing of the Holy Spirit (1:26–35). Yet Mary now refers to Joseph as Jesus' father and she is bewildered by Jesus' reference to God as Father (2:48–49).

Jesus punned in his native Aramaic tongue when he nicknamed Peter, as we noted earlier. His pun on Cephas (Aramaic for "rock," *kepha*) is also conveyed in the Greek of the New Testament: "You are Peter [*petros*], and on this rock [*petra*] I will build my church" (Matt. 16:18). The punny petrifaction remark might be paraphrased in English as: "Simon, your name from now on is Rocky, and on your rock-like character I will construct my church." Stimulated by this comment, Victor Hugo wrote: "The most noble, sublime, and charming persons in humanity, and perhaps beyond humanity, have played on words. Jesus Christ made a pun on Saint Peter, Moses on Isaac."[24]

Again, Jesus punned in Aramaic in this preposterous description of some fastidious Pharisees: "You strain out a gnat [*kalma*] but you gulp down a camel [*gamla*]!" (Matt. 23:24). Faithful to their dietary law, which prohibited the eating of swarming insects (Lev. 11:41), they meticulously poured their wine through cloth to remove tiny bugs. But at the same time, the Pharisees outperformed a hinged-jaw python by consuming a camel. Without blinking, Jesus says they ingested an entire monstrous "unclean" animal! (Lev. 11:4). The religionists consumed camel-size evils, such as slander and prejudice, and thought nothing of it. Terrot Glover helps English readers sense how a camel would be swallowed:

> The long hairy neck slid down the throat of the Pharisee—all that amplitude of loose-hung anatomy—the hump—two humps—both of them slid down—and he never noticed—and the legs—all of them—with the whole outfit of knees and big padded feet. The Pharisee swallowed a camel and never noticed it. It is the mixture of sheer realism with absurdity that makes the irony and gives it its force. Did no one smile as the story was told? Did no one see the scene pictured with his own mind's eye—no one grasp the humor and the irony with delight? Could any one, on the other hand, forget it? A modern teacher would have said, in our jargon, that the Pharisee had no sense of proportion—and no one would have thought the remark worth remembering.[25]

Jesus wanted to get legalists to laugh at their misdirected scrupulous behavior. Here is another example: "You tithe mint and rue and every herb, and neglect justice and the love of God" (Luke 11:42). According to the Bible, the tithe pertains to giving the Lord one tenth of the principal crops—grain, wine, and oil (Deut. 14:23). No mention is made of tithing on garden herbs in the law of Moses. But in Jesus' day conscientious Pharisees desired to spell out in great detail the implications of those laws. As Josephus states: "The Pharisees have transmitted to the people many regulations . . . which are not written in the Law of Moses."[26] The Mishnah likewise indicates that one of their main aims was "to make a fence around the Law,"[27] that is, to protect its decrees by erecting rules that will halt possible violators before they come close to transgressing. Hence, the devout were not only to carry out the 613 commandments of the Pentateuch, but were also to observe the voluminous, more recent specific formulations of those laws. One ancient rabbi cautioned: since the rewards for obeying light and heavy regulations are often not known, one should be meticulous toward them all.[28] The Mishnah asserts that dill and cumin are among the herbs to be tithed, and that rue is exempt.[29] Even in the rabbinical regulations filled with trifling details, mint is not mentioned. Thus Jesus needles those who are even more exacting than the picayune oral traditions in observing rules pertaining to tithing. He points out that they have overlooked practicing much more important principles pertaining to human relationships.

More than once Jesus made hilarious humor out of the gangling camel, whose funny appearance is sometimes considered evidence of the Creator's humor! Jesus referred to the camel when he wanted to reject the close association in folk morality between possessing many goods and having much goodness. "Riches reward the righteous" is a recurring theme of the Hebrew Bible (Deut. 28:1–14; Pss. 1:1–3; 112:1–3; Prov. 13:21; 15:6). Regarding rabbinical Judaism, Winston Davis asserts: "Wealth was a sign of divine approval and poverty was thought to be the result of sin. The identification of wealth and righteousness, sin and poverty was disputed by only a few religious leaders, such as the prophet Amos."[30] To disturb this conventional assumption, Jesus used this grotesque image: "It is easier for a camel to go through the eye of a needle than for a rich person to enter the kingdom of God" (Mark 10:25). Speaking of an enormous animal going through a needle's aperture was a Jewish idiom for impossibility. In Mesopotamia, the elephant was used in the figure,[31] presumably because Jews living there were familiar with the colossus from India. In Palestine, however, the dromedary was the largest animal.

We know that the intended point of the camel image was understood, because Jesus' disciples "were exceedingly astonished, and said to him, 'Then who can be saved?'" Jesus then indicated, in effect, that what is impossible to achieve by human effort can be bestowed by divine grace. In a subsequent episode, he associated salvation with a wealthy man named Zacchaeus who became generous (Luke 19:1–9). Had Jesus blandly said that it is extremely difficult for the wealthy to have a healthy perspective on life, it is doubtful that this insight would have been remembered and recorded a generation later.

Jesus' camel and needle hyperbole has an amusing history of interpretation. Some apologists for the concentration of wealth in the hands of an elite have engaged their hermeneutic talents in assisting rich persons through the pearly gates. Literalists have dismissed the thought that Jesus would have spoken in a ridiculous manner. Since a length of twisted fiber is properly associated with needles, Calvin comments: "The word *camel* denotes, I think, a rope used by sailors, rather than the animal so named."[32] That forefather of capitalism imagined the possibility of a very thin rope and a huge needle! While diminishing Jesus' droll wit, Calvin also gave the rising moneyed class at least a sporting chance to enter the kingdom. However, even the editor of that Calvin commentary admits that the Protestant reformer had no textual basis for his rope interpretation. Economic commitments can so influence commentators on the Gospels that pretense exegesis can sometimes "exit Jesus"!

Calvinists have continued to be solicitous over the salvation of the wealthy. William Barclay, in his popular commentary, suggests this interpretation:

> Beside the great gate into Jerusalem through which traffic went, there was a little gate just wide and high enough for a man to get through. It is said that that little gate was called the needle's eye, and the picture is that of a camel trying to struggle through that little gate.[33]

Thus a way is provided for Andrew Carnegie and other wealthy Scotsmen from Barclay's culture to squeeze through to heaven after giving away their huge moneybags!

The so-called needle's eye gate in ancient Palestine has no historical basis, and is purely the concoction of a European expositor several centuries ago.[34] Walter Rauschenbusch, a pioneer in applying the gospel to modern economic life, acknowledges that "it gives a touch of cheerful enjoyment to exegetical studies" to read of a gate through which camels pass by crawling on their knees! He observes that a sympathetic treatment has been given to only one of Jesus' two camel analogies: "There is a manifest solicitude to help the rich man through. There has not been a like fraternal anxiety for the Pharisee; he is allowed to swallow his camel whole."[35]

Gentile Christians have learned the hard way to recognize Jesus' indulgence in conscious exaggeration to make a point. One outstanding example is related to his exhortation to cut off any sin-stimulating part of the body. In teaching about sexual sin, Jesus said: "If your right eye entices you to sin, tear it out and throw it away! . . . If your right hand is your undoing, cut it off and throw it away! You do less harm to lose one part of your body than to have the whole of it cast into hell" (Matt. 5:29–30). This dramatically worded advice to get rid of bad habits was misinterpreted by young Origen, who thought Jesus was prescribing actual surgery. In Edward Gibbon's circumlocution, "The learned Origen judged it most prudent to disarm the tempter."[36] However, after becoming castrated, this third-century theologian had misgivings over literal interpretation and became the foremost biblical allegorist![37] Patches over empty eye sockets, arm stumps without hands, and the like are not apparent in congregations, so it seems that devout Christians have learned to reject literalism with respect to at least one saying of Jesus!

Here is another example of Jesus' hyperbolic shock treatment: "If anyone comes to me and does not hate his own father and mother and wife and children and brothers and sisters, yes, and even his own life, he cannot be my disciple" (Luke 14:26). New Testament critic Bruce Metzger comments: "Here Jesus states a principle in a startling, categorical manner, and leaves his hearers to find out whatever qualifications are necessary in the light of his other pronouncements."[38] Since Jesus found hate unacceptable even toward enemies (Matt. 5:43–44), and since he emphasized the commandment to honor one's parents (Mark 7:9–13), he is clearly not literally advocating hate toward one's family. Rather, he is establishing priority in relationships: although family loyalty has its importance, the ultimate center of security for his disciples should be elsewhere. Preferring the prosaic to the picturesque, another Gospel writer records Jesus this way: "Whoever loves father or mother more than me is not worthy of me; and whoever loves son or daughter more than me is not worthy of me" (Matt. 10:37).

Jesus also deals with filial priorities in this exchange: "'Follow me,' Jesus said. 'Lord, first let me go and bury my father,' the man replied. But Jesus said to him, 'Let the dead bury their own dead; but as for you, go and proclaim the kingdom of God'" (Luke 9:59–60). Since there are no physically dead undertakers, Jesus intriguingly gets the would-be disciple to reflect on a double meaning of "death" that is as old as the Eden story. The apparent harshness of Jesus' advice is removed on realizing that he is engaging in conscious exaggeration. He used words like a stick of dynamite to break up the lethargic Judaism of his day. Some had forgotten that the First Commandment should take precedence over the Fifth. Jesus states sharply that religious impulses deserve even more consideration than hallowed family obligations, and that prompt action should sometimes be taken to leave spiritually dead surroundings.

Jesus once drew a verbal cartoon of a fellow Jew contributing to charity (Matt. 6:2). Worried that someone might not notice his generosity, he hires a trumpeter to walk before him and play a fanfare whenever he gives a handout on a street or a contribution in a synagogue. Our language has been enriched by the hyperbolic pin with which Jesus attempted to pop the bloated ego. When accused of "blowing his own trumpet" (or "tooting her own horn"), the wise think critically but not literally about their conduct. Christians who are unaware of the ways of Judaism might presume that Jesus was being descriptive rather than ludicrous in this comment on Jewish piety. Also displayed here is Jesus' preference for a delightful concrete image rather than a dull abstract idea. Had Jesus said, "Avoid ostentation," how far would that have been orally transmitted?

Jesus ridiculed the prestige seeker by this story:

When someone invites you to a wedding feast, do not sit down at the place of honor. A more distinguished person than you may have been invited, and the host who invited both of you may come and say, "Give this person your place." Then, to your embarrassment, you would have to go and take the lowest seat. Instead, when you are a guest, go and sit in an inconspicuous place, so that when your host comes, he may say, "Friend, move to a better place." Then all the other guests will see the respect in which you are held. For all who promote themselves will be humbled, and those who humble themselves will be promoted. (Luke 14:8–11)

The scriptures affirm that "humans judge by appearances but Yahweh judges by the heart" (1 Sam. 16:7). Jesus also shrewdly perceived that applause from their fellows is what some people are really seeking when they act religiously. He observed persons who pray publicly and disfigure their faces when fasting, "to be praised by others." By way of assessing this vanity, he declares: "Believe me, they have had their reward!" (Matt. 6:2, 5, 16). For those aiming at impressing others by praying, fasting, and almsgiving, he acknowledges that they get what they want and nothing more. While making a parade of their piety, they are oblivious of God who looks inwardly and recognizes their phoniness.

One hyperbole of Jesus is so ridiculous that translators have blunted the absurdity. He said, "If someone takes your outerwear, let him have your underwear as well" (Luke 6:29). (Compare that with the King James Version, which presumes two layers of outerwear: "Him that taketh away thy cloak forbid not to take thy coat also.") A Palestinian peasant in the warm Mediterranean climate wore simply an outer garment and a loincloth. A creditor was permitted to take a cloak as a loan guarantee only in the daytime, for it was needed for sleeping comfort (Ex. 22:26–27). Thomas Manson points out that if Jesus' teaching is taken literally rather than seriously the issue would be nudity. Manson finds this "a sufficient indication that it is a certain spirit that is being commended . . . not a regulation to be slavishly carried out."[39] Norman Perrin likewise observes that persons could be charged with indecent exposure if they behaved in exact accordance with the injunction.[40] Both scholars agree that Jesus' meaning is that there are situations when gracious acquiescence is better than insisting on one's own rights. Somewhat more prudently, philosopher Epictetus advises regarding one's donkey: "Do not resist if a Roman soldier seizes it; otherwise you will be beaten as well as lose your ass."[41]

Jesus tells twin parables pertaining to eye problems. In the first, Jesus asks: "Can the blind lead the blind? Will not both fall into a pit?" (Luke 6:39). This ludicrous image has inspired artists for centuries. Dutch master Pieter Brueghel painted blind men following in sequence, one holding a shoulder and another touching the one in front with a cane, not realizing that they are headed into the ditch with their leader. Stanley Bleifeld, a modern American sculptor, showed a similar satirical scene involving a politician, an intellectual, an ad man, a superpatriot, a social worker, a soldier, and a priest leading one another but without seeing the perils ahead.[42]

The other widely recognized humorous parable about seeing could have been triggered by Jesus' remembrance of a happening in Nazareth when his eye was reddened by sawdust. A fellow carpenter, unaware of a more perilous situation of his own, might have expressed eagerness to operate on Jesus' trivial problem. Typical of humorists, Jesus may have expanded that experience into this zany cameo:

> Why do you see the sawdust that is in your neighbor's eye, but do not notice the log in your own eye? Or how can you say to your neighbor, "Let me take the speck out of your eye," when there is a log in your own eye? You hypocrite, first take the log out of your own eye, and then you will see clearly to take the sawdust out of your neighbor's eye. (Luke 6:41–42)

Elton Trueblood tells how laughter from his young son on hearing this story motivated him to write a book on Jesus' humor.[43] After reflecting on the response of a child, he came to realize that he had erred in accepting the conventional picture of a somber Jesus.

The eye trouble episodes display a human tendency which Hebrew literature utilizes. The Garden of Eden story provokes the hearer to blame human failings on persons presumed to be the first created. Even as the alleged male named Adam blamed spouse and God, and the female taken from Adam blamed the serpent, so hearers of the story also "pass the buck" in an attempt to relieve guilt. Some overcome this self-deception by discovering that *ha adam* is the generic name for humankind of both genders and that the myth is ahistorical. To be indignant toward the Eden couple is to incriminate ourselves.

A historical example in Hebrew scriptures of our propensity for shifting blame is an account of David and Nathan. The very human king was incensed when Nathan told him a story of a rich rancher who stole a poor shepherd's only ewe. Then, to reveal the allegorical nature of the story, the prophet proclaimed, "You are the man!" (2 Sam. 12:1–7a). The Hebrew literary tradition understood well the human proclivity to recognize evil in others but not in ourselves, and to define sin as anything bad someone else does. When the index finger is pointed judgmentally at the accused, how many are aware of the three fingers pointing back at the accuser?

The illustrations gleaned of Jesus' exhilarating exaggerations should not be interpreted to mean that he laughed indulgently at legalism and haughtiness. He hoped that after self-awareness was heightened and foibles were laughed at, a more wholesome pattern of conduct would result. Jesus, as a healer, used this Hebrew prescription: "A cheerful heart is good medicine, but a gloomy spirit dries up vitality" (Prov. 17:22).

Recent research has rediscovered that both physical and mental therapy can be a laughing matter. Even as stress suppresses the immune system and increases vulnerability to disease, fitness accompanies mirth. Norman Cousins reported on studies showing that laughter quickens breathing, enhances circulation, ignites expectations, and activates certain health-promoting chemicals in the body. As Cousins put it: "Hearty laughter is a good way to jog internally."[44]

The merriment of Jesus was so pronounced that some of his contemporaries invidiously contrasted his life-style with that of the more sober and stern John the Baptist (Luke 7:33–34). But Jesus was no buffoon, and he did not give unqualified approval to all laughter. He promised laughter to his disciples while cautioning them against laughing scornfully (Luke 6:21, 25).

Jesus engaged in irony but not in sarcasm (literally, flesh-tearing). He was comic without being cruel, for his attacks were not directed at individuals. He intended to drive home points constructively; hence, destructive venting of gall was not part of his style. Like Horace, a Roman critic, Jesus "spoke truth with a smile,"[45] hoping that those who heard him would chuckle at their own folly. Those who can laugh at themselves have acquired a perspective that often leads to personal change.

Consider Jesus' irony with respect to the Pharisees. He pretended to accept their own valuations and then encouraged others to laugh gently up their sleeves at such judgments. Many of the Pharisees presumed they were in top shape spiritually and that any who shared their condition should not risk contamination by associating with the "unclean." So they asked: "Why do you eat and drink with tax collectors and sinners?" One of Jesus' ironical responses is: "Those who are healthy have no need of a physician, but those who are sick" (Luke 5:30–31). In other words, he cannot help those who presume they are perfect; those who are unwilling to admit shortcomings are impossible to improve. Another ironical comment by Jesus is: "There will be more joy in heaven over one sinner who repents than over ninety-nine righteous persons who need no repentance" (Luke 15:7). Some Pharisees classified themselves with the virtuous who have no need of inward change, but Jesus was a meliorist, believing that perfecting is a lifelong process. He subtly tried to show the self-righteous that they have more spiritual problems than some disreputable characters (Luke 15:2, 25–32).

Jesus did not travel on the characteristic low road of ethnic humor, which boosts in-group feelings of superiority by insulting out-groups. Justin Miller observes that Jewish wit follows the prophetic thrust, which primarily faults fellow Jews for tolerating a chasm between high ideals and everyday behavior. The wisecracker provides a temporary release from the tension brought on by a recognition of the incongruity. Jews thereby enjoy self-criticism while acknowledging their own limitations.

Jewish jokesters expose viewpoints in their community that seem odd to outsiders. By way of illustration, Miller offers this riddle: How do we know Jesus was a Jew? The answer is that he thought his father was God and his mother was a virgin. Targeted by the joke are those Jews who place their parents on a pedestal of piety that is far above ordinary mortals. The effect is similar to the psalmist who views parents in this manner: "The Lord commanded our ancestors to teach [the law] to their children. . . . In this way the next generation will put their trust in God . . . and not do as their stubborn and rebellious ancestors did" (Ps. 78:5–8).

Miller comments: "The psalmist urges us to be disillusioned with the generation of our parents even while it is our parents' generation which is teaching us the laws and the ways of God. . . . It is in that way that children are reminded not to do as the parents *did* but as they *said* and *taught*."[46] Jesus likewise wittily encourages his disciples to heed the Pharisees' teaching, but not to imitate their deeds (Matt. 23:3).

In spite of funny sayings in the Gospels, no explicit mention is made there of Jesus laughing. This can best be understood by recognizing that a person's departure from the norm is more likely to be recorded in a biographical sketch. The absence of evidence of a common characteristic is not the same as evidence of its absence. Everyone takes for granted that humans smile, get sick, have sexual desire, and have bowel movements. Silence on those matters in anyone's historical record cannot provide the basis for a valid argument that there was a lack of such in the person concerned. However, there have been some who have maintained that Jesus ate but never defecated, was always healthy, never had sexual passion, and never smiled, on the absurd presumption that the Gospels describe all his human characteristics.

Kenneth Latourette, the famed historian, thinks that Jesus comes off well in a mirth comparison with his earliest followers. He writes:

> Jesus had a keen sense of humor which again and again bubbles out irrepressibly, all the more strikingly because it is in contrast with the complete absence of humor in those writings of the Christians of the first century which have been preserved in the New Testament. He had a keen eye for the ridiculous and could make startling what he saw.[47]

Latourette exaggerates, because humor can be detected in the sayings of other early Christians. Jakob Jonsson's monograph on humor in the New Testament shows that Paul, especially, displays a sense of humor.[48] Yet Jesus' speech was more seasoned with salty wit than were the writings of the apostle who recommended spicy words (Col. 4:6).

Christian Responses

In the postbiblical era, some Gnostic Christians kept "the laughing Savior" tradition alive. Actually, mirth is one of the few human qualities of Jesus recorded in the Nag Hammadi scrolls discovered in 1945. Some of those scrolls, buried since the early centuries of Christianity in an Egyptian cemetery, may contain authentic biographical information. In the "Sophia of Jesus" tractate, for example, Jesus responds to his disciples in this way: "The Savior laughed and said to them, 'What are you thinking about?'"[49]

Beginning in the third century, Christianity was impacted by a movement from which it has never fully recovered. With the coming of hermits and monasteries—probably from paganism[50]—Jesus became the role model for self-mortification. On the presumption that laughter and other pleasurable activities were products of the devil's workshop, strenuous efforts were made to exorcise enjoyment from religion. Basil, the father of Greek monasticism, in writing on the alleged wickedness of laughter, pointed to Jesus who he claimed never laughed.[51] Soon afterward John Chrysostom, the most outstanding of the Greek church fathers, told his congregation that, according to the New Testament, Jesus never laughed or smiled. Thus, he concluded, "This world is not a theater in which we can laugh. We have not assembled together to burst into laughter, but to groan for our sins."[52] This Bishop of Constantinople described what will happen on judgment day to those who do not follow his long-faced Jesus: "When you see persons laughing, reflect that those teeth that grin now will one day have to sustain that most dreadful wailing and gnashing."[53]

The leaders of early Latin Christianity also depreciated

laughter. In the fourth century, Bishop Ambrose advised the clergy to avoid all jokes, for they "break down manly dignity."[54] Jerome, his monastic contemporary, stressed that Christians "leave to worldlings the privileges of laughter."[55] That most famous of translators twisted the Hebrew text to advance his austere outlook. "The Lord has placed us in a vale of tears," is the English rendering of his total mistranslation of Psalm 84:6 in Latin. Jerome comments: "This world is the place for weeping, not for rejoicing."[56] Since laughter in his thinking erupts from the spleen, it is a defiling "work of the flesh." Tears, however, are seated higher on the body and are closer to the soul!

Jerome, along with other Christians, was influenced by pagan philosophers who disapproved of laughter. Roman church leaders often appreciated the Stoics more than the Jews. Epictetus, an admired Stoic, taught: "If there is ever a proper occasion for going to the theater, abstain entirely from shouts and laughter."[57] In accordance with their ideal of passionless rationality, Stoics tried to remain stone-faced regardless of whether they were viewing a comedy or a tragedy. Their model was Plato who, according to one ancient source, was "so modest and orderly that he was never seen to laugh outright."[58] This account probably was based on these words of Plato: "Persons of worth . . . must not be represented as overcome by laughter, and still less must such a representation of the gods be allowed."[59]

The pagan Roman Empire ended with Emperor Julian, who allegedly acknowledged on his deathbed, "You have conquered, Galilean."[60] Those words stimulated nineteenth-century poet Algernon Swinburne to add: "Thou hast conquered, O pale Galilean; the world has grown grey from thy breath."[61] Typical of a number of interpreters, Swinburne viewed Jesus through the distorting lens of the church fathers. Consequently, he assumed that the historical Jesus was a pallid Palestinian who was uninterested in the simple joys of life.

During the Middle Ages, a clumsy forgery was even more effective than the church fathers in obliterating from the minds of Christians a laughing Jesus image. A description of Jesus' features is attributed to one Publius Lentulus—the presumed governor of Jerusalem during the reign of

Tiberius Caesar. It alleges that Jesus was tall, long-haired, and bearded; he had unblemished skin, a high forehead, and blue eyes. The apocryphal record also states: "He never laughed."[62] When the medieval monks began to paint scenes from the Gospels, they had no genuine historical writings about the appearance of Jesus. Nor was there any artistic tradition that extended back to the century in which Jesus lived. Understandably, the painters and writers readily accepted an account that was presumed to have been written down by Lentulus, a contemporary of Jesus.

The commonplace image of Jesus in the minds of Europeans no doubt contributed to the discipline expected of those in holy orders. The Benedictine monasteries had this rule: "The monk should speak slowly, softly, gravely, and without laughter."[63] In the period of bubonic plagues, Jesus' morose image accentuated the melancholy of worshipers. Hyers's comment on the ethical outlook of that era is apropos: "It was a most unfortunate omission on the part of medieval Christianity not to have included humor and humorlessness in its moral glossary of the seven cardinal virtues and the seven deadly sins."[64] Ignatius Loyola, the founder of the Jesuit order, laid down for each member this vow: "I should not laugh or say anything that would cause laughter."[65] The virtue of joy was neglected, even though the apostle Paul made "Rejoice in the Lord always" the theme of one of his letters (Phil. 1:4; 2:17–18; 4:4, 10) and included joy among the nine fruits of the Spirit (Gal. 5:22).

Martin Luther attempted to revive the image of a robust Jesus when he said: "He was sad and happy; he wept and laughed."[66] However, a survey of contemporary Lutherans displays how little Luther succeeded in changing the prevailing stereotype. Most Lutherans in America believe that Jesus never told a joke.[67]

Other Protestants also have done little to reverse the medieval caricature of the founder of Christianity and the accompanying depreciation of laughter. Consider, for example, Francis Asbury, the founder of American Methodism. A biography written by an adoring relative states: "Laughter and play he considered affronts to the Lord; he hated them, and often condemned both himself and others for occasional lapses into joviality."[68] Another illustration comes from Greek novelist Nikos Kazantzakis, who visited England in the early twentieth century. He reported on this conversation:

> "Just hear what we've to say," my Puritan friend repeated through his anaemic, unkissed lips. "My ancestors for generations have not smiled. My father was a pastor. When I was still a small boy I asked him one day why we never laughed at home. He looked at me in amazement. 'Have you read the Bible?' he asked me. 'Yes.' 'Does it mention anywhere that Christ ever laughed?' I was silent in shame."[69]

Reflecting on British religious life, George Bernard Shaw quipped: "Unfortunately this Christian Church, founded gaily with a pun, has been so largely corrupted by rank Satanism that it has become the Church where you must not laugh."[70] Generally, the settled opinion has become: the more solemn, the more holy; the more hilarious, the more profane. In discussing "grave" for contemporary Americans, *The Winston Dictionary* explains that a grave person is against what is lively and colorful; clergy lead its illustrations of professionals who are apt to display that trait. If the church has fallen, it may be due to the force of gravity! Nevertheless, were Shaw observing congregations in the last decades of the twentieth century rather than in the first decades, he would probably detect more balance; he might note that clergypersons now, like a certain ancient ecclesiastic, find occasions for laughing and dancing (Eccl. 3:4).

In the modern era, the alleged somberness of Jesus has been a point of agreement by some distinguished friends and foes of Christianity. Philosopher Friedrich Nietzsche writes of Jesus: "He knew only tears and the melancholy of the Hebrew. . . . Would that he had remained in the wilderness and far from the good and the just! Perhaps he would have learned to live and to love the earth—and laughter too." Nietzsche thinks that a true prophet should exclaim: "Laughter I have pronounced holy; superior persons, learn to laugh!"[71] On the other hand, poet Francis Thompson, in a lugubrious essay, alludes admiringly to the Lentulus depiction of Jesus. "Though many had seen him weep, no man had seen him smile" is treated as godly example for Christians to emulate.[72]

The Lentulus fabrication pertaining to Jesus' appearance is still published as authentic in nonscholarly books. The absence of even a smile on the face of Jesus in virtually all art of the past millennium has been due to the iconographic tradition established by that pious fraud and by the imaginations of ascetic monks. Portraits of Jesus collected in art books show him tight-lipped with no smile.[73] A composite of seventeen images of Jesus dating from the sixth century appeared on a cover of *Time*.[74] Although there is some variety in the portraiture, he is solemn in all. Again, Marion Wheeler has published a representative selection of pictures of Jesus' face as depicted by many of the world's greatest painters from the twelfth to the twentieth century. None of the seventy-nine reproductions of the adult Jesus shows him smiling, and his teeth appear in only one painting, depicting the agony of dying.[75]

Why do artists presume that the One who said "Do not look dismal" (Matt. 6:16) did not practice what he preached? The sad countenance of the paintings of Jesus illustrate the well-known hymn of a gloomy medieval monk: "O sacred head, now wounded, with grief and shame weighed down." Bernard of Clairvaux's accurate depiction of the last scene of Jesus' earthly life has been taken as representative of his looks throughout life. Indeed, some third-century Christians relied on Isaiah's prophecy of a Suffering Servant for a sketch of Jesus' appearance.[76] Contained there in poetry written centuries before the Christian era is reference to an uncomely "man of sorrows" who is "acquainted with grief" (Isa. 53:2–3).

Only in recent decades has Jesus' defaced image been partly restored. Dudley Zuver stated that a main purpose he had in writing *Salvation by Laughter* was to show that Jesus "deserves a chief place within any circle of wits howsoever exclusive it be."[77] Cal Samra features several contemporary drawings of a smiling or guffawing Jesus in *The Joyful Christ*.[78] Marvin Hayes's etching of *Jesus Laughing*[79] and like images by other artists are indebted to commentators such as Barclay, who observes:

Too often in Christian teaching laughter has been a heresy and seriousness has been identified with gloom. Jesus knew that often the way to the heart of an audience is through a smile; and he said things which at the moment made men laugh, but which, when they thought about them, left them face to face with the gravity of truth.[80]

Henri Cormier tells of a formal debate on the subject: "Did Jesus laugh?" Among the negative arguments were: (1) Jesus was always serious, so he did not jest; and (2) laughter presupposes an abandon, but Jesus was in control of himself. The affirmative arguments were found to be more substantial: (1) Being serious does not necessitate being glum; (2) laughter does not imply a loss of self-control; (3) Jesus was aware of a pleasant reality within, and laughter accompanied this joy; and (4) laughter is characteristic of wedding parties, and Jesus took part in at least one.[81]

Jesus' divine/human perspective on the world enabled him to see profoundly both the comedy and the tragedy of life. Reflecting on the crucifixion tragedy and the resurrection triumph, Nevin Vos writes:

The clown and Christ are . . . both victims and victors: they both bear both these roles at one and the same time, for they are victors because they have accepted their role as victims. They fall; then they emerge from difficulty and reconstitute their positions; finally, they continue happily on their way—this is the essential rhythm of the clown's career. And we are now laughing not so much at him as with him.[82]

Harvard religion professor Harvey Cox carries this analogy to a greater depth:

In the biblical portrait of Christ there are elements that can easily suggest clown symbols. Like the jester, Christ defies custom and scorns crowned heads. Like a wandering troubador he has no place to lay his head. Like the clown in the circus parade, he satirizes existing authority by riding into town replete with regal pageantry when he has no earthly power. Like a minstrel he frequents dinners and parties. . . . The clown is constantly defeated, tricked, humiliated, and tromped upon. He is infinitely vulnerable, but never finally defeated.[83]

Thus, to call Jesus a clown is not to trivialize his ministry. Sociologist Peter Berger makes us aware of this when he gives his judgment on the ultimate meaning of comedy:

A Christian understanding of human existence would reverse the common belief that tragedy is more profound than comedy. . . . It is comedy that gives us the more significant insights into the human condition. . . . There will be no tragedy in heaven—by definition, as it were. But man will remain funny for ever. . . . The tragic thus shows us man in time, but the comic may well give an intimation of what man is and always will be, even in eternity.[84]

Jesus stands out as a religious leader in part because he was "truly man," complete with both tear ducts and funny bone. By means of laughter he combated hypocrisy and promoted humility. Since his ultimate values were not connected to secular success, he was not sullen when faced with apparent failure. He communicated his deep joy to his distressed disciples at the Last Supper when he said, "In the world the squeeze is on, but cheer up, I have conquered" (John 16:33). Some artists have penetrated beneath the medieval distortions and have recovered the characteristic exuberance of Jesus in the New Testament portrayal.

Carl Sandburg's famous biography of Abraham Lincoln contains a chapter entitled "Lincoln's Laughter—and His Religion." The juxtaposition of laughter and religion was even more uncommon in Lincoln's day than in our own. Sandburg quotes a tribute from Lincoln's friend Isaac Arnold. The description could apply also to Jesus:

Mirthfulness and melancholy, hilarity and sadness, were strangely combined in him. His mirth was sometimes exuberant. It sparkled in jest, story and anecdote, while at the next moment, his peculiarly sad, pathetic, melancholy eyes would seem to wander far away, and one realized that he was a man "familiar with sorrow and acquainted with grief."[85]

Jesus and Lincoln illustrate Socrates' contention that comedian and tragedian share the same inspiration.[86]

.6.

In Light of Philosophers

Jesus' multifaceted personality can be more fully understood if he is viewed from the varying perspectives of some Western philosophers. How is Jesus similar to Socrates, one of the first to call himself "a lover of wisdom" and one of the most influential philosophers in the past twenty-five centuries? As Karl Marx aptly put it, "Socrates is philosophy personified, as Christ is religion personified."[1] Also, how was Jesus perceived by Friedrich Nietzsche and Bertrand Russell, two exceptionally provocative modern philosophers?

Socrates

Comparing Jesus with Socrates involves moving to a quite different perspective from the one that resulted in concluding that Jesus was a prophetic Pharisee. Since he had much historical awareness of prophets such as Jeremiah, or Pharisees such as Hillel, the consideration of similarities and differences was an intercultural matter. But now a transcultural perspective is needed, such as might be used in comparing Aristotle with Confucius. The cultures involved, from different continents and eras, were isolated from each other. There is no evidence that Socrates was aware of Jewish people or that Jesus knew anything about Greek philosophers. Our basis for comparison is simply that both were Homo sapiens, literally, sapient humans. Thus the discussion will examine how, as wise men and teachers, they interacted with common elements of the human situation.

At the outset, the literary parallel between Jesus and Socrates deserves attention. Since neither wrote anything extant, our knowledge of them is limited to remembrances by their contemporaries. As might be expected, each writer sketched a portrait of Socrates or Jesus that displayed a particular bias. Xenophon saw Socrates as an unimaginative moralist, but Plato viewed him as a brilliant metaphysician. Correspondingly, Matthew the Jew (or, more properly, the anonymous Jewish-Christian editor later identified as an apostle) emphasized Jesus as a fulfiller of Israelite prophecy, while Luke the Gentile interpreted Jesus as a fellow internationalist.

In what significant ways were Socrates and Jesus alike? First, both were similarly commissioned. During the fourth decade of their lives, they felt divinely constrained to enter new careers. Socrates was open to a revelation from Apollo, which one of his friends brought back to Athens from the central Greek shrine at Delphi. The oracle affirmed that no one was wiser than Socrates. That prophecy motivated him to turn away from an earlier pursuit of natural science in order to devote his full attention to engaging his fellow Athenians in philosophical discussion. He described his vocation in this self-depreciating manner:

> Real wisdom is the property of God, and this oracle is his way of telling us that human wisdom has little or no value. It seems to me that he [Apollo] is not referring literally to Socrates, but has merely taken my name as an example; as if he were to say that the wisest of humans is the one who has realized, like Socrates, that he is really worth nothing as regards wisdom. This is why I still go about searching and investigating in obedience to the divine command, if ever I think a citizen or foreigner is wise; and whenever I do not find the person wise, I try to help the cause of God by proving that he is not.[2]

According to the Gospel writers, Jesus was divinely inspired to leave his carpentry trade to teach in synagogues, or wherever else he could find interested people. His main oracle was the prophecy of a "servant" who would patiently enlighten people regarding the meaning of justice (Isa. 42:1–4). When someone addressed Jesus as "Good Teacher," he responded in a humble, Socratic manner: "Why do you call me good? No one is good but God alone" (Mark 10:17–18). Both philosophers affirmed objective standards, and did not identify goodness with their own qualities or gifts.

Disciples were later to heap superlatives on their role models: Plato honored Socrates as "the most noble, wise, and just" person he had known, while Xenophon testified: "To me he seemed to be all a truly good and happy man must be."[3] Paul called Jesus "the wisdom of God" (1 Cor. 1:24) and the Fourth Gospel writer found him "full of grace and truth" (John 1:14).

Both the Athenian philosopher and the "Socrates of Galilee"—as Voltaire called Jesus—were unswervingly devoted to transcendent values. While careful of eternal truth, they were careless of temporal safety. When on trial for his life before the Athenian court, Socrates' testimony might well have been expressed in this declaration of Jesus to Pilate: "For this I have come into the world, to bear witness to the truth" (John 18:37). Both "lovers of wisdom" forsook personal security and endured harsh accusations in allegiance to what they believed to be ultimate reality. Socrates admitted: "My service to God has reduced me to extreme poverty."[4] Xenophon points out that Socrates discouraged the love of money by his own life-style.[5] Jesus claimed that he had fewer material comforts than wild animals had: "Foxes have holes, and birds of the air have nests; but the Son of man has nowhere to lay his head" (Matt. 8:20).

In temperament, Socrates and Jesus were alike. Both were gregarious and were often walking or dining with their friends. Balanced with this was a need for private reflection. Once Socrates was observed spending an entire day and night meditating, before saying prayers at dawn and rejoining his companions. His prayer for self-integration is on record: "Give me beauty in the inward soul, and may the inward and outward person be at one."[6]

In a similar manner Jesus one day engaged in extensive social activities, but "the next morning, long before daybreak, he went out to a lonely place, where he prayed"

(Mark 1:35). Going to particular shrines was not, for either individual, considered essential for recharging one's energies. Worshiping "in spirit and truth," Jesus said, has little to do with climbing to the top of a sacred mountain or making a pilgrimage to the Temple in Jerusalem (John 4:21–24).

Classicist Edith Hamilton uses Gospel language to convey Socrates' similarity to Jesus' "temper of mind." Regarding Jesus' Athenian "forerunner," she writes: "His own mission, he believed, was to open blind eyes, to make men realize the darkness of their ignorance and evil and so to arouse in them a longing for the light; to induce them to seek until they caught a glimpse of the eternal truth."[7] Both Socrates and Jesus regarded hypocrisy as a sure sign of corruption. They hoped to free humans from the shackles of their psychic cave, fan into flame their dimly burning internal wicks, and assist them in their struggle toward the light above.[8]

Socrates and Jesus were both storytellers. They presumed that parables can disclose truth too subtle to be grasped by ordinary discourse. In the *Republic*, for example, Socrates conveyed his basic metaphysics by means of a story about escaping from the cave of materialism. In the *Meno* he told a myth about humans recollecting concepts learned by their souls in the immortal realm subsequent to their previous physical deaths. Likewise, Jesus used his longest parable about "a man who had two sons" (Luke 15:11–32) to convey his understanding of the divine-human relationship.

Mental insemination and midwifery were Socrates' distinctive methods of teaching. Those knowledgeable of the "facts of life" realize that two different types of individuals interacting together are needed for a physical conception. Presuming that it also takes an outside stimulus to produce ideas in a student, Socrates engaged in intellectual intercourse, called dialectic. The ancient "obstetrician" then assisted in bringing to birth the implanted conceptions.[9] Socrates' instructional style was in contrast to the Sophists, the first European paid lecturers. Disregarding gestation, they assumed that fully developed ideas can be transferred effectively to passive receptacles.

Socrates' method of delivering ideas, and returning them to their grateful mother, was also used by Jesus. However, due in large part to the Sermon on the Mount, an editorial stringing together of discrete sayings, Jesus has been associated more with preaching than with dialogue. The Gospel of Luke, which distributes those sayings over a variety of settings, probably comes closer to accurately describing the original situation. For example, Jesus talks about prayer after his disciples have observed him praying and asked him to teach them how to pray (11:1). He characteristically provided impromptu responses to inquiries that arose in the midst of different situations, and resisted doing other people's thinking for them. To emphasize active inquiry, he said to his disciples: "Continue to seek and you will find" (11:9).

An excellent example of Jesus' dialectical method of instruction is found in a passage recorded only by Luke. A student of the law of Moses asks Jesus: "Teacher, what shall I do to inherit eternal life?" (10:25). Jesus avoids giving a direct answer to this basic question about ultimate commitment. Rather than attempting to transfer knowledge to the lawyer, he skillfully works to extract the answer from the lawyer's pregnant mind. Jesus, recognizing that the lawyer has sufficient knowledge to answer his own question, asks, "What is written in the law?" The lawyer responds by citing a law from Deuteronomy about loving God—a verse he regularly recited in his synagogue—and then he creatively couples it with a law from Leviticus about loving one's neighbor. Jesus commends the lawyer for answering his own question, whereupon the lawyer, puzzled over the definition of a word in the Levitical law, asks the key question, "Who is my neighbor?"

In order to confront the lawyer with an answer he might not be prepared to accept, Jesus tells him about a priest, a Levite, and a Samaritan who separately encountered a battered person. Only the Samaritan had love that extended to acting compassionately. After his parable, Jesus inquires: "Which of these three do you think proved neighbor to the man who fell among muggers?" From an inquiry about a legal text, Jesus has shifted the issue to acting like a neighbor. He transposed the situation so that it is no longer an academic matter of defining a term. The inquirer is cleverly guided into recognizing that a member of a generally despised ethnic group could be a neighbor. He answers Jesus' question by confessing, "The one who showed mercy." The lawyer shows that he got the point, even though his prejudice is so strong that he avoids using the distasteful word, "Samaritan." Jesus then urges the one who wants to "inherit eternal life" to act like a neighbor even to persons who may be held in contempt by his culture. Where in the history of pedagogy can a better example be found of existential truth being conveyed by the question-and-discussion method?

Another Gospel dialogue echoes both the form and content of Socrates' philosophy. Some Pharisees are disturbed by the conduct of Jesus and his disciples on the Sabbath—as they pass through a field, they pluck ripe grain, rub it in their hands, blow away the chaff, and then consume the kernels. The Pharisees demand an explanation, because the travelers are engaged in a form of reaping, threshing, and winnowing—three of the dozens of kinds of work prohibited by Pharisees' interpretation of the Sabbath law. They have held their view in an inflexible manner, on the presumption that it was anchored in God's inerrant word as expressed in the hallowed scrolls. Jesus counters the Pharisees' criticism by volleying the dialectical ball back into their court. He cogently asks why David's soldiers satisfied their hunger by eating consecrated bread at the Israelite tabernacle (1 Sam. 21:1–6). According to the Torah, only priests were permitted to eat holy bread at the shrine (Lev. 24:5–9). Jesus presents this parallel case pertaining to a revered ancestor in order to goad the Pharisees into realizing that human need should take priority over even sacred law. Jesus concludes: "The sabbath was made to serve humans; they were not made to keep the sabbath" (Mark 2:27).

The humanitarian principle that emerges from that Sabbath episode, and from similar conversations of Socrates, is that entrenched traditions, whether Homeric or Mosaic, should be continued only if they can be defended as enhancing contemporary life. Socrates tried to show a young fanatic named Euthyphro that right action cannot be determined solely by what a deity has allegedly commanded, but by whether it is in accord with the highest human good. Euthyphro was rushing to prosecute his father, who had violated a religious law, without pondering whether the consequences would enhance life in the Athenian community.[10] Both Socrates and Jesus thought an unexamined religion was not worth having. They were often out of step with authoritarian religionists because they marched to the drumbeat of the God of wisdom.

While Socrates was a patient midwife to serious inquirers, he was a stinging fly to the complacent. He used this famous analogy: "The city is a big . . . lazy horse that needs the stimulation of a gadfly to awaken it."[11] The sayings and questions of Jesus also often had a piercing thrust. He acknowledged the sharp and penetrating quality of his teaching when he exclaimed: "I have not come to bring peace, but a sword!" (Matt. 10:34) and "I have come to kindle a fire!" (Luke 12:49).

Socrates irritated many by questioning some traditional values. For example, justice was then, as now, commonly understood as rendering to everyone what he or she is due. But Socrates believed that retaliation was unworthy behavior, and with regard to his own situation he said: "One ought not to return a wrong or an injury to any person, whatever the provocation."[12] In his last recorded public words, Socrates acted on this conviction. He said to the Athenian jury after they had unjustly voted to give him the death penalty: "I bear no grudge at all against those who condemned me and accused me."[13]

When Socrates advised against retaliation, his scope was limited to Greeks, or even to fellow Athenians. A combat hero himself,[14] he considered hostility by those in a panhellenic league against the "barbarians" (non-Greeks) a necessity even in an ideal commonwealth.[15] A professional caste of warriors should be trained to be gentle toward comrades and fierce toward enemies. The combination of such traits is not unnatural, Socrates argued, for guard dogs are taught to be kind to those they know and vicious toward strangers.[16]

Jesus likewise criticized those who craved to get even after suffering injuries (Matt. 5:39–44). While being executed, he recited the "My God, why have you forsaken me?" psalm, which describes, without a trace of vengeance, the excruciating pain an Israelite was receiving from tormenters

(Ps. 22; Mark 15:34). Jesus prayed with regard to his crucifiers, "Father, forgive them; for they know not what they
do" (Luke 23:34). This prayer echoes Socrates' belief that
moral knowledge leads to virtuous conduct. Lack of such
knowledge is optimistically presumed to be a contributing
cause of the execution of an innocent person.

Extending reconciliation beyond the bounds of his own
Jewish people was a fundamental aim of Jesus. Although
Socrates accepted foreign war as natural and inevitable, such
violence is irreconcilable with Jesus' urging that those declared to be national enemies be treated in a loving manner
(Matt. 5:44). He had "a gospel of peace" (Acts 10:36). Consequently there is no record of Christians serving as soldiers for
the first century of church history.[17]

During his last week in Jerusalem, the gadfly from
Galilee used a counterquestion to handle an inquiry from religious leaders about his credentials. The Gospel of Mark
records this exchange between Jesus and his adversaries:

> "Tell me, did John's right to baptize come from God or
> from man?" This started them arguing among themselves.
> "If we say, 'From God,' he will ask, 'Then why did you
> not believe him?' [John the Baptist had declared Jesus to
> be a more significant prophet than himself.] But how dare
> we say, 'From man'?" They were afraid of the people, for
> all were convinced that John was a real prophet. So they
> replied to Jesus, "We do not know." Jesus then said,
> "Neither will I tell you by what authority I act." (Mark
> 11:30–33)

Socrates and Jesus lived in considerable danger of imminent death, and this impacted their general outlooks. According to Socrates, the philosophical life focuses on such
immortal qualities as wisdom and justice and is therefore a
proper preparation for death. Jesus also shows that the good
life involves withdrawing from dependence on material values. Whereas Socrates told a disciple that "true philosophers
are always occupied in the practice of dying,"[18] Jesus urged
anyone who would follow him to "deny himself and take up
his cross daily" (Luke 9:23). For neither man did self-denial

mean self-contempt, but rather a prioritizing of values, setting long-term spiritual values over immediate physical gratifications.

After both Socrates and Jesus were falsely convicted of blasphemy and corrupting the people, they faced death voluntarily. At his trial Socrates vowed not to alter his objectionable life-style: "I owe a greater obedience to God than to you, and so as long as I draw breath and have my faculties, I shall never stop practicing philosophy."[19] By philosophy, Socrates meant the serious questioning of all cultural values, to discern if they were reasonable and worthy of continued acceptance. The Athenian could have evaded death by compromising his principles and by escaping to live in exile. In responding to Crito, who had a guard-bribing scheme for securing his friend's freedom, Socrates said of his scheduled execution, "If this be God's plan, so be it."[20] He chose to lose his life in order to save his integrity.

Likewise, were it not for the courage of his convictions, Jesus could have left Jerusalem and relieved the authorities there of having a martyr on their hands. "No one takes my life away from me," he said; "I give it up of my own free will" (John 10:18). Both Socrates and Jesus, after they pledged to submit to God's will, were executed while surrounded by a few sympathizers. In his *Death of Socrates* masterpiece, French artist Jacques-Louis David portrays Socrates in the midst of a dozen friends, while the jailor—like the centurion in the Gospels—reluctantly administers the death penalty to one whom he recognizes to be a good man. Xenophon comments regarding Socrates: "There is no record of death more nobly borne. . . . He had been admired above all men for his cheerfulness and serenity."[21]

Although victims of local injustices, Socrates and Jesus ultimately became victors. Throughout Western history, they have disturbed more people than any other two teachers. One changed the course of European philosophy; more significantly, the other one divided the calendar. Francis Cornford's book *Before and After Socrates* tells of the pivotal position of Socrates in ancient Greek culture.[22] Focus on the external cosmos by the "pre-Socratics" was largely replaced by attention to the internal psyche. Psychology was born when Socrates and his followers took seriously the Delphic maxim, "Know thyself." Historian Arnold Toynbee notes: "Almost every post-Socratic school of Hellenic philosophy looked back, and up, to Socrates as its patriarch." The Greco-Roman culture became skeptical of the traditional sky gods, but Socrates prepared it for a new ideal. He became, in Toynbee's words, the historic exemplar of "a god incarnate, not in a community, but in an individual human being."[23] Cicero, living a century before Christianity began, assessed Socrates' impact in this way:

> Ancient philosophy up to Socrates . . . inquired carefully into the magnitude, intervals, and courses of the stars, and all celestial matters. But Socrates first called philosophy down from the sky, set it in the cities and even introduced it into homes, and compelled it to consider life and morals, good and evil.[24]

Ironically, Socrates' execution helped to disseminate his personal and political ideas. In John Stuart Mill's words, "Socrates was put to death but the Socratic philosophy rose like the sun in heaven and spread its illumination over the whole intellectual firmament."[25]

The prologue to the Gospel of John tells how the Logos, the voice of divine reason, came down to earth and "dwelt among us." Christians were convinced that the Logos's enfleshment in Jesus made the ultimate intimate. They also believed that the unextinguished "light" of Jesus had survived death and was radiating among nations of the earth. In the second century Justin appropriately claimed that the same Logos inspired both Socrates and Jesus. That church father regarded Christians as among those who practice "philosophy." After delving into various schools of Greek philosophy, Justin became a Christian, finding "this philosophy alone to be sure and profitable."[26]

In modern history, comparisons of Socrates and Jesus have occasionally been made. Thomas Jefferson's interest in Jesus was revived after reading Joseph Priestley's comparison of the two teachers. As a result, Jefferson took time even while in the White House to compose what he called "The

Philosophy of Jesus."[27] Jefferson joined Goethe, his contemporary, in viewing Jesus as "a true philosopher." In the eighteenth century Rousseau compared Socrates and Jesus, and in the nineteenth century Hegel did the same. Vincent McCarthy examines these and other European philosophers of that era in his *Quest for a Philosophical Jesus*. He claims that "for Kant, Jesus is a superphilosopher."[28] Vernon Robbins, a contemporary classical and biblical scholar, has shown similarities between the teaching methodology of Socrates and Jesus.[29]

No one would now object to honoring Socrates as at least an emeritus doctor of philosophy, but only rarely does anyone refer to Jesus as a philosopher. What can explain this difference in evaluation? Perhaps it shows that the profession of philosophy has shifted greatly since ancient times. How few philosophers since Socrates have opted for death rather than compromise what they believe to be true! There are few ranking Western modern philosophers who, like Pascal, believe they are guided by divine revelation and attempt to combine mystic and rational approaches to truth. Also, civil authorities now seldom regard philosophers as alarming disturbers of the established order; most of them will die unmolested in their beds. Today's philosophers may be more akin to the Sophists, who were paid to lecture, answer questions, and conform to cultural expectations. Thus, in temperament, methodology, and goal, Socrates is more accurately seen as the precursor of Jesus and some of his martyred followers than as the harbinger of many of the present career philosophers. But regardless of the current outlook, both of those ancient Logos personifications left indelible marks on subsequent culture.

This focus on the similarities between Socrates and Jesus should not be interpreted as an attempt to gloss over major differences between the two men. Their central purpose was different: Socrates aimed at developing logical thinking and reasonable actions; Jesus aimed at reviving devotion to the God of Hebrew history while displaying concomitant ethical actions. Jesus made theological claims pertaining to his mission that go beyond anything in the record of Socrates. Jesus identified with the marginalized—the poor, the sick, the handicapped, the aliens, the slaves, the women—whereas Socrates associated with the educated male elite of Athens. These and other differences are so obvious that a full discussion of them is not needed here.

Nietzsche

Throughout the century since Nietzsche lived in the German culture, he has been widely recognized as the most formidable philosophical adversary of the Jesus movement. "This man launched what may be the most merciless assault upon Christianity in our time," Karl Jaspers comments.[30] Yet, Jaspers points out, Nietzsche signed himself "The Crucified" shortly before he became completely insane; he saw in Jesus "the anticipated realization of his own idea of what is more than morality."[31] Intuiting the shocking role he would play posthumously, Nietzsche proudly declared, "I am the Anti-Christ." Even so, he also observed that "the most earnest Christians have always been favorably disposed to me."[32] John Bernstein has stated in his book on Nietzsche: "I would unhesitatingly call him the subtlest Christian of modern times."[33]

Nietzsche's brilliant but unsystematic treatment of Jesus deserves what it has never received: a careful examination and evaluation. His style is often striking—even in translation—so his thoughts will be quoted whenever possible. As a philosopher of culture he was interested in showing the relationship of Jesus to the Judaism that preceded and to the church that followed.

According to Nietzsche, the religious leaders of ancient Israel were deceitful to the core in the values they championed. Slave morality began with the Israelite prophets who identified the rich with the godless and the poor with the godly.[34] Also the Israelite priests produced scrolls which, by their allegation, revealed "the will of God." Actually, Nietzsche believed, they engaged in a "literary forgery" to exalt themselves.[35] They declared, for example, that the tastiest pieces of meat offered at sacrifices should be given to the priests to eat. They interpreted "all misfortune as punishment for disobeying God" and "invented sin" in order to produce guilty clients.[36] The priests attempted to make themselves indispensable by means of their so-called sacred scriptures, declaring that God forgives those who obey their dictates.[37]

Jesus rebelled against the priestcraft of his culture, and for such audacity he was crucified. Regarding Jesus' response to the Jewish establishment, Nietzsche writes: "The holy anarchist . . . summoned the lowly, the outcasts and 'sinners', the *pariahs* within Judaism . . . to oppose the ruling order."[38] "One could call Jesus a 'free spirit'—he cares nothing for what is fixed. . . . The *experience* of 'life', in the only way he knows it, is opposed to any kind of word, formula, law, faith, dogma. He speaks only of the innermost—'life' or 'truth' or 'light'."[39]

Nietzsche expresses clearly what he considers to be the basic thrust of Jesus' teaching:

> What is the "good news"? True life, eternal life has been found—it is not promised, it is here, it is *within you*: as life lived in love, in love without subtraction and exclusion, without regard for status. Everyone is a child of God— Jesus definitely claims nothing for himself alone—as a child of God everyone is equal to everyone else.[40]

For Nietzsche, "the Kingdom of God" or "the Kingdom of Heaven" is synonymous with "eternal life." Hence, "the Kingdom of God does not 'come' chronologically-historically, on a certain day in the calendar. . . . It is an 'inward change in the individual,' something that comes at every moment."[41] Likewise, "the 'Kingdom of Heaven' is a condition of the heart—not something that is to come 'above the earth' or 'after death'."[42] Nietzsche assumes that Jesus rejected the dominant theme of apocalyptic Judaism of his day, which viewed the ideal society as a future event that the faithful should wait for expectantly.

In contrast to the synagogue teaching, the gospel is that there is no divine punishment, because "'sin'—any distance separating God and man—is abolished."[43] Nietzsche states: "Jesus denied any chasm between God and man; he *lived* this unity of God and man as *his* 'good news'."[44] The Jewish concept of "faith" or "belief" is replaced by a new life-style: "He makes no distinction between foreigner and native. . . . He is not angry with anyone, does not disdain anyone."[45]

The crucifixion of Jesus shows that he sincerely practiced the revengeless gospel he preached:

> This "bringer of good news" died as he lived . . . to demonstrate how one ought to live. What he bequeathed to mankind is his practice: his behavior before the judges, before the guards, before the accusers of every kind of slander and mockery—his behavior on the *Cross*. He does not resist, he does not defend his rights, he takes no steps to avert the worst; on the contrary *he provokes it*. And he begs, he suffers, he loves *with* those, *in* those who do him evil.[46]

This gospel was best comprehended, Nietzsche thinks, by a man who was crucified with Jesus. "The criminal undergoing a painful death declares: 'The way this Jesus suffered and died, without rebelling, without enmity, graciously, resignedly, is the only right way.' By that he affirms the gospel and is in Paradise."[47] The thief received not personal immortality—for there is none—but a state of blessedness.

Nietzsche claims that Jesus did not resort to rational arguments or to supernatural wonders. The only validation of his teaching was the integrity he exhibited through a life climaxed by his crucifixion.[48] In this regard, Nietzsche states:

> [The gospel] does not prove itself, either by miracles or by rewards and promises, and certainly not "by the Scriptures": it is every moment its own miracle, its own reward, its own proof, its own "Kingdom of God." . . . The idea is lacking that a faith, a "truth" could be proved by reasons (his proofs are inner "lights," inner feelings of pleasure and self-affirmations).[49]

Displaying considerable perspicuity, Nietzsche argued that falsifications about the real Jesus have abounded from the earliest Christians onward. Most church members have portrayed

Jesus as a miracle worker, and have accepted as historical even such "a dreadful corruption" as Jesus cursing a fig tree because fruit was not found on it out of season.[50] Such crudities were attributable to Christians who vulgarized the noble message of Jesus in order to win converts from uncouth pagan cults.[51]

According to Nietzsche, the milieu into which Jesus' disciples were immersed also caused them to misinterpret Jesus as an apocalyptic ruler. Even though Jesus had proclaimed that the "Kingdom" was present, "the popular expectation of a Messiah came once more into the foreground: . . . the 'Kingdom of God' is coming to sit in judgment on its enemies." The disciples wanted their foes destroyed, not forgiven, so they introduced a "Second Coming" doctrine which declared that the Messiah would take vengeance on their enemies. Although Jesus had no hatred of the Jewish rulers who persecuted him, his disciples "*failed* to understand the main point—the exemplary element in his manner of dying, the freedom from, the superiority *over* every feeling of resentment."[52]

Nietzsche faults the apostle Paul for being "the inventor of Christianity." Without the confusions of his mind "there would be no Christianity; we would hardly have heard of a small Jewish sect whose master died on the cross."[53] As Nietzsche puts it:

> In Paul was embodied the opposite type to the "bringer of good news." . . . Paul singly shifted the center of gravity . . . *beyond* this existence—in the *lie* of the "resurrected" Jesus. In fact he had no use at all for the Redeemer's life. . . . He makes of a hallucination the *proof* that the Redeemer is *still* living.[54]

Paul superstitiously fabricated a dogma of personal immortality, Nietzsche claims, and announced a resurrection for everyone.

Paul was the one mainly responsible, Nietzsche thinks, for the Jewish doctrine of slave morality being continued in Christianity. Due to that "frightful impostor," Christianity "has been from the beginning a collective movement of outcast and refuse elements of every kind."[55] Paul's contempt for culture and intellect is allegedly displayed in this Corinthian letter:

Not many wise according to worldly standards, not many
mighty, not many noble, are called. God chose what the
world considers foolish and weak to shame the wise and
mighty. He chose what the world looks down on and de-
spises and thinks is nothing, in order to destroy what the
world thinks is important. (1 Cor. 1:26–28)

Nietzsche, seeing here a revengeful attitude toward the
powerful rulers who crucified Jesus, claims that Paul reversed the "good news" with a message filled with "bad
news." As regards theology, Nietzsche asserts: "God, as Paul
created him, is the negation of God."[56]

Nietzsche held that it was not Jesus, but the subsequent
counterfeit Christianity that "made of sexuality something
impure; it threw *filth* on the beginning, on the prerequisite of
our life."[57] In accord with the New Testament, "the Church
combats the passions with excision in every sense of the
word: its practice, its 'cure' is *castration*."[58] Nietzsche asks,
"What follows from all this? That one does well to put gloves
on when reading the New Testament. The proximity of so
much uncleanliness almost forces one to do so."[59] Nietzsche
is severe in his judgment on the church's treatment of sex as
sin: "Every expression of contempt for the sexual life, every
befouling of it through the concept 'impure,' is *the* crime
against life—is the essential sin against the holy spirit of
life."[60]

Only once does Nietzsche acknowledge a continuity between Jesus and Christians. He states: "I do not like at all
about Jesus of Nazareth or his apostle Paul that they put so
many ideas into the heads of little people, as if their modest
virtues were of any consequence."[61] Torn down was the
"morality of breeding, of race, of privilege," and raised up
were "the poor and lowly, the collective rebellion of all the
downtrodden, the wretched, the failures, the less favored."[62]

According to Nietzsche, "democracy is Christianity made
natural."[63] "The French Revolution is the daughter and continuation of Christianity," he wrote; "its instincts are against
caste, against the noble, against the last privileges."[64] A de-
fender of elitism, Nietzsche was outraged by the success of
Christian values:

The poison of the doctrine *"equal* rights for all"—this has been more thoroughly sowed by Christianity than by anything else. . . . The aristocratic outlook has been undermined most deeply by the lie of equality of souls. . . . Christianity is a revolt of everything that crawls along the ground directed against that which is *elevated.*[65]

By way of evaluating Nietzsche's assessment of Jesus, we may say that he rightly assumes that the historical Jesus is not to be identified with a composite of the values held by Christians. Nietzsche is appropriately remembered widely for this aphorism: "There has truly been only one Christian, and he died on the cross."[66] In 1864, as a young scholar, Nietzsche "savored the work of the incomparable Strauss," who maintained that Jesus was an extraordinary personality but was different from the accounts written by the earliest Christians. That same year David Strauss's *Life of Jesus for the German People* popularized the results of radical biblical scholarship. Although Nietzsche later attacked some of Strauss's ideas, he continued to share the view that the real Jesus should be separated from the untrustworthy Gospel reports. Nietzsche wrote: "What concerns *me* is the psychological type of the Redeemer. This *could* be contained in the Gospels despite the Gospels, however mutilated or embroidered with alien features: as that of Francis of Assisi is contained in the legends about him despite the legends."[67]

Like Strauss, Nietzsche presumed that "Christianity can be understood only by referring to the soil out of which it grew."[68] He accepted Strauss's argument that the Gospel accounts of a supernatural Jesus have resulted from early admirers who were convinced that Jesus must have done more marvels than any Israelite hero. Hence they created stories of Jesus performing miracles of raising the dead, multiplying food, and ascending into heaven, as in the Elijah-Elisha legends. Nietzsche attributed "faith in unbelievable things"[69] only to Jesus' followers; the Jesus hidden under the literary accretions did not claim to have power to intervene in nature's orderliness. In the next chapter I will show that there is much substance in Strauss's interpretation of Jesus' miracles.

To agree that the New Testament writings and subsequent Christian literature do not accurately preserve the image Jesus cast during his lifetime would not satisfy Nietzsche. He goes much farther in his shrill denunciation by assuming that some Christians—Paul especially—deliberately and maliciously "pronounced holy precisely what the 'bringer of the good news' felt to be *beneath* and *behind* himself."[70] Nietzsche perversely calls Paul "the genius of hatred" and the establisher of "a priestly tyranny."[71] However, on the basis of Paul's ode to love in 1 Corinthians 13 and his expressions of affection in a number of letters, a better case can be made that the apostle was generally faithful to Jesus' teaching and practice of love. But Paul might have agreed with Nietzsche that the Gospel accounts of Jesus as a supernatural miracle worker and eschatological judge are corruptions invented after Jesus' death.

Nietzsche claims that Paul was anti-intellectual and that Christianity from the beginning has been accepted exclusively by the simpleminded. Yet Paul writes, "Among the mature we do impart wisdom" (1 Cor. 2:6). In the same letter in which he describes the appeal of Christianity to the common people of Corinth, he stresses that both "spirit" and "mind" are needed for worship (1 Cor. 14:15).

Nietzsche's Jesus resembles his "superior person" (*übermensch*) ideal. The philosopher's fictional Zarathustra spoke of Jesus in this admiring way:

> One man once saw into the hearts of "the good and the just" and said, "They are Pharisees." . . . The *creator* they hate most: he breaks tablets and old values. . . . They call him lawbreaker. . . . They crucify him who writes new values on new tablets.[72]

Jesus embodied *übermensch* values: independence, courage, sincerity, hope, guiltlessness, and self-discipline. "Even today such a life is possible," Nietzsche suggests.[73] "Caesar with the soul of Christ"[74] is the way Nietzsche describes the ideal ruler.

Scorn for the oppressed masses is one *übermensch* quality that Jesus lacked. Nietzsche inconsistently admired Jesus for having been "in mutiny against the social order"[75] while criticizing him for showing compassion on those whom the social leaders neglected. Those who do not share Nietzsche's view that democracy is decadent may find in his criticism an unwitting tribute not only to Jesus but to the Christian movement which "lives and struggles for '*equal* rights'."[76]

"The errors of great men are. . . more fruitful than the truths of little men."[77] Schopenhauer was in Nietzsche's mind when he penned that epigram, but it applies to himself as well. To appreciate the truth of some of Nietzsche's insights, while recognizing significant errors that historical scholarship has revealed, is to honor Nietzsche in the manner he most desired. He wrote impishly to encourage independent thinking; he had no interest in producing dependent followers.

Russell

Bertrand Russell is the most notable English-speaking philosopher of the twentieth century. The wisdom and wit of his *History of Western Philosophy* won him the Nobel Prize for literature. Russell evaluates Jesus' character in several pages of his widely distributed *Why I Am Not a Christian*. Written in 1927, at a time when Russell was devoted to pacifism and after he had been imprisoned for interfering with the British military, the work first expresses admiration for three of Jesus' alleged principles: do not physically resist evil; do not seek law-court remedies; and do give all possessions to the poor. But then Russell inconsistently claims that "it is quite doubtful whether Christ ever existed at all, and if he did we do not know anything about him."

Even after Russell decided that nonresistance would be a disastrous policy against the Nazis, he admired Jesus' love-your-enemies teaching. He comments: "The Christian principle does not inculcate calm, but an ardent love even towards the worst of men. There is nothing to be said against it except that it is too difficult for most of us to practice sincerely." Contrasting himself to Nietzsche, who allegedly despised universal love, Russell affirms: "I feel it the motive power to all that I desire as regards the world."[78]

Russell alleges that Jesus fell short of superlative wisdom or goodness in several ways. This is his first charge:

He certainly thought that his second coming would occur in clouds of glory before the death of all the people who were living at that time. There are a great many texts that prove that. He says, for instance, "Ye shall not have gone over the cities of Israel till the Son of Man be come.". . . When he said, "Take no thought for the morrow," and things of that sort, it was very largely because he thought that the second coming was going to be very soon, and that all ordinary mundane affairs did not count.[79]

Ironically, Russell reads the Gospels with as little scholarly sophistication as the simpleminded fundamentalists he scorns. He naively presents as the "obvious" viewpoint of Jesus what is a highly debated matter. New Testament critics argue cogently that it is unlikely that the verse Russell cites regarding the "second coming" was an authentic teaching of Jesus. Because the saying presumes Jesus to have ascended to heaven, it was probably a creation of the early church after the alleged event occurred.[80] Also, we know Jesus claimed that the end would not come until the gospel had been spread "throughout the whole world, as a testimony to all nations" (Matt. 24:14).

Russell displays even less scholarly caution in attributing to Jesus an idea that actually comes from a change in the English language since the seventeenth century. When William Tyndale and the King James Version translated the Greek phrase *me merimnate* as "take no thought," the English injunction then meant "Do not worry." This meaning has long been obsolete, and all contemporary translations recognize that it would be wrong to convey that Jesus meant "Do not think about." The British Revised Version, which was available to Russell, shows that a modern translation for the original Greek is "Be not anxious." Thus Jesus' maxim pertains to overcoming anxiety about the future; in no way does it presume there will be no distant earthly future.

As we have seen, Jesus encouraged prudent planning ahead. One of Jesus' parables gave special attention to the need for forethought. He told of bridesmaids who were supposed to provide a torchlight entrance for the bridegroom. The wise ones displayed preparedness, whereas the foolish

ones did not think ahead and were faced with an unantici-
pated fuel shortage (Matt. 25:1–13).

Russell's second reason for rejecting Jesus as "the best
and wisest of men" is contained in this comment:

> There is one very serious defect to my mind in Christ's
> moral character, and that is that he believed in hell. I do
> not myself feel that any person who is really profoundly
> humane can believe in everlasting punishment. . . . This
> doctrine, that hell-fire is a punishment for sin, is a doc-
> trine of cruelty.[81]

Here Russell shares Mark Twain's outlook. Russell states
that Jesus had "a vindictive fury against those people who
would not listen to his preaching" and consigned them to
hell. Virtually the only fault that Twain found in Jesus was
that he was "the inventor of hell."[82]

If this charge by Russell and Twain is true, then there is
indeed a basic moral problem in Jesus' teaching. Did he believe in a schizophrenic God, who is both an infinite forgiver
and an everlasting torturer? Or did he believe in a loving but
weak God who is not in control of evil? According to Jesus'
doctrine, are the wicked punished sheerly "for the hell of it"
when there is no possibility of repentance? This matter deserves careful investigation.

Russell unjustly compares Jesus with Socrates on this
point. He thinks that Socrates' sagaciousness exceeds that of
Jesus because the Athenian did not believe in hell. Yet, one
of Socrates' speeches describes a horrible place where murderers are thrown after death and remain till they have obtained the forgiveness of the souls of those they wronged.[83]
Also, he tells of souls who suffer tenfold for their earthly
wickedness by being beaten with scourges and pulled across
thorns.[84] Moreover, Socrates accepted the Greek myth about
Sisyphus, who was punished in the afterlife by being assigned the endless task of rolling a huge stone up a hill only
to have it roll back on its own.[85]

Just what was Jesus' view of punishment after death? In
order to evaluate Russell's interpretation, an excursus is needed
to examine Jesus' eschatological outlook. He continually

taught his disciples that God should be thought of as a caring parent, so any notion of a cruel Omnipotence devising ever-lasting punishments must be rejected. Fiendish humans have created ingenious instruments for tearing apart bodies so as to maximize pain, but Jesus would have considered it blasphe-mous to assume that God does the same. Rather, his theology echoes that of this psalm:

> Yahweh is compassionate and gracious,
>> long-suffering and abounding in steadfast love.
> He will not always accuse,
>> nor will he bear a grudge.
> He does not treat us as our sins deserve,
>> nor punish us according to our offenses.
> As high as the sky is above the earth,
>> so vast is his steadfast love for those who revere him.
> As far as east is from west,
>> so far does he remove our sins from us.
> As kind as a father is to his children,
>> So kind is Yahweh toward those who revere him.
>
> (Ps. 103:8–13)

That psalmist articulates a frequently reiterated doctrine of the Hebrew Bible (Ex. 34:6; Neh. 9:17; Joel 2:13; Jonah 4:2). In regard to the fatherhood of God, Jesus presented some lesser-to-greater logic:

> Is there anyone among you who, if your child asks for bread, will give a stone? Or if the child asks for a fish, will give a snake? If you then, bad as you are, know enough to give your children what is good for them, how much more will your heavenly Father give good things to those who ask him! (Matt. 7:9–11)

Jesus' view of eschatology is rooted in the traditional He-brew view that eternal life is natural to God alone. By con-trast, death is the natural final end for mice and men. According to the Garden of Eden story, humans lose spiri-tual life forever when they separate themselves from God. Due to self-determinism, there is nothing in their future but

127

dusty death (Gen. 3:19, 22–23). God shares the realm of deathless life with those who desire godly virtues. Thus, each human has the option of "passing on" or passing out of existence. Those who devote themselves to spiritual growth during their physical lives will be given the opportunity for further development after physical death. Life after death is seen as a continuance of the eternal or spiritual life which one can begin to enjoy during her or his mortal life.

The consequences of religious commitment are well expressed in the Johannine writings and in the Pauline letters. The "hell" metaphor is not used in either group of books, which together make up more than half of the New Testament. In the Fourth Gospel, "eternal life" is contrasted with personal perishing (3:16–21). Jesus speaks of self-judgment that operates through life-styles, causing some to "love darkness rather than light." Believing that God values individual freedom, Jesus did not think that anyone is compelled to participate in spiritual fellowship. As the "free-doom" pun suggests, the concept of freedom has hidden within it the liberty to self-destruct.

Jesus and Paul shared the Hebrew view that the soul is not inherently immortal. The soul (*psyche*) can be destroyed (Mark 8:36; Luke 2:35; John 3:16). Regarding those who have not cultivated religious values, the apostle says: "Their end is destruction" (Phil. 3:19). He succinctly states: "The wages of sin is death [not hell], but the free gift of God is eternal life" (Rom. 6:23). Comparing harvests in the agricultural and spiritual realms, Paul asserts: "A person reaps what he sows: sow in the field of self-indulgence and the crop is death; sow in the field of the Spirit and the crop is eternal life" (Gal. 6:7–8).

The ultimate result of rejecting the divine gift is personal destruction of immor*table* potentiality, which concludes at death. Jesus pictures this in several different ways. First, some passages in Matthew refer to people being "cast out into the outer darkness" because of their bad behavior. Such will be the end of those who do not invest the talents with which they have been entrusted (25:27, 30), or of those who do not meet the conditions for participating in an international banquet hosted by the Hebrew patriarchs (8:11–12).

Those who do not become infused with the immortal light of God and who do not accept the ensuing responsibilities of that relationship have nothing within them capable of surviving biological death. If they function habitually on the sensate level of animals, they ultimately share the subhuman destiny of animals.

A second metaphor used by Jesus for the outcome of unwise use of choices is "weeping and gnashing of teeth." For example, Jesus tells of a trusted servant who becomes dissipated and acts in a cruel manner during his master's absence. When the time of accountability arrives, there is personal anguish from realizing how much better it would have been if he had been faithful (Matt. 24:45–51). The poignancy of poor choice or no choice is well expressed in this poetic couplet:

> Of all sad words of tongue or pen,
> The saddest are these: "It might have been!"[86]

There is similarity between Jesus' gnashing-of-teeth accounts and Jean-Paul Sartre's salutary look at self-damnation in *No Exit*. In order to encourage a more responsible life before an irredeemable situation arises, Sartre wrote a drama about the after-death confrontation of three persons. While condemned to live forever in the same room, the prisoners torment one another by expressions of emptiness and lovelessness. Each attempts to transfer his or her guilt to the others. Sartre's description of the reverse of what he calls authentic existence resembles the way Jesus portrays the opposite of salvation. Here is a sampling of the exchange in the hell of atheist Sartre:

INEZ: We've had our hour of pleasure, haven't we? There have been people who burned their lives out for our sakes— and we chuckled over it. So now we have to pay the reckoning.

GARCIN [*raising his fist*]: Will you keep your mouth shut, damn it! ... So this is hell. ... You remember all we were told about the torture-chamber, the fire and brimstone. ... There's no need for red-hot pokers. Hell is—other people![87]

Jesus' third picture for the final outcome of the ungodly was borrowed from the Judaism of his day. Frequently he used a Hebrew term, *Ge hinnom*, which becomes *Geenna* in the Greek Synoptic Gospels. This word, usually translated into English as "hell," referred in the time of Jeremiah to the valley (*ge*) belonging to the sons of Hinnom. Located on the southern outskirts of Jerusalem, it was considered defiled because children of pre-Israelite Jerusalem residents had been sacrificed there to the god Molech (Jer. 32:35). The ravine became a trash dump, where unburied corpses were incinerated (Jer. 7:32–33; Isa. 66:24). Fire was continuous there, accounting for the rapid decomposition, and worms were ever feasting on the organic wastes. The Jews drew from the geographical *Ge hinnom* a metaphor for the final liquidation of the unrighteous. In the Mishnah, for example, murderers and deceitful persons "inherit *ge hinnom* and go down to the pit of destruction," whereas the righteous "inherit the Garden of Eden and the world to come."[88] The Jews did not presume that an everlasting paradise for the good must be balanced by an everlasting torment for the bad. Jesus also used *Ge hinnom* as a figure for extinction, and once he explicitly associated it with the complete destruction of all that makes one a human being (Matt. 10:28). It is unlikely that Jesus intended to describe a literal spot on earth, beneath the earth, or separate from the earth, where the damned are perpetually fried.

In *Jesus Before Christianity*, Albert Nolan writes perceptively:

> The imagery of fire and worms is derived from the rubbish dump of Gehenna. It should be noted that according to this imagery it is the worms that never die and the fire that is perpetual or eternal. Everything and everybody else in Gehenna dies, decomposes and is destroyed. Gehenna is the image of complete destruction, the extreme opposite of life.[89]

One of Jesus' uses of the fire metaphor for judgment is separate from the *Ge hinnom* image. His wheat and weeds parable pertains to final accountability after divine tolerance throughout a human's life. Weedy growth is permitted to flourish, but at the end of the season the reapers bind the weeds in bundles to fuel ovens. Casting stubble in fire is a figure of immediate annihilation, not of continued punishment. At the same time, the reapers gather the good grain in barns for storage (Matt. 13:24–30, 41–42).

This extended exploration of Jesus' eschatology shows that he did not have a cruel doctrine of eternal torture. Had Russell studied closely the meaning of Jesus' metaphors, he might have realized that Jesus was far from believing that sinners would forever be roasting over an open fire in the devil's barbecue pit. The point of honest difference of opinion between Russell and Jesus is on the continuation of any form of life after death. Russell states for himself a position that he thinks is universal: "I believe that when I die I shall rot, and nothing of my ego will survive."[90] For Jesus, the destruction of the ego, or self, is the fate only of the godless.

Russell adopts some of the traditional eschatological language to apply to human relationships before death. Somewhat like Jesus, Russell pictures a future scenario that would be inevitable if moral responsibility is shunned. With righteous indignation, he describes policies pertaining to nuclear warfare that can exterminate the human species. In line with the biblical prophets, Russell extrapolates on cultural tendencies that can well lead to a "doomsday" worse than black death.[91] Prophets of every generation hope that their grim forecasts will cause people to swerve from their present fatal course. Both Jesus and Russell believed that humans are accountable and that they need to be shown graphically in images appropriate to their cultures that there is a momentousness in individual and group choice that can lead to disaster. Both hoped to rouse conscientiousness and to encourage the wise exercise of freedom.

In addition to criticizing the idea of an eternal hell ordained by divine power and to appraising the danger of earthly annihilation by international superpowers, Russell takes issue with another alleged viewpoint of Jesus. He states: "There is not one word in the Gospels in praise of intelligence."[92] That categorical statement of Russell displays either ignorance or perversity. In the Gospels, intelligence is commended and its practice is frequently expressed. When

Jesus urges his disciples to "Be wise" (Matt. 10:16), the Greek verb is the same one Aristotle used for expressing practical reasoning. When Jesus quotes from Deuteronomy what he calls the first commandment, he adds to the Hebrew original and to the Septuagint translation the phrase italicized in this passage: "You shall love the Lord your God with all your heart, and with all your soul, *and with all your mind*, and with all your strength" (Mark 12:30). Seemingly, Jesus wished to make explicit what is implicit in the original Hebrew, that devotees to God should not substitute affectionate gushing or ritualistic frenzy for mental discipline.

For Jesus, a full heart was not an acceptable replacement for an empty mind. He was not in favor of the hyperemotionalism that was commonplace in some Greek cults. It was soon to infiltrate Christianity and would come to be known as glossolalia.[93] Due to a second-century spurious ending to Mark—which has unfortunately been preserved without warning in the King James Version, to which most fundamentalists look for authority—Jesus has been thought to encourage speaking in tongues, as well as snake handling and drinking poison! (16:17–18). However, Jesus' only authentic teaching regarding such fanaticism is this: "Don't use a lot of meaningless words as pagans do" (Matt. 6:7).

Russell accepted the self-serving stereotype that religion is the territory of the dim-witted while philosophy is the preserve of the enlightened. Yet Jesus thought of himself as belonging to the tradition of those sages who valued intellectual insight (Luke 11:31). He never condemned a doubter or dodged a critic. For example, Jesus recognized the conceptual difficulties of his disciple Thomas and encouraged him to express his doubts (John 14:5–7). The fact that Jesus did not aim to produce clones of himself is displayed in traditions preserved in the New Testament. The wide variations in the testimony of what Jesus actually said shows that his disciples had minds of their own.

For a balanced perspective, the outlook of Russell on Jesus should be weighed against that of Luther Weigle. He wrote:

We are impressed with the reasonableness as well as the directness of Jesus' appeal to those who heard him. His tone was not that of a lawgiver, who commands; nor that of a despot, who threatens punishment or cajoles with promises of reward. Jesus spoke as one who discerns the truth, and sets it before others that they too may see it and in its light decide the issues which impend. He challenged his hearers to think for themselves, in the light of the relevant facts. He was no propagandist, capturing the minds of people by appeals to prejudice or passion. . . . His appeal was to intelligence, conscience, will.[94]

The rationality of Jesus and Siddhartha, the Buddha, are similar. Both men rejected some dogmatic pronouncements of the religious leaders of their cultures and they encouraged their disciples to do likewise. According to Buddhist tradition, Siddhartha said to a disciple:

Don't believe traditions because they happen to be old and have been passed down through many generations. . . . And don't believe anything on the mere authority of your teachers or priests. What you *should* accept as true and as the guide to your life is whatever agrees with your own reason and your own experience after thorough investigation, and whatever is helpful both to your own well-being and that of other living beings.[95]

Sharing the stance of Siddhartha and Jesus, Russell appealed to reason, experience, and sympathy. He constructed an argument between Nietzsche and Siddhartha in which the latter states:

You are mistaken, Professor Nietzsche, in thinking my ideal is a purely negative one, . . . the absence of suffering. . . . I, too, have my heroes: my successor Jesus, because he told men to love their enemies; the men who discovered how to master the forces of nature and secure food with less labor; the medical men who have shown how to diminish disease; the poets and artists and musicians who have caught glimpses of the Divine beatitude. Love and knowledge and delight in beauty are not negations; they are enough to fill the lives of the greatest men that have ever lived.[96]

Russell, despite his criticisms of Jesus, ended up championing a secularized version of Jesus' love principle. This confession opens his autobiography, written in his tenth decade: "Three passions, simple but overwhelmingly strong, have governed my life: the longing for love, the search for knowledge, and unbearable pity for the suffering of mankind."[97] Elsewhere he summed up his ethics in this way: "The good life is one inspired by love and guided by knowledge."[98] Russell readily admitted that a person needs "love, Christian love, or compassion." After asserting this, he added:

> If you feel this, you have a motive for existence, a guide in action, a reason for courage, an imperative necessity for intellectual honesty. If you feel this, you have all that anybody should need in the way of religion. Although you may not find happiness, you will never know the deep despair of those whose life is aimless and void of purpose; for there is always something that you can do to diminish the awful sum of human misery.[99]

Philosopher George Santayana may have been thinking of Russell, his contemporary, when he analyzed the outlook of the typical atheist. That master of prose wrote:

> Experience has repeatedly confirmed that well-known maxim of Bacon's, that "a little philosophy inclineth man's mind to atheism, but depth in philosophy bringeth men's minds about to religion." . . . [Atheists] yearn mightily in their own souls after the religious acceptance of a world interpreted in their own fashion. So it appears in the end that their atheism and loud protestation were in fact the hastier part of their thought, since what emboldened them to deny the poor world's faith was that they were too impatient to understand it. Indeed, the enlightenment common to young wits and worm-eaten old satirists . . . is not nearly enlightened enough: it points to notorious facts incompatible with religious tenets literally taken, but it leaves unexplored the habits of thought from which those tenets sprang, their original meaning, and their true function.[100]

Socrates, Nietzsche, and Russell are representative of the pivotal philosophers of Western civilization. Although coming from different centuries and nations, each man admired the shimmering intellect and lamented that its potential is little used. They tended to caricature the religiously oriented as lamebrained bigots who make little use of thought in the pursuit of good goals. But they all did share some of the wisdom of Jesus in spite of their viewpoints on religion. All of them displayed sincerity and courage in their words and actions. Socrates shared with Jesus the value of humility toward an immortal and just deity. The pedagogy they championed has left a lasting legacy. While rejecting the God to whom Jesus was devoted, Nietzsche and Russell found ideas of great significance in the Gospels. The German philosopher admired Jesus' independence as a value creator. The British philosopher appreciated Jesus' devotion to love in the pursuit of world peace. Understanding these three philosophers can help us to clarify, in a dialectical manner, the abiding significance of Jesus' wisdom.

.7.

Supernatural and Other Signs

The ambiguous term "supernatural" is here used to describe alleged happenings that are presumed to be unexplainable by the ordinary operations of nature, whether physical or psychic. Supernaturalism is the belief that for such events a divine causation interrupts the regular natural order. Did Jesus accept this presupposition, which has been popular throughout history with many other religious personalities?

Fantastic Legends

The stories of Israelite charismatic figures were recorded years—or even centuries—after they happened. In cases where the biographical information is written by the charismatic personalities themselves, or by their contemporaries, the absence of supernaturalism is notable. Thus the fifteen Latter Prophets in the Hebrew canon, from Isaiah to Malachi (Daniel is not counted), perform no supernatural miracles. By contrast, the earlier prophets were remembered not so much for what they did in their lifetimes as for the bigger-than-life caricatures drawn by adoring disciples writing much later.

The saga of Moses illustrates the way in which the biography of a dead hero bloats with the passage of time. The book of Exodus is an editorial mosaic of Mosaic traditions. Recorded there are several fragmentary accounts of different vintage, which had been circulated orally for many generations. The literary structure of the entire Pentateuch resembles a mound left by an ancient town, in which the different levels of artifacts reveal to the archaeologist the succession of peoples who lived there over the centuries. Likewise, textual scholars have painstakingly probed the Pentateuchal documents to ascertain chronological development. The earlier recorded traditions are less supernatural than the supplements made by the Priestly editors of the Pentateuch, who lived about seven centuries after Moses.[1]

The first two chapters of Exodus, for example, which mainly record early traditions about Moses, contain no reference to unnatural happenings. There the Israelite slave resistance is portrayed as instigated by a number of women who are armed only with compassion and cleverness. Hebrew midwives and an Egyptian princess engage in civil disobedience against a pharaoh, with the help of Moses' mother and sister. Providence is expressed through human resourcefulness, not through direct divine intervention.

In the later traditions of slavery in Egypt, emphasis is placed on the plagues wrought by the magical powers of Moses' staff.[2] His rod is turned into a snake at a performance in the pharaoh's palace. However, using other rods, "the magicians of Egypt did the same by their secret arts." To top the snake "sign" of divine power, the Nile is allegedly turned to blood: Moses' rod strikes the river and all the fish die from lack of water (Ex. 7:3–24). That is just the first of ten incredible plagues. Thus Moses becomes more of a wand-wielding wonder-worker than a believable human. In Judeo-Christian history, more have been impressed by superman Moses than by the ordinary women who actually started the rebellion against the pharaoh.

The subsequent course of Israelite religion was affected by the latest level of the Mosaic literary "mound," where appeal is made to signs as proof. Those with little depth of faith looked for what seemed supernatural in visual manifestations. To illustrate, consider Jesus' trial centuries later in the Jerusalem palace of his king. There is this confrontation: "Herod was delighted to see Jesus because he had heard about him and had long desired to meet him. The king was hoping to see a miracle performed by him" (Luke 23:8). The outlook of Herod has been well depicted for contemporary audiences by the rock opera *Jesus Christ Superstar*. The Jewish king urges Jesus to walk on his swimming pool and thereby provide a spectacular demonstration. The Jews eagerly wanted a miracle-man messiah who could perform divine tricks like the legendary Moses.

Elijah and Elisha, ninth-century contemporaries, also were transformed into wizards as the legends about them grew. Elijah allegedly did mighty marvels, including announcing the beginning and ending of a drought, killing hundreds of pagan prophets, and raising the dead. Before he ascended to heaven in a fiery chariot, his cloak was powerful enough to divide the Jordan River twice. That enabled Elijah and Elisha to walk to the east side together, and then it helped Elisha to return to the west bank without the inconvenience of getting wet or using a boat (2 Kings 2:8, 14).

According to Jewish reckoning, Elisha performed sixteen miracles after receiving the Spirit. By Mark's account, Jesus also performed the same number, and some are quite similar. In one story, Elisha takes a small amount of food, divides it among a large number of people, and has some left after everyone is filled (2 Kings 4:42–44). The parallel in Mark is the two multitude feedings (6:30–44; 8:1–10). Again, like Elisha, Jesus gains fame by curing a leper (2 Kings 5:10–14; Mark 1:40–45) and by opening blind eyes (2 Kings 6:20; Mark 10:46–52). Elisha's levitation magic in making an iron ax head float is matched by Jesus' walking on water (2 Kings 6:4–7; Mark 6:48). Stories are told of both Elijah and Elisha restoring young persons to life after shutting themselves up with their dead bodies (1 Kings 17:21–23; 2 Kings 4:32–37). Accordingly, Mark writes that Jesus, after arranging for privacy, restores a dead child (5:35–43); after this act some Jews conclude that Elijah has returned in the person of Jesus (6:15).

There is a scholarly consensus that Matthew and Luke were written approximately a decade after Mark and about half a century after Jesus' public ministry. These later Synoptic Gospels borrow heavily from Mark and occasionally heighten the supernaturalism of the earlier record. Gerd Theissen finds seventeen instances where the miraculous is enlarged in the transmission from Mark to Matthew.[3] In Mark's account, for example, Jesus curses an unfruitful fig tree, and a day passes before Peter notices its withered condition (11:13–14, 20–21); in Matthew's account, the tree withers "immediately" (21:19). Both accounts agree that Jesus destroyed life in a tree in order to display that faith in God can accomplish the most absurd happenings imaginable. Jesus allegedly said: "If you have faith and never doubt, you will not only do what has been done to the fig tree, but even if you say to this mountain, 'Be taken up and cast into the sea,' it will be done" (Matt. 21:21). In one of Mark's stories, Jairus describes his dying daughter to Jesus and requests that she be healed (5:22–23); but in Matthew, the father states she has died and requests that she be resurrected (9:18). Embellishment may also be detected in a miracle performed at Jericho, for Matthew mentions two men, not one, whose sight is restored (20:29–34; see also 9:27–31). Alleged miracles enlarge with time like fermenting dough; the yeasty rise in the decade between the writings of Mark and Matthew illustrates this phenomenon.

In Luke's portrayal, Jesus cures at least ten more Gentile lepers than did Elisha (2 Kings 5:8–14; Luke 5:12–15; 17:11–14). Occasionally miracles embellish stories obtained from Mark's Gospel. For example, Mark simply tells of two brothers leaving their fishing nets at the Galilean lake after Jesus invites them to join him (1:16–18). Luke adds that Jesus told Peter to cast out his nets again at a time when the fisherman was convinced no fish were around. When he followed Jesus' instructions, the nets began to break from the enormous catch and the boat began to sink (5:4–7). Again, according to Mark, one of Jesus' disciples cut off an ear of the high priest's slave in Gethsemane (14:47). Luke adds that Jesus "touched his ear and healed him" (22:51).

The writer of John—the latest of the canonical Gospels—retells the feeding-of-the-multitude miracle, found five times in the Synoptic Gospels, but he alone explicitly compares the account with the Moses saga. Jesus declares he is greater than Moses because he provides "the true bread from heaven" and not just physical "manna" (6:31–51).

Several "signs" in the Fourth Gospel also echo Elisha legends. Water transformation is the first miracle performed by both Elisha and Jesus. After receiving a double portion of Elijah's spirit, Elisha manipulated water in a magical manner while near the Jordan River. He asked for a new bowl containing salt and then cast the salt into a spring to prevent the water from causing death or miscarriage (2 Kings 2:9–22). Jesus turns water into wine after returning from the Jordan, where he was baptized. Some had questioned if John the Baptist might be a new version of an old prophet with miraculous powers; he denies this while giving high tribute to Jesus (John 1:19–36; 2:1–11). Elisha and Jesus restore a son to health (2 Kings 4:32–37; John 4:46–54), and they both cure by having a man wash in a designated place (2 Kings 5:1–14; John 5:2–9). Reviving a buried corpse is the last miracle for both prophets (2 Kings 13:20–21; John 11:38–44).

A comparison of some teaching of the Synoptic Gospels with the first and last "sign" of the Fourth Gospel suggest that the later writer may have transformed them in a bizarre manner. In the Synoptics, Jesus contrasts the old wine of Jewish fasting ritual with the new wine of the gospel (Mark 2:22). Also, he tells a fictitious story about life after death, in which Abraham refuses to permit the resurrection of Lazarus because such an unnatural happening would not change uncaring persons into caring persons (Luke 16:19–31). Although Jesus' parables are omitted from the Fourth Gospel, allusions may be found to some. In the Cana wedding "sign," water for Jewish rites is contrasted to the superior new wine allegedly produced by Jesus (John 2:1–11). After the Bethany tomb "sign," his alleged resurrection of Lazarus made the Jewish leaders even more determined to eliminate Jesus (11:53).

Some ancient rabbis were also presumed to have supernatural powers like the prophets. Rabbis Gamaliel and Tanchuma, at different times, were at sea when a tempest threatened to sink their boats. After they prayed, the waters immediately quieted down.[4] In a similar manner, Mark's Jesus calms a sea so his disciples can cross to the other side (4:35–41).

The Jews did not have a corner on the magic market of the ancient Mediterranean world. "Divine men" were a common feature of Hellenistic hero cults. Legends attribute to Greek philosopher Empedocles the power to resurrect the dead and to arrest violent wind.[5] Asclepius was reputed to have the power to correct physical deformities as well as to raise the dead.[6] Apollonius, a contemporary of Jesus, traveled from town to town performing miracles. He restored a blind man, cured a man with a paralyzed arm, and ascended bodily into heaven after his own death.[7] About the time the Gospel of Mark was written, it was claimed that Vespasian had performed miracles to authenticate his sovereignty. Roman writers report that their emperor instantly healed a lame man and cured a blind man after applying spittle to his defective eyes.[8] Jesus' saliva is also alleged to have magical powers to correct speech impediments and restore sight (Mark 7:32–35; 8:22–25). A man blind from birth received his sight after washing from his eyes an ointment Jesus placed there made of his spittle and clay (John 9:1–12).

Milo Connick observes: "Miracle stories clustered like grapes about the stem of historical personages. Their aim was to inflate the personal status of the hero. It was even considered legitimate to manufacture miraculous tales for this purpose."[9] In prescientific cultures, people have generally believed that the more contrary an event is to the perceived natural pattern, the greater its importance.

Classicist E. R. Dodds points out that "miracles were both commonplace and morally suspect" in late antiquity.[10] Lucian, a Greek satirist living in the second century of the Christian era, introduced the term "superman" (*hyperanthropos*) to refer to pretenders who claim to be wizards. He lampoons the credulity of simple people who are exploited by charlatans who pose as supermen. Lucian records a number of instances of trickery, including an account of a sick man rising up and carrying his bed away after receiving magical words and gestures. He tells of these phony claims: an incantation that resuscitated a corpse and a Pythagorean who could walk on water or fly over it.[11]

Magnification through the process of transmission has also happened to the central figures of some other religions. For example, the earlier stories of the Buddha contain no suggestion of miraculous powers. He reacted negatively to the levitation claims of gurus in his parent Indian religion. Siddhartha taught: "There is no path through the air; one does not become a holy man by outward acts."[12] He judged appeals to supernaturalism as devoid of spiritual significance as conjurers' tricks. In one story he meets an ascetic who claims he can cross a river by walking on water. The Buddha amusedly judges walking on water a waste of effort, because riding a ferry is inexpensive. In spite of the Buddha's distaste for the miraculous, legends arose regarding his ability to vanish and reappear, to pass through walls, and to fly like an eagle.[13]

In the Qur'an, Muhammad affirms that the performance of signs and wonders is not a part of his mission, and he criticizes those who demand such. To that prophet, the superlative wonder is the internal revelation that God has given his messengers across the centuries.[14] Even though Muhammad repeatedly disclaimed miraculous powers, tales of supernatural feats began to be told of him soon after his death. Included in the lore are accounts of his power over nature: he caused trees to move at his command to provide himself shade, and he multiplied one family's dinner to feed a multitude. The most spectacular legend to infiltrate the post-Qur'anic tradition was that of Muhammad's nocturnal ride from Mecca to Jerusalem on his winged steed, and thence through the seven heavens.[15]

The craving for signs continues to be found in our own time, even among some with a scientific education. Indeed, positivists who have the presupposition that all things real are empirically in evidence may be more oriented than others toward physical proofs. Championing what might be called the immaculate perception dogma, they contend that if there are no supernatural signs, there is no God. For example, Robert Ingersoll, "the notorious infidel" of the nineteenth century, traveled all over America attacking Christianity.[16] Its impotence could be demonstrated, he claimed, by its failure to provide visible signs. Ingersoll seemed to presume that an alleged divine power would appear on terms he dictated. He began his "Why I Am an Agnostic" oration by demanding that God strike him dead within the next minute. He then held out his pocket watch and dramatically announced the countdown by seconds. Those listeners who were devoted to supernatural signs were impressed that he did not have a stroke or get struck by a bolt of lightning.

In the twentieth century, Bertrand Russell also presumed—like Elijah at Sinai, until he learned better (1 Kings 19:11–12)—that a convincing God should be revealed in extraordinary rather than in ordinary experiences. Russell asserted: "I think that if I heard a voice from the sky predicting all that was going to happen to me during the next twenty-four hours, including events that would have seemed highly improbable, and if all these events then proceeded to happen, I might perhaps be convinced at least of the existence of some superhuman intelligence."[17] Russell here discloses that he might be persuaded of the reality of a voice from the blue if a kind of irrational parapsychology could be verified. By contrast, those oriented toward rational religion would find in such precognition *less* evidence for divine "intelligence."

Jesus' Viewpoint on Miracles

The earliest Christian writings contain no supernaturalism as the term is here defined. Paul's letters, which were written about a decade before the earliest Gospel, do not suggest that God interferes with the natural order.[18] Supernatural stories about Jesus, from virginal conception to physical resurrection, are absent from Paul's "gospel"—a term he uses much more often than the writers of the later "Gospels." The miracles that developed in Jewish Christianity, which are first recorded in the Gospel of Mark, were probably circulated by people whom Paul opposed.[19] They testify to a common expectation in folk religions, that of experiencing the divine in supernatural occurrences. Had Jesus been one more wonder-worker—one of those whom the Greeks called thaumaturges—he would not have been revolutionary. There were shamans and wizards galore in ancient folk culture. Theissen documents that supernatural stories were immensely popular in the Roman era.[20]

Paul disappointedly wrote that most "Jews demand signs" and do not recognize what is marvelously dynamic (*dynamis*). The apostle proclaimed the crucified Christ as "the miracle [*dynamis*] of God and the wisdom of God" (1 Cor. 1:22–24). That "miracle" was "scandalous" to many, Paul admits, because it portrays one who did not supernaturally zap those who would crucify him. For Paul, however, the wonder-working of God is not displayed in erratic spectaculars but in Jesus' suffering humanity. At the heart of Christianity there is a transformation of values, rendering potent what was commonly regarded as impotent. Paul was convinced that God chooses the weak and despised, not those who are strong by ordinary standards (1 Cor. 1:26–31). Paul writes of the basic shift in religion with the coming of Christianity: Jesus paradoxically shows that God's action is best displayed in situations of lowly oppression, not lofty splendor. "The word of the cross is foolishness to those who are perishing," Paul claims, "but to us who are being saved it is the miracle of God" (1 Cor. 1:18).

The importance of Paul's rejection of supernaturalism is illustrated by Paul Tillich's theology. A frequently sounded leitmotiv is that an antisupernaturalism approach is needed for an in-depth understanding of Christianity. He wrote: "Today we know what the New Testament always knew— that miracles are signs pointing to the presence of a divine power in nature and history and that they are in no way negations of natural laws." So central are those words to Tillich's thought that they are carved in stone in the park established to memorialize him.[21]

In addition to the letters of Paul, another pre-Gospel written source for earliest Christianity is called Quelle (German for "source") and abbreviated "Q." Although the original Q is not extant, it can be reconstructed by determining what non-Markan material is quoted by both Matthew and Luke. Q shows that some Christians who lived in the first decades after Jesus' death remembered him primarily because of teachings, not miracles. Jesus criticizes those whose faith rests on alleged miracles:

This is an evil generation: it seeks a sign, but none will be given it except the sign of Jonah. For as Jonah became a sign to the Ninevites, so will the Son of man be to this generation. At the judgment, the queen from the South will stand up and accuse you, because she traveled from afar to hear the wisdom of Solomon. Look, there is more than Solomon here! At the judgment, the Ninevites will stand up and accuse you, because they repented when Jonah preached. Look, there is more than Jonah here! (Luke 11:29–32; cf. Matt. 12:38–42)

In this Q passage, some Gentiles are commended for being open to nonsupernatural expressions of power and wisdom. The city of Nineveh repented because of Jonah's "sign," that is, his demonstration of God's power through preaching. Likewise, the Queen of Sheba was attracted by Solomon's wise teachings. Neither Solomon nor Jonah performed supernatural wonders. Jesus lamented that his fellow Jews longed more for miraculous proof than for the self-authenticating teaching he was imparting. They missed the point of the book of Jonah by literalistically focusing on the monstrous fish in which a human could survive for days. The fish in this story is a red herring! The symbolic story aims at comparing Jonah's hatred toward the Assyrian capital—located near where Baghdad is today—with the wideness of God's mercy on a warring people who repent.

Ernst and Marie-Luise Keller find importance in Jesus' distancing himself from the traditional demand for miraculous signs. Regarding his criticism of those Jews who demanded additional legitimation, they write:

Conviction should rest on what he says and it is on this basis that they should decide whether he is speaking the truth, i. e., whether he is of God or not. External miracles do not take one any further in this matter; indeed they distract from the real point at issue. Inner conviction through the truth of his words is the only criterion which Jesus has to offer in response to the question as to his credentials. . . . If one describes Jesus' views, as reflected in his rejection of the demand for signs, from the point of view of the history of thought, it may be said that his proclamation liberated man's personal power of judgment by appealing to his personal conviction and individual conscience. In this way Jesus declared man to be of age, autonomous.[22]

The four Gospels, dating from the last third of the first Christian century, inconsistently mix traditions of a limited human Jesus and an unlimited supernatural Jesus. Embedded in them all, Günther Bornkamm points out, is the theme that real faith is not built on supernatural miracles (Matt. 12:38–39; Mark 8:11–12; Luke 11:29; John 4:48; 20:29). That leading New Testament scholar asserts: "Jesus will not allow miracles to be considered a proof of God's working and power, which could be demanded as the prerequisite to faith. Such a demand is a challenging of God. Trust and obedience have both been destroyed at the roots."[23]

A parable in Luke reinforces that Jesus rejected the notion that supernaturalism can transform a person. A rich man in hell, as the story goes, requests that he be resurrected in order to warn his brothers of what will happen to them if they persist in an attitude of indifference to human suffering. His request is denied for this reason: "If they do not listen to Moses and the prophets, neither will they be convinced if someone should rise from the dead" (16:19–31). Thus Jesus did not think that individuals can be amazed into a life-style of ethical concern. According to his parable, those who are unresponsive to the social justice teachings of the Israelite prophets will not be converted by a display of supernaturalism.

Why did some early Christians tell of a superman Jesus if, in fact, the historical Jesus functioned as an inspiring leader, an enlightening teacher, and a compassionate physician? The Gospel writers found themselves in a competitive religious market, and they seemed determined to demonstrate—at the expense of consistency—that the founder of Christianity was as spectacular as any of the acclaimed wonder-workers of antiquity. They were especially eager to meet the resistance from Judaism by recording legends displaying that Jesus could match or even surpass the tall stories recorded of the prophets Moses, Elijah, and Elisha. They did not consider that Hosea, Isaiah, and Jeremiah—the prophets Jesus most admired—were not associated with contrary-to-nature acts.

Fyodor Dostoevsky comments on a perennial human craving: "Man seeks not so much God as the miraculous. And as man cannot bear to be without the miraculous, he will create new miracles of his own for himself, and will worship deeds of sorcery and witchcraft." In order to set in bolder relief the intention of the founder of Christianity, the Russian novelist portrays the human obsession for suspending natural causality. In the Grand Inquisitor story, he expresses this trenchant understanding: "You [Jesus] did not want to bring man to you by miracles, because you wanted their freely given love rather than the servile rapture of slaves subdued forever by a display of power."[24]

Without intending his action to be a sign of his supernatural power, Jesus assisted some sick people. He pointed out that his therapy was not unlike what other Jewish physicians were administering (Luke 11:19). He tried to make people aware of the psychosomatic causation of some maladies, yet he recognized that he was powerless to effect cures among any who lacked confidence that they could regain health through the help of God (Mark 1:40–42; 5:25–34; 6:5–6). Frequently Jesus informed those who felt healed that their faith was the cause. Even though he did not seek public acclaim as a healer, he and his disciples did gain some notoriety as faith healers.

Signs of the Times

Jesus encouraged people to look for *natural* signs, while maintaining that reliance on *supernatural* signs is "adulterous"—that is, a display of unfaithfulness to God (Matt. 16:4). In this regard, consider his response to some adversaries:

> The Pharisees and Sadducees came, and to test him they asked him to show them a sign from heaven. He replied, "In the evening you say, 'It will be fair weather, for the sky is red.' And in the morning, 'It will be stormy today, for the sky is red and overcast.' You know how to interpret the appearance of the sky, but you cannot interpret the signs of the times!" (Matt. 16:1–3; cf. Luke 12:54–56)

Weather prophets with no formal training can, over a period of time, examine the sky and discover regular patterns. With more sophistication, scientists do the same with meteorologic phenomena. Their recognition of past patterns are *sign*ificant because extrapolations can be made about probable happenings in the future. Galilean fishermen took precautions when there was a red glow in the eastern sky. They accepted the folk wisdom that has come down in this proverb: "Red in the morning, sailors take warning." Jesus thought that past experience should also *sign*ify what would likely happen in society. The "signs of the times" come from analyzing past history and discerning what is likely to happen if the same conditions persist in the future. This is the methodology that both simple people and social scientists use in making intelligent forecasts.

As a boy, Jesus was probably disturbed by a bloody experience that provided him with a lifelong conviction about political realities. Josephus provides this information: "A Galilean, named Judas, incited his countrymen to revolt, upbraiding them as cowards for consenting to pay taxes to Rome and tolerating human rulers, after having God for their sovereign."[25] Luke also tells about a forerunner of the Zealot party: "Judas the Galilean arose during the days of the tax registration [6 C.E.] and raised a popular following. He was killed, and all his followers dispersed" (Acts 5:37). This was probably the same Judas who sparked an insurrection at Sepphoris, the capital city of Galilee. Judas seized the arsenal at the royal palace, took control of the city, and aspired to become the Moses of an Israelite theocracy. However, Roman troops commanded by Varus soon crushed the extremists. Thousands of the rioters were either crucified or enslaved.[26] Could anyone in Galilee during the reign of Caesar Augustus not remember what happened when this guerrilla action was followed by devastation?

Later, two of Judas's sons were crucified as political assassins, but another son named Menahem continued to attract those who liked to express their zeal for God by hating the Roman conquerors.[27] Many thousands approved of terrorist actions and holy war against the pagan Romans, hoping for the kingdom of God after liberation. Eventually this group of freedom fighters stirred up the rebellion of 66 C.E., which resulted in Rome's bloodiest clash with any colony. The total destruction of Jerusalem was caused not only by the Roman army but also by the Zealots, who preferred to burn everything possible rather than turn it over to the victors.

The spirit of ultranationalism had been brewing for generations before the Zealot party arose in Palestine. That spirit motivated the writer of Esther, one of the latest books in the Hebrew Bible. With exquisite literary style, the novella tells of vehement vindictiveness against a Gentile nation that had been generally tolerant toward the Jews. According to the story, a Persian prime minister named Haman was hanged for a scheme that would have resulted in the unjust execution of a Jew named Mordecai. After this, Mordecai was able to get approval for special days when Jews could slaughter their enemies. During two days, the small Jewish minority allegedly massacred more than seventy-five thousand Persians. Although a work of fiction, Esther motivated an annual carnival which gloats over the time when the Jews ran swords through all their opponents, apparently without suffering casualties (Esth. 9:5–19).

Jesus could read the "signs of the times" and see the toll resulting from centuries of unholy bitterness. He lived in the epicenter of Jewish xenophobia and saw at first hand the devastation it had wrought. Growing up in a town only three miles south of Sepphoris, the Nazarene may have provided carpentry assistance during the years of urban reconstruction. Although he had no enthusiasm for Roman control, he appeared to view it as less catastrophic than what had ensued from the Sepphoris rebellion. Indeed, he may have considered the Roman government in Palestine a lesser evil than domination by fanatical Jewish patriots who hated pagans.

This reconstruction of the politics of Jesus has been influenced by specialists on the relation of Jesus to reform movements of his day. Shirley Case has plausibly conjectured that the loss of life and property from the Galilean uprising *signaled* for Jesus throughout his mature years what would be the probable outcome of any subsequent Jewish attempt to throw off Roman colonialism. Case suggested that Jesus shared the moderation of the new residents of Sepphoris:

> The people of Sepphoris and its vicinity were three-quarters of a century earlier than the people of Jerusalem in learning by sad experience the utter futility of a revolution

against Rome. When at the time of his first insurrection Judas had taken possession of the royal treasures and arms at Sepphoris, evidently the citizens were not unsympathetic with his action, for when the Romans suppressed the revolution they burned the city and enslaved the inhabitants. But the residents of the new city were distinctly opposed to all revolutionary movements. Not even its Jewish population could be persuaded to take up arms against Rome [in the rebellion beginning in 66].[28]

More recently, John Riches has discussed why Jesus rejected the Armageddon approach of Judas the Galilean and other holy-war activists of his time. He writes: "The calamities which befell the Jews at Sepphoris and the firm control which Antipas exercised over Galilee may well have led Jesus to the conclusion that *if* God were to vindicate his people, to establish his rule, it would not be through military struggle." Over against the popular apocalypticism, Jesus' intention was strikingly different:

> He points to his own ministry of healing and forgiveness, of association with sinners as the way of redemption for his people. For his contemporaries the way to redemption lay via the destruction of Israel's enemies, not via the forgiveness and invitation to the feast of those who wittingly or unwittingly were their instruments, i.e. those who collaborated with the foreign powers."[29]

As a political realist, Jesus understood that the Jews were no match for the Romans and their Herodian puppets. Even if killing in armed conflict could be justified in some situations, it was imprudent for hotheads to inflame people to rise up against the overwhelming might of the occupation army. Jesus was asked about a massacre of fellow Galileans by Pontius Pilate, probably during an insurrection at the Temple in Jerusalem. Although Jesus rejected the view that those killed had displeased God more than others, he used the inquiry as an occasion to express his view toward the politics of violence. "Unless you change your attitude," he announced, "you will all perish as they did" (Luke 13:1–3).

Jesus was not opposed to resisting Roman policy that conflicted with religious expression, but he sanctioned a peaceful approach. Shortly before the beginning of his public ministry, some Jews engaged in nonviolent resistance which Jesus probably found commendable. Around 26 C.E., Tiberius Caesar ordered Pilate to have troops carry effigies of himself on standards as they marched into Jerusalem. Consequently, a huge crowd went to the governor's headquarters at Caesarea and participated in a sit-in for five days. Pilate then threatened the protesters, but he found among them a courage for which he was unprepared. Josephus writes:

> Pilate declared that he would cut them down unless they accepted the images of Caesar, and nodded to the soldiers to draw their swords. As if by arrangement, the Jews all fell to the ground, extended their necks, and proclaimed that they were ready to be killed rather than transgress their Law. Astonished by the intensity of their religious fervor, Pilate ordered the immediate removal of the standards from Jerusalem.[30]

Unlike some compatriots, Jesus did not believe that a multitude of angelic warriors would fight on the side of God's chosen against the Romans.[31] E. P. Sanders contrasts Jesus' style with that of various messianic pretenders who expected the kingdom of God to come by miraculous intervention followed by a military defeat of the Romans. In his influential study, Sanders states:

> There are prophetic and symbolic actions, but they are not miracles. . . . Jesus saw himself as one who was a servant of all, not their glorious leader in a triumphal march through parted waters. . . . When he decided to go to Jerusalem and to offer symbolic gestures to indicate what was to come (the replacement of the Temple) and his own role in it (a king, but one who rides on an ass), it is unlikely that he realistically thought that the leaders and aristocrats would be convinced that the kingdom was at hand and that he was God's last envoy before the end.[32]

Jesus' accepting attitude toward the Roman army is displayed in this teaching: "If anyone compels [*aggareuo*] you to go one mile, go with him two" (Matt. 5:41). As is frequently the case with sayings of Jesus, Thomas Manson best states the meaning: "The first mile renders to Caesar the things that are Caesar's; the second mile, by meeting oppression with kindness, renders to God the things that are God's."[33] The Greek verb *aggareuo* is a technical term pertaining to a soldier's right to require a civilian to carry a load for a certain distance. That temporary pressing into service is illustrated in the way Roman soldiers acted in taking Jesus out to be executed: "They compelled [*aggareuo*] a passer-by, who was coming in from the country, to carry his cross" (Mark 15:21).

Bearing the burdens of aliens for even the mandatory first mile must have generally caused much resentment. Such work was a bitter reminder to the Jews of the humiliating conquest of their homeland by the Romans. Most Jews probably never realized that providing assistance beyond what was demanded could be a way of destroying enemies. Roman soldiers might be transformed into friends by occasions of unexpected helpfulness.

Out of the crucible of his own experiences Jesus came to this conclusion: "All who draw the sword will die by the sword" (Matt. 26:52). In a study of Jesus' response to the Palestinian political ferment, Sherman Johnson concludes with this sound judgment:

> He took a highly independent attitude toward the authorities, both political and religious, and, like the Old Testament prophets, was keenly aware of the political situation. On the other hand, while he believed that God alone was king, and men were his free children, he rejected the revolutionary movement entirely. . . . Jesus rejected the way of violence, which his compatriots followed to their own destruction.[34]

Consider the interaction between Jesus and the Passover pilgrims who were traveling with him on his last visit to Jerusalem. He was accompanied by a crowd who were filled with yeasty nationalism and religious enthusiasm. They were singing a Hallel psalm, which was used for festival occasions such as this.[35] The last one in the Hallel group (Pss. 113–118) tells of the divine assistance available to Jews as they desperately respond to encompassing enemies. Psalm 118:25 contains the Hosanna (Hebrew, *hoshiah na*) exclamation, meaning "Rescue now!" The exclamations that follow identify the singers as being in the Jerusalem area:

> O Lord, give us success!
> Blessed be the one who enters in the name of the LORD! . . .
> With branches in hand, move in procession
>   to the Temple altar!

Accompanying Jesus was a festive crowd carrying leafy boughs. They hoped he might be God's agent for driving the Romans out of Palestine. According to Mark, they cried, "God bless the coming kingdom of our father David! Hosanna in the highest!" (11:10) Matthew has the demonstrators shouting, "Hosanna to the Son of David!" (21:9). During the Passover—the annual celebration of the Israelite defeat of the Egyptians—there was a fervent longing for liberation from contemporary pharaohs. The pilgrims dreamed that the new savior would be like one of God's anointed kings who never lost a battle. David had removed the Philistine threat and had widened the boundaries of the independent Israelite state to the greatest extent ever. Those along the road with Jesus desired a new David who would behave in a parallel manner.

Jesus decided to show those excited people a dramatic personal sign of the type of messianic hope he wished to fulfill. He discerned two irreconcilable hopes embedded in the scriptures. The popular one was that the Lord's anointed would become king at Jerusalem and "break them [national enemies] with a rod of iron" (Ps. 2:9). The other hope was of a "Prince of Peace" (Isa. 9:6), who would lead people in beating their "spears into pruning hooks" (Isa. 2:4). In order to signal that his mission was the latter type, Jesus acted out a biblical prophecy. In the Jewish tradition, particular individuals thought of themselves, or were thought of by others, as signs pointing to the will of God. For example, a prophecy states that "Ezekiel shall be to you [Jews] a sign," because he witnessed for God to his generation (Ezek. 3:4; 12:6; 24:24). Jesus is referred to at the outset of Luke's Gospel as an extraordinary sign: shepherds are told that an infant in a stable "will be a sign for you" (2:12), and Simeon announces that Jesus is a "sign" whom people will oppose (2:34). Supernatural powers are not associated with Jesus in those stories.

Prophets in Jerusalem had long used crowd-stopping symbolic actions to draw attention to a message that was counter to popular sentiments. To those prophets an event was *sign*ificant if it conveyed God's presence, not if it deviated from the natural order. Thus, Isaiah—on behalf of God—responded to Judah's alliance with Egypt by walking "naked and barefoot for three years as a sign and a warning" (Isa. 20:3). On the basis of historical antecedents, the prophet thought the Assyrians would carry prisoners away naked from towns where the Egyptians had guaranteed protection. Recognizing that the Jewish people treasured stories of the flamboyant acts of earlier prophets, Jesus dramatically proposes an alternative to another insurrection against Rome.

Jesus counters the zealotry of those approaching Jerusalem with him by publicly demonstrating for the first time that he is the promised king. To express the qualities of his reign, he acts out Zechariah's hope by means of a royal entry (Matt. 21:1–11). Jesus liked the symbols of the prophet's poetry:

> Shout for joy, people of Jerusalem!
> Look, your king is coming!
> He is vindicated and victorious,
> But humble and riding on a donkey. . . .
> He will banish the war horse and the battle bow;
> He will make peace among the nations;
> His rule will extend from sea to sea.
> (Zech. 9:9–10)

Jesus may also have had in mind the concluding words of Zechariah's prophecy: "There shall no longer be traders in the house of the LORD of hosts" (14:21).

By riding into Jerusalem on what was then the most common beast of burden, rather than on the mount of a military commander, Jesus acts in a highly *sign*ificant manner. He points to a radically new kind of reign: one in which majesty is combined with meekness; one in which international peace replaces national chauvinism. Marcus Borg describes Jesus' procession into the traditional royal capital in this way: "His entry was a planned political demonstration, an appeal to Jerusalem to follow the path of peace, even as it proclaimed that his movement was the peace party in a generation headed for war. It also implied that the alternative of peace was still open."[36]

Thus, Jesus' immersion in prophetic history enabled him to extrapolate future scenarios from past happenings. During his last week in Jerusalem the parallel between his situation and that of Jeremiah was much on his mind. Jesus' method of parading into the city was as iconoclastic as that of Jeremiah, who wore an ordinary ox yoke in the city streets. The earlier prophet explained to the curious that the freedom-curtailing "yoke" of Babylonian rule should be preferred to the alternative. To picture the alternative of mass destruction by the Babylonian army, he shattered a pottery vase. Jeremiah believed that Jewish nationalists were inviting war, famine, and pestilence because they aimed at political independence regardless of the cost (Jer. 27:2–13). He was convinced that submission was the Lord's will, even though many thought of him as subversive to the Judean religious community (38:4).

When Jesus obtained a panoramic view of the city from the Mount of Olives, he lamented that the people did not understand or endorse a vision for the future which he shared with some earlier prophets. The Jerusalem dwellers rested their security on two things: the presumedly impregnable walls of the mountaintop fortress and the location there of "the house of the Lord," on the verge of completion after decades of construction. Reading the historical signs, Jesus saw parallels between what weeping Jeremiah faced vis-à-vis the Babylonian destruction of Jerusalem six centuries earlier and what might be ahead for those who disregarded the lessons of history. Luke tells of Jesus:

> When he came into full view of the city, he burst into tears, saying, "If only you knew today the path to peace! But it is hidden from your sight. The time is coming

155

when your enemies will build fortifications around you and besiege you. You and the children within your walls will be dashed to the ground. Your enemies will not leave one stone standing upon another because you did not recognize your time of opportunity." (Luke 19:41–44)

Like his mentor Jeremiah (ch. 27), Jesus counseled the Jerusalemites to reject the conventional wisdom that patriotism always meant warring against the foes of one's nation, presuming that such was God's will. At the risk of being called a deserter, he urged: "When you see Jerusalem surrounded by troops, realize that its devastation is near. Then those who are in Judea must run away to the mountains, and those who are inside the city must evacuate" (Luke 21:20–21). Neither prophet performed any miracle to try to convince the people that it is better to be subject to a foreign power than it is to be buried by that power.

Jesus also followed Jeremiah in maintaining that the enemy of the Jewish peasantry was, in considerable part, the Jewish rulers. With that elite group in mind, Jesus laments: "Jerusalem, Jerusalem, the city that kills the prophets and stones those who are sent to it!" (Matt. 23:37). He then uses bird imagery from his scriptures (Deut. 32:11; Ps. 36:7) to convey that God's redemptive activity continues for the fledgling Jewish nation. Yet, in spite of divine oversight and assistance, the ruling "house" in Jerusalem has violently opposed God's messengers. Consequently, both Jeremiah and Jesus declare: "This house shall become a desolation" (Jer. 22:5; Matt. 23:38).

Prophets Jeremiah and Jesus both attempted to deflate the priests' presumption that the Temple was indispensable to God. For them it was unthinkable that God would permit the destruction of his earthly dwelling place which they were commissioned to manage. Jesus infuriated them in supporting Jeremiah's claim that the Temple had become a "den of robbers" and that its destruction was justified (Jer. 7:11–14; Mark 11:17; 13:1–2). Such rashness led to both Jeremiah and Jesus being beaten, and caused the Jerusalem elite to demand their deaths (Jer. 26:11; 37:15; Mark 15:14–15). After Jesus instituted the "new covenant" which Jeremiah had announced (Jer. 31:27–34; 1 Cor. 11:25), he experienced the humiliation of rejection by the Jewish leaders.

To many Jews in Jerusalem, Jesus must have seemed to be more of a traitorous wimp than a triumphant winner. When Pilate gave them a choice between freeing him or Barabbas, a terrorist and a murderer, they chose the latter (Mark 15:7–11). Jesus had seen condemned insurrectionists like Barabbas carrying horizontal beams of crosses on which they would be executed. He may have admired the sacrificial devotion of the rebels, while considering their cause to be misdirected. Jesus advocated that followers endure persecution while "seeking the divine rule and God's justice" (Matt. 5:10; 6:33). At Golgotha, the unpopular Jesus was taunted by those who equated kingship with militant resistance to alien political powers. Jesting among themselves, the Jewish religious leaders said: "He saved others but he cannot save himself. Let us see the Messiah, the king of Israel, come down from the cross now, and we will believe in him!" (Mark 15:31–32).

Discerning Christians have realized that Jesus showed his kinship to God when he was not in any way manifesting irresistible physical power. Martin Luther wrote: "On the cross Christ was powerless, yet there he performed his mightiest work."[37] Similarly, Japanese writer Shusaku Endo sums up Jesus' most profound effect on his disciples. That anti-superman

> possessed no power in this visible world. . . . It was nothing miraculous, but the sunken eyes overflowed with love more profound than a miracle. And regarding those who deserted him, those who betrayed him, not a word of resentment came to his lips. . . . That's the whole life of Jesus.[38]

Jesus was super as in *super*lative but not as in *super*natural. He was the superlative model of suffering love (*agape*) to neighbors far and near. Mouths agape at the alleged supernatural have been characteristic of folk religion throughout history, but the more demanding regulation of life by *agape* has not been as popular. Paul acknowledged that some crave for happenings that go against nature—such as the removal of mountains by means of faith—but the true miracle of God is seen in the life and death of the lowly, loving human Jesus. After devaluating supernaturalism in his famous ode to agape in 1 Corinthians 13, the apostle goes on to describe the ultimate divine/human value. Since the Crucified One is the quintessential personification of agape, a paragraph may be read with this substitution of subject:

> Jesus is patient and kind. He is not jealous or boastful or snobbish or rude. Jesus is not selfish or touchy or resentful; he does not gloat when others go wrong, but is gladdened by the truth. There is no limit to Jesus' faith, hope, and endurance.

.8.

Fulfillment for Everyone

A simple teaching of Jesus has given a theological base for movements toward individual and civil rights in Western civilization. Consider his lesser-to-greater reasoning: "Are not five sparrows sold for two pennies? Yet not one of them is overlooked by God. . . . Fear not; you are of more value than many sparrows!" (Luke 12:6–7). Sparrows—great in number and small in size—provided the cheapest meat in the marketplace. As Jesus watched poor people purchasing sparrows he may have reflected on words a psalmist sang on behalf of God: "I know every bird in the air, and I care for all life in the fields" (Ps. 50:11). Since God is aware of even common birds, Jesus thought, how enormous must be the worth of even plain people, all of whom are made in the divine image.

The affirmation that every individual is a VIP in the sight of God has had monumental significance in subsequent social policy. Georgia Harkness writes: "Jesus' ideal of the infinite worth of persons has lifted child life and womanhood wherever it has gone; it has abolished many forms of slavery; it lies at the root of democracy."[1] When fascism and other collectivisms arise, that ideal of Jesus is suppressed. Look, for instance, at the ideological fight of Adolf Hitler on this issue. One of the most influential German books during Hitler's youth was written by historian Adolf Harnack on the essence of Christianity. He stressed that "Jesus Christ was the first to bring the value of every human soul to light" and that he has motivated equal rights movements.[2] Hitler—arguably history's most dehumanizing tyrant—rejected Jesus' teachings. He declared "the saving doctrine of the nothingness and insignificance of the individual human being."[3] The totalitarian slogan of the Nazis was: "You are nothing, the people are everything!"

Is it fair to world history to claim with Harnack, Nietzsche, and Harkness that the gospel is at the root of some aspects of modern democracy? The Greeks gave us the word "democracy," but they did not treat slaves or women as having any citizen rights. They called foreigners *barbaroi* and treated them with the contempt that still is connoted by the word "barbarian." In Athens, "the birthplace of democracy," citizenship protections were extended to only a small percentage of the residents, namely, to free adult males. Unwanted babies were often "exposed" to die or were raised as slaves. Greek patriarchy diminished woman's role to little more than that of a domestic drudge. The concept of democracy—well encapsulated in America's "liberty and justice for all" slogan—sprang more from Galilee than from Greece.

According to the Fourth Gospel, Jesus came to provide life in its fullness (John 10:10). How did he go about achieving this aim regardless of the age or gender of those he encountered? How did Jesus' view of the preciousness and dignity of each individual affect what he said and did toward achieving fulfillment for others and for himself?

The Childlike Ideal

Among the many paradoxical teachings of Jesus is this: those who desire a fulfilled life must "become like children" (Matt. 18:3). What did he mean when he associated personal development with reviving characteristics of the young? To avoid sentimentality, a distinction between being childish and being childlike is needed. To be childish is to pout, to have temper tantrums, and to be selfishly concerned for one's own pleasure. One of Jesus' parables is about children who sulked, a characteristic he did not admire (Matt. 11:17). He describes some kids who are determined not to join in a musical game unless they can call the tune. They squabble and end up not playing at all. The continuance of that childish habit in adults is displayed among those who will not participate in a situation unless they can dominate. As the eldest of at least six siblings (Mark 6:3), Jesus probably had observed peevishness among his brothers and sisters. He was talking about something quite different from such childishness when he commended childlikeness.

From the accounts of Jesus' interactions with his disciples, childlikeness can be defined negatively and positively. Children lack prestige, which was a dominant social value in Palestine.[4] For example, Rabbi Judah advised that a person should seek "that which is an honor to him and gets honor for him from others."[5] Jesus' disciples attempted to keep children away from their rabbi, presuming that he wanted to spend his time only with significant persons. Angered by their attitude, he told them: "Let the children come to me; do not stop them, for the realm of God belongs to the childlike" (Mark 10:14).

What positive childlike qualities can be extracted from episodes in the Gospels? Consider first that children tend to express themselves spontaneously. The First Gospel tells of boisterous children who were shouting praises in the Temple. The religious leaders were indignant over such loud behavior at the most sacred Jewish shrine, whereas Jesus commended their enthusiasm (Matt. 21:15–16).

A second characteristic of the young is that they seek out fresh experiences and are not likely to be fully satisfied with the religious practices of their elders. Most Jewish adults contentedly sang, in effect: "Give me that old-time religion; if it was good enough for Moses, it is good enough for me." Jesus found the settled religious routines to be as inflexible, dry, and faded in vitality as old leather. He recognized that if the fermenting "new wine" of his message were poured into the old wineskins, an undesirable explosion would occur. "Fresh skins for new wine!" he exclaimed (Mark 2:18–22). Jesus proclaimed "good news" for a new day, as Isaiah had at the end of the Babylonian exile (40:9; 42:9).

Most of Jesus' disciples were probably teenagers, for he addressed them as "children" (Mark 10:24; John 21:5). Also, it is unlikely that students would have been older than their rabbi, and Luke states that Jesus was "about thirty years old" (Luke 3:23). He probably selected youth to launch his movement on the presumption that young minds, like new wineskins, would stretch with challenging ideas. Unfortunately, Christian art has often disguised the age factor, and sometimes Jesus' disciples are portrayed as older than their teacher.

A questioning mind is another common attribute of children. A child's enormous capacity for curiosity is expressed in the ditty: "Twinkle, twinkle, little star, How I wonder what you are." Those who have compared classes of children with classes of adults have found a striking difference in inquisitiveness. In elementary school, the students take most of the initiative in asking questions; in college, the professor asks most of the questions.[6]

A sampling of comments about or by some brilliant modern men shows that childlike inquiry is never extinguished. Regarding Mark Twain, a close friend wrote: "He was a youth to the end of his days, the heart of a boy with the head of a sage."[7] On the eightieth birthday of a comrade, Albert Einstein reflected: "People like you and me . . . do not grow old no matter how long we live. What I mean is that we never cease to stand like curious children before the great Mystery into which we are born."[8] The secret of Albert Einstein's genius was his cosmic awe and search for simplicity throughout life.

Theologian Reinhold Niebuhr finds a place for childlikeness in the area of his specialty:

> The most charming characteristic of childhood is the penchant of the child for simple but profound questions. . . . The child is a theologian rather than a scientist, . . . confused and uncertain about secondary and natural causes; but . . . interested in primary and ultimate ones. . . . They all concern themselves with the problem of ultimate meaning: "Why was I born?" and with the relation of the infinite to the finite: "If God was not born, why did he want me to be born?"[9]

A child's openness to knowledge of the divine and of nature is displayed in Jesus' life-style. He frequently withdrew from social life to contemplate the Creator and creation. He evaluated wildflowers as more splendidly garbed than wealthy King Solomon (Matt. 6:28–29). Jesus viewed the world with the eyes of a child, as William Blake intended when he wrote:

To see a World in a Grain of Sand
And a Heaven in a Wild Flower,
Hold Infinity in the palm of your hand
And Eternity in an hour.[10]

Philosopher Richard Taylor reinforces Jesus' outlook by telling of the peril of getting away from childlikeness. He writes:

To replace the love of pebbles and dandelions with the eagerness for power and name, to replace the need to be tenderly cared for with a frozen acceptance, to replace the simple delight of one's body, of touches, of smells, of soft caress—to replace these with the kind of mantle meant to shut these things out or at least hide them from view, from the view even, sometimes, of their possessor—all these replacements, the steps toward being grown-up, are only steps toward making dying easier.[11]

Another characteristic of children is frankness. They have not acquired the false front where smiles can be switched on and off for effect only. Compare childlike candor with Tennessee Williams's description of cocktail parties: "The horror of insincerity . . . overhangs those affairs like a cloud of cigarette smoke."[12] Sometimes with adults it is almost impossible to get beneath the veneer of artificial sweetness that hardens over the true personality.

Hans Christian Andersen tells of the difference between adult and child perceptions in "The Emperor's New Clothes." The classic story discloses how older folk tend to replace truth with flattery in order to go along with the crowd and to feed authority figures what they most appreciate. But then a candid child punctures their petty pretensions, causing them to admit: "The child is right, the Emperor is unclothed!" Jesus, like the child, spoke sincerely even when it exposed the nakedness of pious paraders.

Children also stand out from adults in the matter of forgiveness. Feelings of fury can suddenly boil up between children, causing mutual clobbering. They easily fall out and easily make up. The fall-out rate of adults is not as high, but when it does occur, haughty pride often burns so deeply that reconciliation is barred. A child can easily and honestly admit to mistakes, but confession of wrongdoing is more difficult for face-saving adults.

Young children are without prejudices, since prejudgments are based on learned behavior. Prejudices come from nurture, not nature. Prejudices against other groups are acquired when guardians place ethnic tattoos on those for whom they are responsible. Lyrics of "You've Got to Be Carefully Taught," by Oscar Hammerstein in *South Pacific*, reveal the source of our tribal markings. According to the song we internalize the repulsion that our relatives have toward outsiders during our early, impressionable years. We are "taught to hate" before we are eight.

By his teachings and actions, Jesus attempted to counter the bigotry of his day and restore the ethnic openness characteristic of the very young. To those who thought the only good Samaritan was a dead Samaritan, he told a story that has been unsurpassed in its social effect. In actions, Jesus was notorious for his assistance to people commonly viewed as disreputable—beggars, lepers, tax collectors, prostitutes, and Gentiles.

Lastly, children have a simple trust. A human infant is the most helpless creature on earth, for the longest period of time. Children naturally ask for basic needs from their parents.

To convey his unsophisticated faith, Jesus unconventionally addressed God as *Abba* (Mark 14:36), the intimate term for father in Aramaic. Consequently, this familiar mode of speaking to God as Daddy became a distinguishing characteristic of the worship of the early church (Rom. 8:15). That the child in Jesus never died is displayed in his last words: "Abba, into your hands I commit my spirit!" (Luke 23:46). He may have recited these words, taken from Psalm 31, as a bedtime prayer in his boyhood home. Thus, while dying on the cross, Jesus relaxed in God's care as he had done nightly over the years, confident that life would be his again when he awakened.

Classicist Terrot Glover points out that you have to read far in ancient literature before you find anything approaching Jesus' appreciation for children.[13] Only in Taoism is a similar outlook advocated. Countering the stiff formalism of

Confucius, that Chinese religious philosophy affirmed: "Wise men hear and see as little children do."[14]

In sync with Jesus' outlook, the distinguished Harvard child psychiatrist Robert Coles claims that a child has many of the qualities needed for full personhood. His lengthy research displays that children's spirituality affects psychic integration throughout life.[15] Sigmund Freud erred in assuming that the secular adult is the only model of the mentally healthy person. For him the religious temperament is like mumps, an expectation for children but a danger for adults who fail to outgrow it.[16] However, the basic Christian virtues of faith, hope, love, and joy are healthy personality qualities, which are often better displayed in children than in adults. Perhaps this is what Jesus had in mind in this prayer: "I thank you, Father, . . . for revealing to little children what you have hidden from the learned and the clever" (Luke 10:21).

Jesus' tenderness with children stands out when seen against the relief of traditional Jewish child training. The book of Proverbs, a manual for instructing youth, emphasizes punishment as a means of instruction. The Israelites considered the whip to be an indispensable obedience training tool for both children and domestic animals (Prov. 26:3). Israelite practice is behind this chronic proverb, "Spare the rod and spoil the child" (cf. Prov. 22:15). They even claimed that "those who spare the rod hate their children" (13:24).

Children in ancient Israel who did not accept discipline submissively were in peril. In the Fifth Commandment, children's longevity is associated with honoring their parents (Ex. 20:12). Unlimited retaliation was permitted toward a child who expressed anger toward a parent in word or action. According to several cruel laws of Moses, capital punishment was decreed for striking or cursing a parent (Ex. 21:15, 17; Lev. 20:9). Parents were expected to have "a stubborn and rebellious son" stoned to death (Deut. 21:18–21). Children were no doubt frightened to learn that disobedience to either parent could result in vultures pecking out their eyes (Prov. 30:17).

By contrast, Jesus was concerned over the harsh treatment that adults often inflict on children. He directed his most outspoken criticism toward verbal or physical abuse: "If any of you puts a stumbling block before one of these little ones who has faith in me, it would be better for you to be drowned in the deep sea with a large millstone fastened around your neck. . . . Be careful not to treat with contempt a single one of these little ones" (Matt. 18:6, 10). In light of the harshness toward children permitted in the Hebrew Bible, it appears that Jesus would have favored a modification of the Fifth Commandment injunction along this line: "Respect your father, your mother, *and your children*." Also, as the inaugurator of the "new covenant" (Jer. 31:9–32; 1 Cor. 11:25), he probably found it objectionable that the only reference to children in the Ten Commandments is the declaration that they will be punished for their parents' iniquities.

The fact that children were attracted to Jesus indicates that they did not view him as the typical unapproachable disciplinarian. His affectionate gesture of taking them into his arms was evidently so overly permissive for rabbinical behavior that Matthew (19:13–15) and Luke (18:15–17) omit it from what they copy from Mark (10:16). Karl Marx, although a caustic critic of religions in history, so admired the abiding influence of Jesus' tenderness toward children that he often said, "We can forgive Christianity much, since it taught us to love children."[17]

In a contemporary setting, Jesus would probably have little interest in proclaiming the "word of God" in a grandiose sanctuary, but would have great interest in informally rapping with youth in a park. That style and setting corresponds more closely to his interactions with his disciples. Among the Bible-thumping televangelists, where is one who shares Jesus' orientation toward children? On children's television there is a person who exudes some of the gracious qualities of Jesus. Fred Rogers, a Christian minister, handles with sensitivity a sad time as well as "a beautiful day in the neighborhood." Yet even his show does not permit a dialogue or a personal relationship with the viewers.

Jesus thought that regaining childlikeness for adults was a difficult but not impossible accomplishment. "Convert" and "conversion" are infrequent terms in the New Testament, but the verb is appropriately used in this traditional translation: "Except ye be converted, and become as little children, ye shall not enter into the kingdom of heaven" (Matt. 18:3).

The Greek verb *strepho*, translated only here in the King James Version as "converted," means to turn and go in a new direction. Jesus was confident that childlikeness can be regained, even by someone as old as Nicodemus, through a transforming spiritual encounter (John 3:3–8).

Gender Liberation

What did Jesus do to dignify the role of women, another belittled group of the ancient world? Far more than any other biblical personality, he put into practice the Genesis affirmation that both females and males share the image of God (Gen.1:27). Several episodes illustrate well the way in which he brought a larger measure of self-fulfillment to women.

The brief account of Jesus' visit in the home of Mary and Martha contains explosive sex-role criticism. In Palestine a woman was admired principally for her food-preparation and baby-production abilities. Thus Martha was preoccupied with housekeeping routines and was determined that her sister should also conduct herself in the traditional manner. Mary had less interest in bustling about to serve a fancy meal than in learning from an intriguing rabbi. Disturbed by Jesus' acceptance of Mary's iconoclastic pursuit, Martha confronts both of them. Moving in on their session together, she rudely blurts out to her guest: "Lord, don't you care that my sister has left me to serve alone? Tell her to help me!" (Luke 10:40).

Mary was in violation of social mores when she assumed the customary posture for a student receiving instruction (Luke 10:39; Acts 22:3). The taboo surrounding any such discussion is seen in the disdainful comments of ancient rabbis. One of them gravely warned: "He who talks much with women brings evil upon himself and neglects the study of the Torah, and in the end will go to hell." Another enjoined: "Let the Torah's words burn up but let them not be transmitted to a woman."[18]

Jesus countered a customary view that the Jews shared with most traditional cultures, namely, that a woman's fulfillment is inseparable from her homemaking role. He encouraged Mary and other women to become disciples—that is, students. Some of those learners were later sent out as agents to convey his message.[19] Those apostolic women were forerunners of Susan B. Anthony, who exclaimed, "What an absurd notion that women have no intellectual and moral faculties sufficient for anything but domestic concerns!"[20]

Jesus implored both men and women to engage in lowly acts of service to others, so there is no reason to think he objected to Martha's busyness with kitchen tasks. Indeed, the Lukan episode of Mary and Martha immediately follows a parable praising anyone who uses his or her hands to perform acts of practical service. However, Jesus did not like to see one person infringe on another person's aspiration to act independently. He did not favor the "brother's keeper" role becoming like a zookeeper's role. Therefore he encouraged Mary to break out of the conventional cage by realizing that a woman could be something other than a homebody. He admired her eagerness for learning and, in effect, her desire to be liberated from the limitations of her gender-defined role. By contrast, Martha's horizons did not seem to extend beyond preparing the perfect meal. Jesus gently admonished her: "Martha, Martha, you fret and fuss about many things; one thing is needful. Mary chose the right thing, and it shall not be taken from her" (Luke 10:41–42).

The Fourth Gospel also portrays Martha in a serving role, with Mary at Jesus' feet. Jesus loved both of the women, according to the account, but he was especially moved by Mary's spontaneity (11:5; 12:2–3). The sisters expressed kindness in different ways: Martha by preparing a dinner to honor Jesus, Mary by showing anticipatory grief in anointing him with perfume customarily used for burials.

Rejecting the double standard in sexual morality was another way by which Jesus witnessed to the belief that all men and women are created equal. As was typical of most societies, a woman in his culture received harsher treatment for sexual infidelity than a man. For example, Jesus' forefather Judah was on the verge of burning to death his widowed daughter-in-law for having sex, until she proved that he himself had impregnated her. Judah thought he had consorted with a prostitute, which was acceptable behavior for a man (Gen. 38:13–26). In the century when the party of the Pharisees was developing, death by fire was prescribed for a woman who engaged in sexual misconduct. Illicit sex by a woman in a family was treated as an evil even more heinous than murder.[21]

Jesus believed it was unjust to treat punitively only one person in a liaison that was adulterating a marriage. Consequently, when some men charged that a woman had been detected in "the very act of adultery," he was indignant that the Pharisees had apprehended only one of the sex partners. The law to which they were appealing gave penalties to both parties (Lev. 20:10; Deut. 22:23–24). It is ludicrous to presume that witnesses would see only one person engaging in sexual intercourse. Obviously the adulterous men had indulgently winked at the male participant. Jesus admonished them: "Let him who is without sin among you be the first to throw a stone at her" (John 8:7). He dealt sternly with the self-righteous male accusers and gently with the adulterous woman—although he did not condone her behavior.

There are several other subtle but telling ways in which Jesus subverted the sexism of his day. First, he avoided the chronic male proclivity toward describing the alleged wiles of women. Rather, he viewed all humans as individuals, without classifying behavior as masculine or feminine. Second, Jesus helped numerous women as well as men regain physical and moral health. To honor one whom he healed, he called her "a daughter of Abraham" (Luke 13:16). Along with the "sons of Abraham," whom others frequently designated as belonging to the Hebrew covenant, Jesus dignified a hunchbacked woman by including her among God's chosen. Some women who traveled with him felt indebted to him for their restored health (Luke 8:2–3).

Third, Jesus had no reluctance to draw examples in his teaching from situations involving either sex. He commended the generosity of both women and men (Luke 19:2–10; 21:1–4). Empathy with various situations faced by women is revealed in a number of Jesus' parables: the ten bridesmaids (Matt. 25:1–13), the woman working with yeast (Luke 13:21), and the widow with an unjust judge (Luke 18:1–5). In one parable he compares God to a woman in search of what she has lost, and tells of her joy in finding it

(Luke 15:8–10). The God of Jesus, although most frequently called Father, was neither all masculine nor all feminine, but embraced and transcended alleged gender characteristics (cf., e.g., Ps. 103:13; Isa. 9:6; Hos. 11:1–4).

Fourth, Jesus attempted to counteract economic discrimination against women. He was angered by those who "devour widows' houses" (Mark 12:40) while pretending to be faithful Jews. Jesus' frequent reference to the plight of widows may have been prompted by his own mother's situation. His father probably died before his public ministry began, because Joseph is last mentioned when Jesus was twelve years old.

Modern scholars have been impressed by the various ways in which Jesus was supportive toward women. While harshly critical of antifeminism in Christian history, Mary Daly admits:

> There is no recorded speech of Jesus concerning women "as such." What is very striking is his behavior toward them. In the passages describing the relationship of Jesus with various women, one characteristic stands out starkly: they emerge as persons, for they are treated as persons, often in such contrast with prevailing custom as to astonish onlookers.[22]

Dorothy Sayers suggests that women were especially drawn to Jesus because he treated them as full humans:

> They had never known a man like this man—there never has been such another. A prophet and teacher who never nagged at them, never flattered or coaxed or patronized; . . . who took their questions and arguments seriously; who never mapped out their sphere for them, never urged them to be feminine or jeered at them for being female. . . . There is no act, no sermon, no parable in the whole Gospel that borrows its pungency from female perversity; nobody could possibly guess from the words and deeds of Jesus that there was anything "funny" about woman's nature.[23]

In order to illustrate this startling way in which Jesus stands out, Charles Carlston quotes many expressions of "wisdom" about dumb and deceitful women which he found in ancient writings. "For a woman, silence is a grace," is one example. Carlston comments:

> This so-called wisdom is totally absent from the traditions about Jesus. And I know of no way of accounting for this phenomenon except on the grounds that Jesus was perfectly at ease in the company of women and that for him equality between the sexes was not so much a distant legislative goal as a rather self-evident fact.[24]

A group of women were loyal to Jesus to the end. At Jerusalem, the male political and religious establishment crushed an innocent person, while some marginalized women responded with acts of affection. During the last hours before his execution, his male disciples were so fearful of their own safety that they did not tarry even to arrange for his burial. The contrasting attitude of the women was well depicted long ago by Irishman Eaton Barrett:

> Not she with trait'rous kiss her Saviour stung,
> Not she denied him with unholy tongue;
> She, while apostles shrank, could danger brave,
> Last at his cross, and earliest at his grave.[25]

The life of Jesus illustrates the artificiality of gender stereotypes. It is significant that the Gospel writers describe the superlative model of Christian morality as having traits that traditionally have been at least as much associated with females as with males. Jesus is especially noted for his tender emotions, for example. The verb "to have compassion"—the standard translation of a Greek term meaning "to be moved in one's viscera"—is used in the New Testament exclusively with respect to Jesus' teaching and life (Mark 1:41; 6:34; 8:2; Matt. 20:34; Luke 10:33; 15:20). Unlike Julius Caesar, who in the century before had announced triumphantly, "I came, I saw, I conquered," Luke reports that Jesus *came* to Nain, *saw* a widow mourning over the corpse of her only son, and *had compassion* on her (Luke 7:13).

Weeping, a particular expression of the tender feelings, is also primarily associated in Western civilization with the female sex. In Shakespearean drama, "to play the woman"

171

means to weep.[26] By contrast, in the biblical culture weeping was associated as much with one sex as with the other. Jeremiah, the most profuse weeper in the Bible, expressed himself in this poignant way: "Would that my head were all water, my eyes a fountain of tears; that I might weep day and night for my people's dead!" (9:1). The grief response of another prophet is summed up in the shortest biblical verse: "Jesus wept" (John 11:35). A New Testament letter cites Jesus' "loud cries and tears" as proof of his humanity (Heb. 5:7). He was emotionally a true "son of David" for there are eight occasions recorded when David wept aloud (1 Sam. 20:41; 30:4; 2 Sam. 1:12; 3:32; 12:21; 13:36; 15:30; 18:33).

Devotion to children was a characteristic of Jesus, even though it is another trait societies generally call feminine. Consider the simile Jesus used in his lament over Jerusalem. Alarmed by violence directed toward the innocent in his nation, Jesus pictured his role as a sheltering mother: "How often have I longed to gather your children around me as a hen gathers her brood under her wings, but you would not let me!" (Luke 13:34). He was no strutting and fighting cock! Jesus also identified with children by announcing that cordiality to them was a way of receiving him (Mark 9:36–37).

Jesus shared with women the trait of gentleness. He was associated with the feminine personification of God, Wisdom [Greek, *Sophia*], in the Gospels (Matt. 11:19; Luke 11:49) and by Paul (1 Cor. 1:24). Wisdom had earlier been described in Jesus' culture as a woman whose "yoke" makes burden-bearing easier.[27] Similarly, he said: "Come to me, all of you who are tired from carrying heavy loads, and I will give you rest. Take my yoke upon you, and learn from me, because I am gentle and humble in spirit" (Matt. 11:28–29). Paul appealed to "the gentleness and kindness of Christ" in writing to a congregation (2 Cor. 10:1).

Serving needy people both in and beyond the home has also been a role more associated with women than with men. Among the qualities that composed an ancient Hebrew's picture of an ideal woman was this: "She is openhanded to the wretched and generous to the poor" (Prov. 31:20). Today it is still the case that there is a high ratio of women to men in the areas of social work and nursing. Regarding Jesus' activity, this summary statement is given: "He went about doing good and healing all who were oppressed" (Acts 10:38). Assisting the social outcasts was a main thrust of his mission.

Suffering is another trait especially associated with women. Before the coming of modern medicine with its painkillers, excruciating suffering was one of the dreads of childbirth. Inspired by the Suffering Servant ideal of Isaiah, Jesus said, "The Son of Man must undergo great sufferings" (Mark 8:31). He exemplifies par excellence the traits of suffering and serving which traditionally have been more associated with females than with males. Also, he warned his followers that they will have to suffer like a woman in labor (John 16:21–22).

Turning to those traits commonly thought to be masculine, let us look at how they are related to Jesus' personality. Aristotle claimed that men by nature are more dominant, courageous, persevering, and rational than women.[28] "Be courageous" is an admonition of Paul (1 Cor. 16:13), according to the usual translation; however, a literal rendering is "Be masculine" (*andrizesthe*). Those stereotypes have been transmitted rather uncritically down through our civilization until the present day. "Bold, resolute, and open in conduct" is the definition that Webster gives for "manly."

Jesus was noted for his leadership, fearlessness, powerfulness, and wisdom. Many were attracted to him by his charisma; some left work, possessions, and home to follow him (Mark 1:16–20). On encountering a storm at sea that frightened even seasoned fishermen, Jesus was not worried (Mark 4:37–38).

The power within Jesus was physical as well as spiritual. For most of his adult life he was in a manual trade that required bodily strength. Since there were no power tools for sawing and drilling, his muscles were probably even more developed than those of carpenters today. When he became an itinerating teacher, he warned those who joined his band that stamina was needed for coping with hardships they would encounter (Matt. 8:20). Like a scoutmaster, he took his young disciples on a trek up the Lebanese mountains (Mark 8:27; 9:2).

Jesus' assertiveness is conveyed by his denunciation of the exploitation by religious leaders. At the risk of his life, he combined verbal criticism with physical force to drive out those who were commercializing the Temple (Mark 11:15–18). Mexican artist José Orozco may have been reflecting on the forceful Jesus in the Temple when he painted the mural lodged at Dartmouth College. He portrays a fierce but triumphant Jesus who has chopped down his cross and shattered the column of a building that represents the established order.

In past times self-confidence has been associated more with males than with females. Jesus displayed assuredness in a superlative manner when he was on trial for his life. Pilate asked him if he thought of himself as a Jewish king. The Fourth Gospel represents Jesus as replying in this bold manner: "I am a king. For this I was born, and for this I have come into the world, to bear witness to the truth; and all who are on the side of truth listen to me" (John 18:37). The Roman procurator remarks: "Surely you know I have power to release you or to have you crucified." To this Jesus affirms: "You would have no power over me unless it had been given you from above" (19:10–11).

In the masculine mystique of ancient Judaism, it was assumed that reasoning power was principally possessed by males and that only they had the ability to become scholars. It was in accord with sex-role expectations for Rabbi Jesus to have an intellectual command of his religious traditions and an ability to communicate fresh insights from that heritage. The keenness of his mind is well illustrated in his handling of criticisms after he drove money changers and animal sellers out of the Temple. Inquiries were made with the purpose of embarrassing him regardless of his answer. Jesus cleverly responded to one loaded question about his authority by tossing back a question that his critics refused to answer. He then dealt astutely with a question involving giving to Caesar or to God by replacing the either/or dilemma with both/and logic. According to Luke, the Jerusalem leaders conceded that Jesus won this battle of wits: "They were unable to catch him in anything he had to say in public; they were amazed at his answer and were silenced" (20:26).

In this survey of some of Jesus' traits, it can be seen that he was free of the pernicious gender polarization of human history. As Elisabeth Moltmann-Wendel rightly observes: "He had himself personally integrated so many male and female behavioral characteristics that one could consider him the first maturely integrated person."[29] Rosemary Ruether expresses a similar assessment:

> Jesus is not so much "feminine" or "masculine" as he is a figure that defies all such sex stereotyping. Although authoritative, he is authoritative in an iconoclastic way. . . . His is an authority that overthrows conventional models of patriarchal, hierarchical, religious and political power systems; that champions women, the poor, the unwashed and outcasts, that rejects the power games of the male leadership classes.[30]

Thus, qualities that many cultures have considered feminine or masculine were harmoniously blended in his lifestyle. Jesus was both a brave, brainy, and brawny he-man and a sensitive, serving, and suffering she-man! He affectionately took children in his arms, but he also indignantly took strong-arm methods to drive out Temple hucksters. He surprised his companions by being both more "feminine" and more "masculine" than others.

Jesus was a revolutionary, but his sphere was more psychological than political. His life-style liberates males and females from sexist molds that can be severely constricting, and encourages persons to consider a broader range of options for temperamental expression. Like Jesus, they can choose from a broad arc of possible human traits and reunite what culture has split asunder. Into their personalities they can combine, as Jesus did, qualities as varied as shedding tears with impunity over the plight of their nation's capital on one day and striking forcefully against corrupt business practice on the next.

Jesus' Emotional Gratifications

How does "Physician, heal yourself," a proverb Jesus once quoted (Luke 4:23), apply to his own relationships? We know he encouraged self-fulfillment for lonely and downtrodden people, appreciating their normal desire for unfettered human relationships. But did Jesus love himself even as he loved others?

On many occasions Jesus enjoyed dining with others, causing some to call him "a glutton and a drunkard" (Luke 7:34). Those slanderers thought that he should follow John the Baptist and renounce simple pleasures. In response, Jesus contrasted John's austere fasting with his own joyful life-style (Luke 5:33–34). To describe one facet of the good life, he pictured a wedding party—where giggling, gabbling, gobbling, and guzzling accompany festive song and dance.

In the biblical era, dance and religion were closely intertwined. The annual high holy days were prime times for folk dancing, even though scriptural translations do not usually make this apparent. The Hebrew term *hag*, usually rendered "feast" in English Bibles, originally meant "a round dance." Israelites often prayed with their bones and muscles at religious ceremonies. One psalm urges people to "praise the Lord's name with dancing, making melody with tambourine and lyre" (Ps. 149:3). Another psalm describes the processional dance: "Singers lead; minstrels come last; in the middle women play on tambourines" (68:25). Worship in the biblical era was associated with both bodily movement and mental exercise. This may be because body language is sometimes more honest than verbal language.

At the Jerusalem Temple, exuberant dance climaxed the Tabernacles festival. The Mishnah describes the gala occasion in this way:

> Pious men danced with torches in their hands and sang songs of joy while the Levites played on harps, lyres, cymbals, trumpets, and other musical instruments on the fifteen steps leading down from the Court of the Israelites to the Court of Women. . . . The man who has never seen the joy of the night of this feast has never seen real joy in all his life.[31]

During a night of one of these fiestas, Rabbi Simeon ben Gamaliel celebrated by dancing and flinging eight torches into the air, one after another, and catching them.[32]

Jesus showed himself to be a true son of Israel by blending the solemn with the festive. His life-style was in accord with an Israelite sage's observation that there is "a time to weep, and a time to laugh; a time to mourn, and a time to

176

dance" (Eccl. 3:4). Jesus contrasted the outlook of his followers with those who, like quarreling children, refuse to dance
(Luke 7:31–34). Dance participation was one way in which
the adult Jesus heeded his own advice to "become like children." The Fourth Gospel affirms that "the Word became
flesh and lived among us, and we have seen his glory" (1:14).
It might also be said that Jesus incarnated his religious ideas
through glorious dance. When his body became the medium
of communication, the flesh became word (*logos*).

"Be glad and dance for joy," Jesus exhorted (Luke 6:23).
Judging by the Greek and Aramaic terms behind Gospel
translations, Jesus leaped for joy after his disciples returned
from a successful mission. Also, they danced when greeted
by pilgrims waving palm branches.[33]

On the night before his crucifixion Jesus may have led his
disciples in a sacred dance. The Gospels indicate that they
participated in a Passover celebration that was concluded on
a musical note. The Hallel psalms customarily sung after the
Passover meal include a call to join in a circle dance. A legend about Jesus, recorded two centuries after that upper
room event at Jerusalem, may suggest what happened:

> Before he was arrested . . . he assembled us all and said,
> "Before I am delivered to them, let us sing a hymn to the
> Father." . . . So he told us to form a circle, holding one an-
> other's hands. . . . He began to sing, "Glory be to you, Fa-
> ther." And we circled round him and answered him,
> "Amen.". . . "He who does not dance does not know what
> happens." "Amen." "If you follow my dance, see yourself
> in me.". . . After the Lord had so danced with us, my
> beloved, he went out.[34]

A generation ago Sydney Carter renewed the tradition of
a dancing Jesus. Carter's inspiration for writing "Lord of the
Dance" came from witnessing Shakers dancing to their
"Simple Gifts" tune at a folk festival.[35] His lyrics, now
widely published, give a first-person rendition of the life of
dance leader Jesus. The common people join him while the
religious establishment scorn him and eventually destroy
him. Defiant jubilance is finally conveyed when, after being

cut down on Good Friday, the "Lord of the Dance" springs up to dance within Christians eternally.

According to some of Jesus' parables, even God is not wholly self-abnegating in loving, but finds joy in love that is returned (Luke 15:7, 10). Jesus' ideal person is quite different from Aristotle's "great-souled" person who "is fond of conferring benefits, but ashamed to receive them, because the former is a mark of superiority and the latter of inferiority."[36] Sheer altruism or selflessness was not idealized by Jesus, even though he taught that giving takes priority over receiving in mature love (Luke 6:35; Acts 20:35).

The mutuality of love is well displayed in Jesus' encounter with "a woman of the city, who was a sinner." Simon, the host, was shocked that Jesus did not shun her after being clued by her loose hair that her morals were also loose. Jesus was pleased when she poured ointment from an alabaster jar on his feet, kissed them, and wiped them with her long hair. Even though Jesus' hand often went out to others, this is the only episode recorded in the Gospels in which he receives the kindly touch of another. He defended her hospitable acts and expressed appreciation for her profuse love. Luke portrays the woman of ill repute as not only more loving but more lovable than the priggish Pharisee who owned the home into which she had entered (7:36–50).

In Mark there is a similar exchange with an unnamed woman in the home of a man named Simon. She lovingly anointed Jesus' head with ointment from an alabaster jar, a gesture associated with a king's coronation. In his typical manner, he came to the defense of the woman against the male critics present. Despite their indignation over her waste of expensive ointment, Jesus remarked: "She has done a beautiful thing to me." Recognizing that ointment was also used on corpses, Jesus ironically commented: "She has anointed my body beforehand for burial." That woman received the highest tribute he gave to any person: "Wherever the gospel is proclaimed in the whole world, what she has done will be told in memory of her" (14:3–9).

Joseph Haroutunian is properly critical of the common assumption that Jesus' love "flowed out of him as water from a spring . . . unmindful of any reciprocation." Haroutunian suggests that those called "sinners" in the Gospels aroused Jesus' affection:

> He saw in them a humanity that escapes the "righteous" and is, in fact, repudiated by them. Sinners, like the adulteress at Simon the Pharisee's home or Zacchaeus the publican, for all their sins and wrongdoings, showed a sensibility that is the love one creature hopes for from another and owes another. . . . Jesus not only loved but was also loved in return by the sinners. It is true that he did not love so that he might be loved in return. But it does not follow that he did not care whether he was loved or not. . . . Nothing but theological prejudice and confusion, accumulated through the centuries . . . would lead a man reading the accounts of Jesus' encounter with people to judge that his love was a one-way affair.

Haroutunian maintains that a basic human quality is hungering for love, and feeling empty when others do not respond to friendship extended. He considers it a denial of Jesus' humanity to believe that he was insensitive to, or unneeding of, love from others.[37]

The best-known of Jesus' female friends is Mary from the town of Magdala, in Galilee. Since the name Mary was as common then as now, this woman is often identified as Mary Magdalene, or simply Magdalene. After Jesus assisted her in becoming healed of a psychic and/or moral disorder, she joined his traveling band and became one of the women who took care of the group (Luke 8:1–2). Magdalene was with Jesus not only during his Galilean ministry but also as he journeyed to Jerusalem (Mark 15:40–41). She was among the courageous women who remained with him until his agony ended. She saw where his body was buried, and returned to that place with ointments and spices after the Sabbath was over (Mark 15:47–16:1).

The Synoptic Gospels place Magdalene first in each listing of women (Matt. 27:56; Mark 15:40–41; Luke 8:2; 24:10), and Peter first in the listing of male disciples. This displays that the evangelists regarded Magdalene and Peter as prominent persons. The church is well aware of Peter's intimate companionship and special importance, but Magdalene's status is generally disregarded. Ruether argues plausibly that orthodox Christianity suppressed the early testimony that Magdalene was the woman closest to Jesus. This was done in order to exalt Mary, his mother, even though the historical sources do not describe him as having much rapport with her.[38]

A generation ago, Nikos Kazantzakis attempted to portray the give-and-take passion of Christianity's central figure. His novel, *The Last Temptation of Christ*, and the more controversial film with the same title, use fiction to convey Jesus' presumed struggle with the bilateral nature of love. In his prologue, Kazantzakis hypothesizes that "Christ passed through all the stages which the man who struggles passes through. . . . If he had not within him this warm human element, he would never be able to touch our hearts with such assurance and tenderness; he would not be able to become a model for our lives."[39]

An examination of Kazantzakis's *Last Temptation* is worthwhile because it tells of the agony of conflicting demands in a religious personality. The Greek artist's effort to rehabilitate Jesus' full humanity has been denigrated by the hyped film which Martin Scorsese directed. Kazantzakis's story line will be treated independent of Scorsese's mediocre production.

Satan presents difficult tests to young Jesus, the ultimate one being sexual. Jesus is placed in seductive situations and is tempted to fulfill his strong desire for having sex. He confesses: "When I see a woman go by, I blush and lower my head, but my eyes fill with lust."[40] According to Kazantzakis, satisfying the conjugal urge was for Jesus the primal and persistent human temptation. On seeing snakes slither together, Jesus reflects: "Men and women couple like this, and that is why God banished us from Paradise."[41]

Jesus' sexual desire is directed toward Magdalene, a daughter of his rabbinical uncle. Kazantzakis tells of their mutual attraction by alluding to an ancient androgynous tale: "They had both sensed the deep dark fact that one was a man and the other a woman: two bodies which seemed once upon a time to have been one; but some merciless God separated them, and now the pieces had found each other again and were trying to join, to reunite."[42]

According to the novel, Jesus and Magdalene are on the verge of betrothal when he is confronted by the "merciless God" who wills to separate their bodies. During that terrifying experience Jesus "shrieked and fell down on his face, frothing at the mouth."[43] Frightened by what he takes to be the divine will, he renounces marriage. He keeps a nail-studded strap in his carpentry shop, believing that he can exorcise his libido by flagellation. After having sexual dreams involving Magdalene, he relieves his shame by scourging himself until his blood spurts out.[44]

This method of rigorous self-punishment leaves Jesus pale and emaciated, but it does not cure his lust. He recalls that Magdalene's father had spoken fondly of a desert monastery to which he belonged before abandoning the holy life to marry. Jesus wants to identify with white-robed monks who abstain from meat, wine, and women while they pray continuously.[45] As he heads toward their community, he expresses this hope: "There I shall kill the flesh and turn it into spirit."[46]

En route to the monastery, Kazantzakis continues, Jesus could not resist stopping by Magdalene's town to greet her. Jilted by her loved one, she has become a prostitute. She explains, "In order to forget one man . . . I've surrendered my body to all men!" Recognizing that Magdalene's plight is due to his unwillingness to marry her, Jesus begs her forgiveness. He finds himself craving her body even while visiting her in "the greatest degradation" at a brothel where customers are outside awaiting their turn. But because of his determination to remain virginal, he resists even his desire to touch her lips.[47]

At the Palestinian monastery, Jesus joins with others engaged in self-mortification. Each monk practiced asceticism "so that his soul might be unburdened of the body, might be relieved of this weight and enabled to ascend to heaven in order to find God."[48] After a while Jesus feels constrained to leave the secluded life in order to prophesy.

While itinerating in Galilee, Jesus happens to enter a village where an infuriated crowd has gathered to execute Magdalene. She has been convicted of polluting the Sabbath by failing to rest from selling her body on that day. Jesus exclaims to those assembled: "Let him among you who is without sin be the first to throw a stone!" He saves her life by making the villagers ashamed of their hypocrisy.[49]

Out of gratitude to Jesus for rescuing her from death, Magdalene renounces prostitution and ministers to him as he travels around Palestine. Consequently, the celibate's erotic desire for his repentant cousin becomes keener than ever. A voice speaks within:

> Take her! God created man and woman to match, like the key and the lock. Open her. Your children sit huddled together and numb inside her. . . . Look how God married the whore Jerusalem. The nations passed over her, but he married her to save her. Look how the prophet Hosea married the whore Gomer.[50]

Jesus came close to succumbing to this temptation to take Magdalene as his bride, especially since it was subtly couched as an argument from scripture. On one occasion when she was hugging his knees, "Jesus bent over, took her by the hand and lifted her up. Bashful and enchanted, he held her just as an inexperienced bridegroom holds his bride. His body rejoiced from its very roots."[51]

In the Kazantzakis novel, Jesus' most poignant sexual temptation strikes in the final moments of his earthly life. While he hangs on the cross, Satan entices him with a "deceptive vision" of marital happiness.[52] In his imagination Jesus confides to Magdalene: "How very many years I've longed for this moment! Who stepped between us and refused to leave us free—God?" Then he caresses her with joyous abandon. "They lay down under a flowering lemon tree and began to roll on the ground. The sun came and stood above them. A breeze blew; several flowers fell on the two naked bodies. . . . Purring, Mary Magdalene hugged the man, kept his body glued to hers." Then Jesus confesses: "Beloved wife, I never knew the world was so beautiful or the flesh so holy. . . . I never knew that the joys of the body were not sinful."[53]

But Jesus comes out of even this last bout victorious over temptation. After the hallucination his conscious mind affirms that marriage is basically a lust of the flesh which a holy man must abhor. Kazantzakis's story of Jesus' life concludes: "The moment he cried Eli Eli and fainted, temptation had captured him for a split second and led him astray. The joys, marriages and children were lies . . . illusions sent by the Devil."[54]

Are these portrayals of Jesus' sexuality anchored in the apostolic testimony to him? Kazantzakis attempted to strip away the perverted interpretations of Jesus which "cassocked representatives of Christianity have heaped upon his figure."[55] Yet the novelist failed in this, for his image of Jesus is more of a caricature originating in postapostolic asceticism than a portrait in line with what contemporary biblical scholarship knows about the historical Jesus.

Kazantzakis, like ascetic Christians, misunderstood a crucial saying of Jesus pertaining to sexual desire. Due to poor translations, most people think that Jesus, in the Sermon on the Mount, evaluated "anyone who looks at a woman lustfully" (Matt. 5:28) as committing a major sin. For example, Pope John Paul II expressed a Catholic outlook as old as Jerome when he asserted on the presumed authority of the founder of the church that "adultery in the heart is committed" when a husband gazes sexually even at his own wife.[56] One wonders how the pope expects a good husband to obtain an erection and pursue propagation with his wife if sexual desire is absent. However, the Greek term *gyne* in the Gospel text should be translated as "wife" with "of another" understood. The Great Bible of the English Renaissance properly translates *gyne* as "another man's wife." The other Greek term here deserving attention is *epithymia*, usually mistranslated as "lust." In English, lust is associated with lechery and generally has a bad connotation. For example, Shakespeare describes lust as "savage, extreme, rude, cruel."[57] However, *epithymia* is a morally neutral term meaning "longing." For example, Jesus tells his disciples, "I have longingly [*epithymia*] desired to eat this passover with you" (Luke 22:15). A better translation of Jesus' saying under consideration would be: "You have heard the commandment, 'You shall not commit adultery,' but I say to you that anyone who looks longingly at the spouse of another has already committed adultery within." Jesus interrelates two commands of the

Decalogue: coveting a neighbor's spouse is the first step toward the act of adultery.

There is no basis for maintaining that Jesus thought sexual desire was in itself bad. Kazantzakis reveals his Hellenistic bias in presuming that Jesus thought that erotic impulses are satanic. Jesus treasured the Creation story in which the celibate condition is the first thing God declares not good. The story concludes with naked spouses expressing their passion for each other without shame (Gen. 2:18–25). Exegete Frederick Grant's judgment about Matthew 5:28 is right:

> It does not forbid the natural desire of a young man for a young woman, or her desire for him, which leads to marriage; for the desire here denounced is one that involves adultery. . . . The fundamental Jewishness of the saying seems certain, and should be understood as forbidding the indulgence of the eyes and of the imagination, the covetous desire for another man's wife.[58]

Martin Luther once encountered some who were puzzled by Jerome's Latin translation of Matthew 5:28. They asked him if it was proper for unattached men and women to have sexual desire for one another. Luther responded by saying that those who ask such "silly" questions do not understand either nature or scripture. He queried, "When would people marry if they had not desire and love for one another?" Trouble comes if the sexual passion between them is weak. He then explained the verse under consideration by offering this terse maxim: "One is not to look at another as every one is to look at his wife."[59]

More recently, David Mace has remarked:

> There have been people of fanatical zeal who have distorted this saying of Jesus. He obviously did not mean that a young man seeking a wife should experience no feelings of sexual desire as he contemplated an eligible young woman. Nor did he mean that the wholesome pleasure a man might feel in admiring a beautiful woman, or the delight with which a woman might look upon a fine specimen of manhood, was evil in itself. What he meant, surely, was

that the best way in which we can all safeguard ourselves
from unfaithfulness is to refuse to let the imagination dwell
upon the thought of a sexual relationship which if it actually took place would violate a marriage, our own or another's.[60]

In Jesus' culture, holiness was allied with marital relations
rather than with sexual renunciation. By no means did the
ancient Palestinian Jews believe lifelong virginity was prerequisite to rabbinical or priestly preeminence. On the contrary, the Mishnah prohibited an unmarried man from being
a teacher.[61] Also, the Mishnah cites the first law of the Torah
as a requirement for all:

No man may abstain from keeping the law "Be fruitful
and multiply". . . : according to the School of Shammai,
two sons, according to the School of Hillel, a son and a
daughter, for it is written, "Male and female created he
them."[62]

Moreover, the *Gospel of Philip* claims that Magdalene was
Jesus' spouse.[63] Excavated in 1945, the gospel may convey a
tradition that is as ancient as the canonical Gospels. In *Was
Jesus Married?*[64] I dealt thoroughly with these matters, and
suggested that Jesus may have married Magdalene.

The historical Jesus differed from Kazantzakis's Jesus in
that he did not see women as a symbol of the sensuous realm
that must be spurned. The moral dualism endemic to Greek
philosophy, and which percolated through Gentile Christianity, was not a part of Jesus' ethic. Kazantzakis the Greek reveals his own heritage in assuming that the carnal is
tainted.[65] Jesus did not impose a dichotomy between a divine spirit and a devilish flesh.

The Palestinian milieu in which Jesus was reared cannot
be characterized as predominantly either hedonistic or ascetic. Likewise, Jesus did not think that the pursuit of pleasure was the goal of life, nor did he identify unhappiness with
the will of God. Kazantzakis's comprehension of the Gospels
is outrageously faulty when he interprets Jesus' desire for joy
as a manifestation of evil temptation. Jesus' inner struggle is

misrepresented by Kazantzakis in passages like this: "At every opportunity he had to be happy, to taste the simplest human joys—to eat, sleep, to mix with his friends and laugh, to encounter a girl on the street and think, I like—the ten claws immediately nailed themselves down into him, and his desire vanished."[66] The Jesus portrayed in the Gospels was noted for his conviviality, for blessing matrimonial unions, and for referring to the wedding feast as a symbol of the highest human happiness. His anguish was over human recalcitrance and refusal to extend love more broadly, not over whether to renounce love of a woman.

By way of positive evaluation, it may be said that Kazantzakis commendably endeavored to describe the struggles of the human Jesus. Judging by several New Testament accounts, his temptations were intensified rather than diminished by the divine power he possessed (Matt. 4:3, 6; 27:41–43; Mark 14:33–38; 15:29–32; Luke 4:3, 9; 23:35–37). One account states that Jesus "is able to help those who are being tempted" because he "was tempted in every respect as we are without committing any sin" (Heb. 2:18; 4:15). The Greek novelist stressed a neglected implication of that affirmation. He did not accept the apparent assumption of the writer of the Fourth Gospel that Jesus never underwent agonizing temptations at the beginning or end of his ministry. Kazantzakis held that Jesus accepted the following logic: Yielding to sexual temptation is evil; I am seeking to be holy; therefore, I cannot engage in coitus, either marital or otherwise. There is some truth in the major premise: although sexual temptation is not intrinsically evil, it is wrong to give in to sexual desire in some situations.

Kazantzakis did not accept the position of Bishop Augustine that Jesus' sublime holiness made it impossible for him to have libidinous temptations. That most influential church father argued: All sexual desire pollutes psychic purity; Jesus was perfect; therefore, he could not have had sexual desire.[67] Augustine's untrue major premise, but valid logic, has become widely accepted in Western Christianity. Accordingly, *The Last Temptation* was placed on the Vatican's Index of Forbidden Books.

In recognizing that sexual desire is a part of the nature of the best of humans, Kazantzakis makes more theological and psychological sense than Augustine. But there is no basis in the ancient Jewish history for the monastic doctrine, which both the novelist and the bishop accepted, that a superlatively moral person shuns a happily married life. Jesus was no monk, and he did not pommel his pleasure drive to death. Thus we need to look elsewhere for a more plausible treatment of the sexuality of Jesus.

Luther, even though he was an Augustinian monk, rejected the view that Jesus had no desire to love in a sexual way. He assumed that Magdalene was Jesus' sexual partner.[68] Few in the Lutheran tradition have been as bold as Luther, but Elisabeth Moltmann-Wendel wonders if he might not have been right.[69]

Lutheran clergyman Richard Langsdale has written a novel about a Jesus who went beyond Kazantzakis's Jesus and did more than dream about marriage. Langsdale relates Jesus' earlier experiences in the carpentry shop to those on his sacramental marriage bed. Langsdale's Jesus reflects on his honeymoon with Magdalene:

> Long ago and in another place I had watched my father Joseph hone and plane and mold the jointure of two olive boards until, with nod of perfection gained and satisfied, he closed the jointure and bound the olive wood from two parts into one. So here in this night I drew this Mary, this handicraft of God, into human jointure with myself, and through the night we honed the union to its height and depth and breadth of intended perfection. We two became one.

This intimate love of a particular person does not diminish Jesus' love for others. On the contrary, he acknowledges: "My life with Mary has turned a new facet of this prism of love into focus."[70] This enriching experience is similar to that of Shakespeare's Juliet, who confesses:

> My bounty is as boundless as the sea,
> My love as deep; the more I give thee,
> The more I have, for both are infinite.[71]

In recent years, the prevailing position of Christians on the humanity of Jesus has deviated widely from judgments by the celibate leadership of the largest Christian church. A survey shows that three fourths of the readers of *U.S. Catholic* believe that Jesus had sexual feelings.[72] The Jesus Seminar, composed of about a hundred Catholic, Protestant, and Jewish scholars,[73] has concluded that Jesus not only had erotic desires but probably expressed them in a heterosexual way. The full results of the Seminar's six-year probe of the Gospels—sponsored by the Westar Institute of California— are now being published. Seminar director Robert Funk reports: "More than half the members of the Seminar believe Jesus probably was not celibate, that he did not advocate celibacy as a lifestyle and that he had a 'special' relationship with at least one woman, but that it might not have been a sexual relationship."[74] Although the Seminar doubts the genuineness of many statements pertaining to Jesus in the Gospels, they unanimously agree that he was followed by a retinue that included women.

It would be presumptuous to maintain that Jesus thought of marriage as prerequisite to a full human life, even though it was highly sanctioned in his Jewish culture. There is no evidence that he believed that one's holiness is either increased or decreased by having sex. Intercourse and marriage are not the only healthy ways of expressing the sexuality that is a fundamental part of human nature. To maintain that Jesus *must* have opted to marry is as curtailing of his freedom as to maintain that he necessarily was celibate.

.9.

The Central Theme

The Glittering Rule

Many cultural leaders have assumed that the core of Jesus' ethics is in this principle: "Treat others as you would have them treat you" (Luke 6:31).[1] They have the encouragement of some biblical scholars: William Barclay evaluates it as "the Everest of all ethical teaching," while Bruce Metzger writes: "The ethical demands of Jesus upon his followers are summed up in what has come to be called 'the Golden Rule.'"[2] However, "glittering" might be the better adjective to modify a maxim that shines brilliantly but often in a misleading manner.

The "Golden Rule" is not distinctively Christian; it is championed in other religions and by persons who have no religion. The Jewish version, which goes back to the second century before the Christian era, reads: "What you hate, do not do to anyone."[3] The Rule is also found in Confucianism, Hinduism, Buddhism, and Islam,[4] as well as in the secular ethics of other people. Richard Busemeyer, an outspoken atheist, endorses the sensible morality that stems from this Rule.[5]

What are the merits of this widely honored "Golden Rule"? Many problems have been ameliorated when alienated groups have cultivated the ability to imagine each group's predicament if situations were reversed. While the Rule has been applied between ethnic groups and nations, it is nurtured and primarily expressed in individual relationships. Children are generally taught to avoid excepting themselves from conduct expected of others.

The Rule has considerable value, but in some applications it resembles fool's gold because of its egoistic orientation. Before using it, a person asks, "How do I want others to treat me?" Some might answer the question almost exclusively in terms of receiving things that satisfy their private appetites. The practice of scratching the backs of those from whom like treatment is expected can be found even among thieves.

Since personal tastes differ, many may be disgusted on receiving someone's expression of the Rule. For example, giving to others things you would like to receive has been promoted by advertisements showing men distributing gift-wrapped Scotch under a "Dewar's unto others" caption. All that is needed is a pun on a phrase from the well-known Rule to suggest that a Scotch drinker should take care of his Christmas list by purchasing a case of Dewar's brand of whiskey. One who finds Scotch distasteful but archaeology books delightful would send something quite different to his Scotch-loving friend!

As a comprehensive principle of morality, the "Golden Rule" also fails to deal with motivation. Immanuel Kant, the most renowned of German philosophers, argues that the Rule is secondary because it does not deal with good intention, the sine qua non of morality. "*Do* as one would be *done* by" focuses on outward actions and can operate apart from the inward attitude of either party. Also, Kant points out, the issue of how to treat one's self is ignored.[6] Indeed, self-deceit can be justified by the Rule. Tact has been deftly defined as lying unto others as we would have others lie unto us!

A paramount consideration in Jesus' teaching was the disposition of the "heart" or mind. He observed: "Figs are not picked from thistles nor grapes from thorn bushes. A person does good from the store of good within or does evil from the store of evil; for the mouth utters what overflows from the heart" (Luke 6:44–45). Rabbi Joseph Klausner contrasted Jesus' inner orientation with that of his contemporaries: "He stood in opposition to the majority of the Pharisees and their followers who made the external act the main object, and the underlying intention only a secondary matter."[7]

The opening of the Sermon on the Mount focuses on inner character:

Congratulations to the humble!
  The rule of God is theirs.
Congratulations to those who sorrow!
  They shall be strengthened.
Congratulations to the patient!
  They shall inherit the earth.
Congratulations to those who hunger
    and thirst for goodness!
  They shall be satisfied.
Congratulations to the merciful!
  They shall be shown mercy.
Congratulations to those with pure minds!
  They shall see God.
Congratulations to the peacemakers!
  They shall be called the children of God.
Congratulations to those who endure
    persecution for the cause of right!
  The rule of God is theirs.
                              (Matt. 5:3–10)

Those Beatitudes (happiness sayings) extol, with enthusiasm, certain character qualities and point to their consequences. Jesus is not describing eight different personality types but many facets of one person. Indeed, the combined portrait is that of Jesus—and one that he hoped his followers would attempt to imitate. Any rule of Christian morality that overlooks those qualities is deficient.

The Beatitudes are followed in Matthew by a probe beneath some outer acts contained in moral codes. For example, Jesus recognizes that most people have a clear conscience with respect to the "You shall not murder" commandment. Treating others as they want to be treated themselves, they avoid acting on urges to kill. Like a surgeon interested in cutting out the cause of symptoms, Jesus exposes the inner disposition that leads to acts of violence. Breakers of the Sixth Commandment are vastly increased in number by his judgment that it prohibits being hateful and insulting (Matt. 5:21–22). Not only should the action of Cain be avoided, but also the envious attitude that prompted that paradigm murder. The purpose of Jesus' analysis is to stir disciples out of their smugness and guide them toward a higher morality.

The main shortcoming of the glittering Rule is that it contains no norm that transcends individuals and cultures; it lacks a standard that can inform persons what they ought to desire. This may be why the apostle Paul does not even mention the Rule in the earliest summary of Christian ethics (Rom. 12) or elsewhere in his letters. Paul Tillich has probed the most glaring defect of the Rule. Displaying a Kantian outlook, that most influential philosopher of religion of the twentieth century reasons:

> For many people the Golden Rule is considered as the real content of Christianity. . . . But we know that this is not the answer of the New Testament. The great commandment as Jesus repeats it . . . infinitely transcends the Golden Rule. It must be transcended, for it does not tell us what we *should* wish that men would do to us. . . . We wish to receive a fortune which makes us secure and independent. We would be ready to give a fortune to a friend who asks us for it, if we had it. But in both cases love would be violated. For the gift would ruin us and him. . . . Our wishes express . . . our foolishness more than our wisdom. This is the limit of the Golden Rule. This is the limit of calculating justice. Only for him who knows what he *should* wish and who actually wishes it, is the Golden Rule ultimately valid. Only love can transform calculating justice into creative justice.[8]

All that glitters is not gold, but a few rare things that sparkle are solid gold. Some pure gold amid much superficial luster can be found in the Rule under scrutiny. It may be an artery of morality, conveying a precious quality, but it is not the heart.

The Highest Good

In the source called Q, which appears in both Matthew and Luke, Jesus states the perennially popular Golden Rule in order to contrast it to the veritable heart of morality. Luke is the better Gospel for a contextual examination of the Rule because it is likely to be closer to the pattern of Jesus' oral teaching.[9] Significantly, the Rule is immediately followed by a criticism of those whose assistance of others is based on self-interest and secular exchange. Jesus asks repetitiously, for emphasis:

> If you love only those who love you, what virtue is there in that? Even the irreligious love those who love them. If you help only those who help you, what virtue is there in that? The irreligious do the same. If you lend only when you expect to get it back, what virtue is there in that? Even the irreligious lend to one another, expecting full repayment. (6:32–34)

The three uses of "only" in those rhetorical questions indicate that the Golden Rule has *some* merit. Obviously it is superior to hurting others preemptively. Consider, for example, a nineteenth-century humorist's expression of the code accepted by some Americans. Edward Westcott puts it this way: "Do unto the other feller the way he'd like to do unto you, and do it fust."[10] Similarly, in the "Peanuts" comic strip, Lucy declares that to survive nowadays, you have to "walk all over others before they walk all over you."

Jesus does not fault the widespread use of the Rule in folk morality, but chides those who exalt it as the quintessential principle of conduct. He criticizes the shallowness of the bilateral assumption on which the Rule is based. Showing its shortcomings is preparatory to entering into an affirmation of what he regards as truly the highest good. Jesus transcends the mediocre Rule with his theological ethics:

> No, you are to love [*agapao*] your enemies; treat them well and lend without expecting any return. Then you will have a wonderful reward: you will belong to the family of God, because he is kind to the ungrateful and the evil. Be compassionate as your Father is compassionate. (6:35–36)

In short, Jesus urges his disciples to go beyond prudential ethics and attempt to imitate the merciful God. Such an aim would give them the satisfaction of participating in God's loving community.

A simple illustration of Jesus' agape principle is found in his teaching on hospitality. He implicitly recognizes that in the usual form of party planning there is a quid pro quo expectation: invited guests are viewed as potential hosts. It would be overly literal to presume that Jesus was against the reciprocation of dinner parties or that he disliked the exchange of presents. Yet such swapping, pleasant though it may be, is not unilateral *giving*. Agape begins when a welcome is extended to those who cannot repay. Jesus urges: "When you entertain, invite the poor, the crippled, the lame, the blind, and so find happiness" (Luke 14:13–14).

Jesus' agape teaching can be placed in bold relief by examining an antithetical outlook held by some in his Jewish community. Some psalmists thought that the ideal ruler would "crush the oppressor" and make "enemies lick the dust" (Ps. 72:4, 9). A king devoted to justice should vow before God: "I will destroy all the wicked in the land" (101:8). Members of the Qumran community pledged "to bear unremitting hatred toward all persons of ill repute."[11] The mentally and physically handicapped were explicitly excluded: "No fool, madman, simpleton, imbecile, blind, maimed, lame, or deaf person, and no minor may enter into the community."[12]

By actions as well as by teachings, Jesus mirrored God's loyal love for all people. He accepted the disreputable: the neurotics and the psychotics, the lepers and the beggars, the tax collectors and the thieves, the prostitutes and the adulterers. Jesus taught that helpfulness "to the least" of his neighbors was the way of showing allegiance to him (Matt. 25:40).

Walt Whitman has captured in flaming poetry the compassionate projection encouraged by the gospel. His involvement with frail humans is expressed in this way:

> I walk with delinquents with passionate love,
> I feel I am of them—I belong to those convicts
>   and prostitutes myself,
> And henceforth I will not deny them—
>   for how can I deny myself?[13]

In encouraging an open hand instead of a clenched fist in dealing with those generally treated as the dregs of society, Jesus did not condone reverse exploitation. To avoid sentimental coddling, wariness was to go with acceptance and generosity. If no change from laziness, meanness, and other vices resulted, other ways of effecting genuine repentance were encouraged. In this regard, it is instructive to look at consecutive verses in the *Didache,* the earliest collection of apostolic teaching outside the New Testament. "Give to everyone who begs from you, and ask for nothing in return" is followed by "Let your donation sweat in your hands until you know to whom to give it." Both maxims are represented as coming from Jesus and they may be as authentic as some of his teachings recorded in the New Testament. Following up on this combination of kindness with caution, the manual commends extending hospitality to visiting Christians, but warns that even so-called apostles and prophets may be scheming deadbeats.[14]

Jesus' love principle has often been misinterpreted because the typical ancient way of instructing by proverbs has been misunderstood. In this regard consider Proverbs, a book written in Hebrew but containing a collection of crisp sayings from several cultures. The maxims have varied thrusts, and were intended to be applied to a variety of different situations. To make this obvious, these proverbs are placed together:

> Give not a dumb answer to a dumb question,
>   or you will become like the fool.
> Give a dumb answer to a dumb question,
>   or the fool will think himself wise.
>   (Prov. 26:4–5)

Just as "Absence makes the heart grow fonder" and "Out of sight, out of mind" succinctly express antithetical ways in which separation can affect individual relationships, so each of those contrasting Hebrew proverbs contains a partial truth. Likewise, in Matthew's summary of Jesus' teachings, the proverbs "Give to him who begs" (5:42) and "Judge not" (7:1) are followed by others encouraging judgment making and withholding from beggars. In a traditional parallelism of couplets, Jesus says:

Give not what is holy to dogs,
  lest they turn and attack you.
Throw not pearls to pigs,
  lest they trample them underfoot.
                                    (Matt. 7:6)

An illustration of that porcine principle is found in Jesus' response to his Galilean ruler. He called Herod Antipas a cunning fox (Luke 13:32), probably because he had unjustly beheaded John the Baptist. Jesus judged him to have no more appetite for moral and spiritual matters than swine would have for pearls. Consequently, he gave the silent treatment to Herod's inquiries when on trial before him in Jerusalem (Luke 23:6–9).

An outlook of Leo Tolstoy displays the foolishness of extracting one saying from a teacher prone to hyperbole without examining the contextual balance. The key to all religion, Tolstoy maintained, is Jesus' categorical injunction: "Resist not one who is evil" (Matt. 5:39). The Russian writer accepted that saying without qualification, with all its implications. Whereas the verses that follow in the "Sermon on the Mount" pertain to personal injury—being slapped or swindled—Tolstoy applied nonresistance also to governmental matters. Thus police, prisons, and the legal system are contrary to true religion and should be abolished.[15] Pacifist Tolstoy conveniently overlooked Jesus' self-defense injunction: "If you have no sword, sell your cloak and buy one" (Luke 22:36). Also he disregarded the implication of the episode about Jesus forcing money changers and animal sellers out of the Temple (Mark 11:15–16).

Tolstoy's understanding of Jesus' ethics is similar to that of Max Weber. That influential sociologist thought that "Resist not one who is evil" was the central theme of the gospel. Weber, in contrast, found some merit in the reverse proposition, "You *shall* resist evil by force."[16] Weber did not realize that Jesus' position was far from the passive and irresponsible stance of acting so as to allow evil to win out.

A more balanced treatment of Jesus' core teaching can be found in Richard Horsley's study of Jewish resistance in Roman Palestine. He concludes:

It would be difficult to claim that Jesus was a pacifist. But he actively opposed violence. . . . He mediated God's liberation to a discouraged Jewish peasantry and offered some fundamental guidance for the renewal of the people. "Love your enemies" turns out to be not the apolitical pacific stance of one who stands above the turmoil of his day, nor a sober counsel of nonresistance to evil or oppression, but a revolutionary principle. It was a social revolutionary principle insofar as the love of enemies would transform local social-economic relations.[17]

There is truth in the punny adage: "A text without a context is nothing but a pretext." The only sensible way of understanding the meaning of Jesus' "Love your enemy" injunction is to examine its cultural context. Jesus belonged to the larger culture of Western Asia, where the "law of the tooth" was the basic principle of jurisprudence. The Mosaic law adapted it from the Code of Hammurabi as the standard of justice. It established a limit on retaliation—*no more than* an eye for an eye, tooth for tooth, wound for wound, or life for life (Ex. 21:23–25). That principle was intended to curtail the unequal retaliation of earlier times. For example, one of the first bits of poetry preserved in the Bible tells of Lamech avenging "seventy-sevenfold" by killing a youth who hit him (Gen. 4:23–24).

Jesus thought that revenge, limited or unlimited, was not sweet but bitter. He inverted the hyperbole of Lamech's vendetta by advising an injured person to extend occasions of forgiveness of another member of the church to seventy times seven (Matt. 18:22). Jesus reduced to an absurdity the notion that a quantitative limit can be placed on reconciliation efforts. In this regard, there is another hyperbolic teaching that also becomes ridiculous if taken literally: "If anyone hits you on the right cheek, turn the other cheek also" (Matt. 5:39). Interpreters miss the point if they assume that those who are struck on the left cheek or receive some other bodily injury can retaliate as they like! "Turn the other cheek" was Jesus' concrete imagery for expressing the abstract notion of nonretaliation. The apostle Paul found a proverb in scripture for expressing Jesus' way of behaving toward opponents: "If your enemy is hungry, give him bread to eat" (Rom. 12:20; Prov. 25:24).

Inspiration for the difficult task of removing vindictiveness ought to come, Jesus believed, when persons reflect on what God has done for them. In one parable, God is pictured as a creditor who agrees to liquidate an enormous debt owed by a servant. This generosity is displayed with the expectation that the servant will show a similar attitude toward others. However, the creditor learns that the pardoned servant has treated harshly a pleading borrower who needed longer to repay a relatively insignificant debt. The creditor then becomes angry and cancels his agreement to be merciful (Matt. 18:23–25). The parable shows the peril of isolating God's nonretaliation from human relationships. John Meir states the point of this parable in this way: "A Christian cannot win God's forgiveness; but he can lose it, by refusing to extend it to a brother."[18] Those who receive the reconciliation lifeline from God are bound to pass it on to others.

In the Lord's Prayer, the most influential prayer ever uttered, Jesus coupled divine forgiveness with human forgivingness. One petition contains a weighty conjunction: "Forgive us our sins, *for* we forgive everyone who does us wrong" (Luke 11:4). Jesus provides this illustration: "If, as you come to worship, you remember a falling out with your neighbor, first go and make peace with him" (Matt. 5:23–24). Jesus is indebted to the wisdom tradition of his people in forging a link between devotion and ethics. Jesus ben Sirach said:

> Forgive your neighbor his wrongdoing;
> then your sins will be pardoned when you pray.
> If a grudge is harbored against another,
> can healing be expected from the Lord?[19]

The dynamics of reconciliation that Jesus taught is explained by Ernest Saunders in this way:

> The man who shuts his heart against an erring brother and nurses his grievances will soon discover that he has likewise barricaded the way against the inflow of God's forgiveness. Such is the corrosive power of hostility rankling in the human heart that it destroys both the power to accept as well as to give pardoning love.[20]

Jesus was perturbed by the rancorous animosity of his fellow Jews toward foreigners, as well as toward groups and individuals within his own culture. Consequently, he aimed at widening the scope of neighbor love of traditional Judaism to include other ethnic groups. To this end he told a story about a Samaritan who expressed agape toward a Jew. The viewpoint of the "good Samaritan" is ably conveyed by Edwin Markham:

> He drew a circle that shut me out—
> Heretic, rebel, a thing to flout.
> But Love and I had the wit to win:
> We drew a circle that took him in![21]

David Flusser, a Jewish authority on Christian origins, finds the "definitive characteristic" of Jesus' ethic distilled in these three words: "Love your enemies."[22] This ethic is also distinctive when compared to pagan moral philosophy in the Greco-Roman civilization.[23] Prior to Jesus, no one had been quite so bold in expanding the concept of neighbor to include enemies. He carried out that radical love in practice by praising the religious concerns of a Roman centurion. Jesus found exemplary "faith" in the attitudes and actions of an officer of the foreign army that had humiliated the proud Jewish people by conquering their homeland (Luke 7:1–9).

The most original theologizing in the Sermon on the Mount is the likening of ideal human inclusiveness to the operations of the God of nature. Jesus states: "Love your enemies and pray for your persecutors, so that you may show yourselves true children of your Father in heaven. He makes the sun shine on bad and good people alike, and sends rain on the just and on the unjust" (Matt. 5:44–45). Even as the cosmic sun does not discriminate as to what it shines on, so the heavenly Father shows no favoritism among his multiethnic children. This teaching on the boundlessness of agape concludes with an idealistic imperative: "Be all-embracing, as your heavenly Father is all-embracing" (Matt. 5:48).

Jesus accepted what subsequent theologians have called a doctrine of general providence, meaning that God looks ahead and plans broadly for the needs of the various components of creation. Divine *provide*-ance for organic nature is exquisitely expressed by Jesus in these words:

> Consider the birds; they neither sow nor reap. They have neither storehouse nor barn, yet God feeds them. . . . Consider the flowers; they neither toil nor weave. But not even Solomon in his royal splendor was robed like one of them (Luke 12:24, 27).

Jesus' teachings were in harmony with those poetic composers of hymns and epics in his culture who believed that the structure of nature displays the intricate "handiwork" of God (Pss. 19:1; 104:1–30). According to Genesis, the Creator repeatedly affirms that all parts of nature, including sea monsters and human sexuality, are "good"—using the customary translation (1:4, 10, 12, 18, 21, 25, 31). *Tob*, the Hebrew term used here, not only connotes a moral quality but also points to a natural loveliness (Gen. 6:2; 24:16; Esth. 1:11). Thus, the Creation account might be concluded in this way: "God saw everything he had made and exclaimed, 'How very beautiful!'" A corollary of that affirmation is found in the Eden story. "Not *tob*" is the Lord's evaluation of human life lived without fulfillment of the natural craving for sexual partnership (Gen. 2:18). Echoing the Genesis leitmotiv, a psalmist declares: "Yahweh is *tob* to all" (145:9). Accordingly, Jesus saw God's beauty and power in the ongoing natural processes. The sustaining and devouring web of life was for him within God's will. Jesus' custom of giving thanks before meals illustrates his awareness of God's perennial goodness, a sentiment that has been captured in the hymn "This Is My Father's World."

Jesus departs from much of his Jewish tradition, however, as well as from most spokespersons for Christianity and other religions, in what has been called *special* providence. Suggesting that God's general governance of creation is not sufficient, many presume that interruptions occur that show favoritism or vindictiveness. God allegedly intervenes to protect those who engage in religious behavior but gives calamity to the impious. For example, when small boys made fun of Elisha's bald head, he "cursed them in the name of the Lord, and bears from the woods mauled forty-two of them" (2 Kings 2:23–24). Mark Twain, presuming Elisha's chagrin over the harm he indirectly effected, comments:

> There is this trouble about special providences—namely, there is so often a doubt as to which person was intended to be the beneficiary. In the case of the children, the bears, and the prophet, the bears got more satisfaction out of the episode than the prophet did, because they got the children.[24]

In Jesus' day it was popularly believed that holy men could change the local weather, in imitation of Elijah (1 Kings 17:1; 18:1, 41; James 5:16–18). A Galilean named Hanina ben Dosa allegedly caused rain to cater to his own convenience. When that righteous man was caught in a downpour while walking home, he prayed that he not get soaked, and the rain stopped at once. On arriving home dry, he prayed and the shower began again! His experience illustrates this affirmation from an Aramaic Targum: "If the clouds are filled with rain, on the earth they pour their waters on account of the purity of the righteous." On the other hand, rain will not fall where impure humans want it.[25]

A comment of John Calvin illustrates the way special providence has often been treated in the Christian tradition. He asserts: "It is certain that not one drop of rain falls without God's sure command." Thus a grainfield consumed by drought or struck by hail displays God's "special vengeance." Calvin thought that creatures cannot count on nature to function regularly, so to farm without the "singular blessing of God" could result in disastrous harvests. That Protestant Reformation leader believed that such "special providence" was sanctioned by Jesus when he declared that even the fall of a small and insignificant sparrow is governed by God's particular plan.[26]

Jesus did say that no sparrow or hair escapes God's notice (Matt. 10:29–30; Luke 12:6–7). But those sayings should not be interpreted to mean that God micromanages the movements of each bird or counts hairs on each scalp. Such

201

hyperboles pertaining to divine omniscience are only trivialized when interpreted literally. In the text they follow Jesus' comment about thanatophobia: those who make physical threats should not be feared as much as those who can destroy both soul and body. Thus, Jesus did not teach that his friends would be protected from bad happenings. Rather, he observed that God sees both birds and humans fall in the natural world; the latter "are of more value than many sparrows" because they possess immortal souls that can transcend death.

Shakespeare treats Jesus' sparrow comment in a manner that harmonizes with the gospel context. In his masterpiece, Hamlet acknowledges: "There's a special providence in the fall of a sparrow."[27] Before the duel that ends the drama, Hamlet has resolved the turmoil churning within him pertaining to "the slings and arrows of outrageous fortune." He serenely recognizes that persons should respond to their limited understanding of the "divinity that shapes our ends" and be ready for their time to die.[28] Hamlet interprets "special providence" not as a deus ex machina reversal of his mortal situation, but as an awareness that there is a divine plan in tragedy that humans cannot fathom.

Jesus' teachings as well as his crucifixion show that being chosen by God does not exempt one from the created order. He found the equality of divine concern reflected in the impartiality of the weather. Jesus observed that the natural order established by the Creator does not favor acreage owned by worshipers of the true God while crops are destroyed on the land of the wicked. Contrary to rain-god devotees in every age, Jesus perceived that holiness is no guarantee of harvests. He referred to floods and hurricanes as witnesses to nonpreferential nature because they hit all in their path with equal intensity. More security will be attained by those persons who choose to construct their lives on a firm foundation than by those who are unconcerned about such (Matt. 7:24–27). The natural order operates independently of human "just deserts," so life-sustaining or life-destructive forces are no respecters of persons. Jesus' conviction that the rain descends on virtuous and vicious alike is, as theologian Reinhold Niebuhr points out, a graphic expression of his rejection of special providence, in which God guarantees safety and prosperity for the good guys.[29]

Jesus' outlook on the relation between human needs and weather phenomena coincides with that of eminent men of scientific orientation living both centuries before and centuries after him. Aristotle observed that rain falls without regard either to giving growth to a farmer's grain or to spoiling it on the threshing floor.[30] Sigmund Freud ironically held that religion cannot stand up against the scientific spirit, which holds that "earthquakes, tidal waves, conflagrations, make no distinction between the virtuous and pious and the scoundrel or unbeliever."[31] Jesus, while having a theological outlook sharply different from the pagan Athenian philosopher or the atheistic Viennese psychoanalyst, nevertheless shared their viewpoint on the moral neutrality of natural processes.

Once Jesus was asked if the eighteen who were killed with the collapse of a Jerusalem tower were more immoral than those in the area who did not perish (Luke 13:4–5). The questioner reveals a typical presumption which the biblical people share with the many people of every culture. The Jews treasured this proverb: "Nothing bad happens to good people, but the wicked have nothing but trouble" (Prov. 12:21). Eliphaz, in debating Job, rigidly connected individual suffering with that person's sin. He challenged Job to name a single case where an innocent person has perished in a disaster (Job 4:7). Jesus, like Job, was fully aware that good people are not necessarily protected from bad happenings. On encountering a man who was born blind, Jesus asserted that the handicap was not caused by either the sin of the man or that of his parents (John 9:1–3). Jesus could have used the example of Herod Antipas to show the defectiveness of the doctrine that bad things happen only to bad people. Throughout Jesus' life that killer of John the Baptist had lived luxuriously on the taxes of Palestinian peasants. Jesus no doubt had frequent confirmations of an observation by an earlier Jewish sage: "There are good people who perish doing justly, and there are wicked people who grow old in their evildoing" (Eccl. 7:15). While recognizing that suffering is sometimes due to sin, Jesus could not find in human experience a necessary invariable causation between the two. He did not attempt to give an elaborate explanation, although he tacitly recognized that accidents operate in accordance with the impersonal regularity of natural forces. God's governance of nature does not include special intervention to reward or punish people for their various deeds.

Philosopher George Santayana's description of a religion integrated with reason helps to clarify the viewpoint of Jesus:

> In rational prayer the soul may be said to accomplish three things important to its welfare: it withdraws within itself and defines its good, it accommodates itself to destiny, and it grows like the ideal which it conceives. . . . The prayer, "Thy will be done," . . . must not be degraded from its original meaning, which was that an unfulfilled ideal should be fulfilled; it expressed aspiration after the best, not willingness to be satisfied with anything. Yet the inevitable must be accepted, and it is easier to change the human will than the laws of nature. To wean the mind from extravagant desires and teach it to find excellence in what life affords, when life is made as worthy as possible, is a part of wisdom and religion. . . . Prayer, *in fine*, though it accomplishes nothing material, constitutes something spiritual. It will not bring rain, but until rain comes it may cultivate hope and resignation and may prepare the heart for any issue. . . . The believer knows . . . that a material efficacy is not the test of his faith. His faith will survive any outward disappointment. In fact, it will grow by that discipline and not become truly religious until it ceases to be a foolish expectation of improbable things and rises on stepping-stones of its material disappointments into a spiritual peace.[32]

Jesus' outlook on nature and enemies is radically different from what is contained in a strand of the foundational tradition of the nation Israel and in folk religion everywhere. According to the exodus saga, Moses extended his magic rod with this result:

Yahweh thundered and sent a hailstorm, . . . which struck down everything outdoors throughout the whole of Egypt—including people and animals. It beat down every plant and shattered all the trees. The only place where there was no hail was in the Goshen region, where the Israelites lived (Ex. 9:23, 25–26).

Those alleged Egyptian plagues climaxed with selective destruction indoors. While sparing all Israelites, one midnight the Lord killed a child in every pagan family, causing loud crying throughout the land. This massacre of the innocents was done, Moses claimed, "that you may know that Yahweh discriminates between Egypt and Israel" (Ex. 11:4–7; 12:29–30).

Even though certain aspects of Jesus' inherited theology presumed that nature smiled benevolently on the chosen Israelites at the expense of others, the theology also contained a doctrine of equal human status, which was based on the opening chapter of the Bible. To convey the unity of peoples everywhere, the Talmud asks, "Why did the Creator form all life from a single ancestor?" The reply: "So that the families of mankind shall not lord one over the other with the claim of being sprung from superior stock; . . . that all peoples—saints and sinners alike—may recognize their common kinship in the collective human family."[33] Jesus may well have found a truth embedded in the Creation story similar to this talmudic interpretation.

An examination of a basic term in the Hebrew Bible also makes it evident that God does not sanction unfair treatment. The term is *awen*, which designates social injustice resulting from an abuse of power.[34] The Hebrew term and its Greek equivalent in the New Testament are usually translated as "iniquity" in English. Jesus criticized leaders who were guilty of extortion and other forms of iniquity (Matt. 23:28; Luke 13:27). The modern spelling for this word is "inequity." Thus Jesus was distressed over deceptive dealings among his fellow Jews. His theological ethics appears to have been this: Since the Creator and Preserver acts evenhandedly toward all people, those people, who are made in the divine image, should go and do likewise. He would join the psalmist in praise of the divine Ruler "exalted over all the peoples" who "loves justice and has established equity" (Ps. 99:2–4).

Philosopher John Dewey, after equating equity with "impartiality" and iniquity with "using uneven measures of judgment," integrates this concept with loving enemies:

> Equity demands that when one has to act in relation to others, no matter whether friends or strangers, fellow citizens or foreigners, one should have an equal and even measure of value. . . . In an immediate or emotional sense it is not possible to love our enemies as we love our friends. But the maxim to love our enemies as we love ourselves signifies that in our conduct we should take into account their interests at the same rate of estimate as we rate our own.[35]

Love as equity is well expressed in Jesus' story of a *graceful* employer. He hires vineyard workers from the marketplace labor pool, contracting some early in the day and others at later hours that day. Apparently he underestimated at the beginning of the workday how many it would take to complete the harvest. Recognizing that all showed a willingness to work a full day and that all have the same basic needs, the employer promises each the usual daily wage.

Those who began work early in the day regarded their wages as just until they learned that those employed later were also receiving a living wage. Then those lucky enough to get hired first, having no sense of solidarity with their fellow workers, now thought they should be paid several times more than those who found no work until late in the day. Forgetting that their full employment was due to good fortune, they thought that payment should be strictly on a quid pro quo basis. To one of them the employer responds: "Friend, I am not cheating you. Did we not agree on the usual wage? Take your pay and go home. I choose to give the last man hired the same as you. Have I no right to do what I like with what belongs to me? Why do you begrudge my generosity?" (Matt. 20:1–15).

The grumbler here is like jealous Jonah, who was disgusted that God was kind to some who had not worked earnestly for him. In the parable, the spokesperson for the dissatisfied advocates a common economic outlook. He thinks that compensation should be based exclusively on individual productivity, without any consideration of needs. This principle is in contrast to that of the earliest Christians, who distributed their possessions "to each as any had need" (Acts 4:32–35).

The theology of grace is also found in another parable, which likewise deals with soured labor relations. The essence of the gospel is contained in Jesus' story of the broken family (Luke 15:11–32). Toiling through many long days for the father, who represents God, is the begrudging elder brother. Focus on his character, central to the story, has popularly been eclipsed by attention to his younger brother.

The best-known member of the family is the prodigal son, the brother whose story moves through three phases: sick of home, homesick, and home—sick. He misused his personal freedom by demanding his inheritance while his father was still alive and then by living irresponsibly in "a far country." After "he squandered his wealth in dissolute living," he became a fellow scavenger with pigs while working for a Gentile. The prodigal then realized that he was destroying himself and considered how even his father's servants were better off. Motivated by prudence, he took the initiative to return home and admit that he had done wrong. The father, who had patiently waited for the alienation to end, ran to meet his son and profusely expressed forgiveness. He dressed him in fine clothes, gave him a ring, and prepared a party to herald the homecoming.

Treatment of the relationships of the lost son who strayed sets the stage for examining the relationships of the lost son who stayed at home. That elder brother articulates the same values as the Pharisees who provoked the lost-and-found trilogy of Luke 15. Jesus provides parables of the lost sheep, the lost coin, and the lost sons in response to "the Pharisees and the scribes," who objected to his associating with undeserving people. Those religious leaders had little place for mercy in their relationships; they felt, rather, that one should receive from God and from others punishment that balanced bad conduct exactly. Like Jonah after his life was spared, their religion was largely a joyless matter of carrying out what they perceived to be difficult rules. Had they not assumed that God was bound by the conventional rewards-and-punishment system of justice, they would have been resentful. Absent was the childlikeness that Jesus sought.

The fairness of the extravagant celebration by the father probably puzzled both sons. The siblings both alike found that their father's eagerness for status restoration exceeded their expectations. The one who had failed while away from home thought his father would have been fully justified in not accepting him back as a son. Had he become a household servant, the elder brother might not have complained.

By means of a paraphrase, I have attempted to convey the sibling rivalry as expressed by the elder brother:

> During the banquet, Frank Brown returns from a long day at the family firm. As he comes into the courtyard, he asks what all the big beat is about. "Haven't you heard?" the cook responds. "Your brother Joe came back safe and sound, and your daddy's having a ball!" Frank shouts contemptuously as he stomps away from the house. On hearing his elder son's burst of resentment, Mr. Brown goes out to conciliate him.
>
> Frank harshly complains: "It isn't fair. I've always been a clean and decent person. For years I have slaved for you and have never disobeyed an order. You take me for granted while doting on that bum. If there ever was someone deserving something special, I am the one. But when that decadent son of yours turns up after blowing your money and fornicating with whores, you knock yourself out to be nice to him. He made his bed and now he ought to be forced to lie in it. But what do I get for behaving myself?"
>
> Mr. Brown gently counsels Frank: "Remember, I gave you the larger, elder son's share of my property at the time your brother wanted his portion. He decided to convert his into money, and you were content to keep yours in the family property. You surely realize that you will inherit anything else I have left, so your jealousy is inappropriate. Joe, who is your brother as well as my son, has been in a predicament where for all practical purposes he has been

dead. But now he has found himself and his conscience is alive. It is only fitting that we should make merry."

The central love theme of all Jesus' teachings contains priorities which the *Didache* faithfully states. That second-century church manual opens with these lines: "This is the way of life: first, you shall love God who made you; secondly, your neighbor as yourself; and whatever you would not like done to you, do not do to another."[36] The truly golden rule is placed in the primary position, and the neighbor-love silver rule follows. Christian catechumens were taught to place in a tertiary position what might be called the bronze rule, to treat others as one would like to be treated. The latter does not express the essence of Christian morality, but has value when viewed in its derivative position.

The positive way in which Jesus expressed the basic principles of life is significant. He generally avoided the negative laws that predominate in the Pentateuch. The "just say no" approach to moral issues had not proven to be highly motivational in changing outlooks. To sum up the portion of the Ten Commandments dealing with duties to God—all but one being thou-shalt-nots—he selected a positive law from Deuteronomy 6:5 about loving God wholeheartedly. Then, to sum up the portion dealing with duties to humans—all but one also being negative—he selected a positive law from Leviticus 19:18 about loving neighbors. Israelite morality was, one might say, tied up in nots. Rabbi Hillel had summed up the entire law in a maxim from his Jewish heritage: "What you hate, do not do to anyone."[37] But Jesus insisted that morality lies more in what a person does than in what the person does not do. In his parable of the talents, the person criticized was the one who did nothing with what he was given—even though he was neither dishonest nor greedy (Matt. 25:14–27). In another parable, a rich man was excluded from paradise not because of deliberate cruelty but because he was unconcerned to do anything to relieve his neighbor's dire need (Luke 16:19–25).

Jesus maintained that a morality of subtraction is ineffective. In a dramatic way he traced the odyssey of a bad habit that was temporarily swept out:

209

When an unclean spirit goes out of a person, it wanders over uninhabited country seeking a place to rest. Finding none, it says, "I will go back to the home I left." When it returns, it finds the house unoccupied and tidy. Then it goes and brings seven other spirits more evil than itself, and they enter and settle down. In the end that person's plight is worse than before. (Luke 11:24–26)

In the course of history, many have been content with a negative morality. The hear-no-evil, see-no-evil, speak-no-evil dictum of the Shinto code is known worldwide. "Swearing off" is a common approach of folk morality, but it may fix one's thought on the bad habit. Bertrand Russell joined Jesus in criticizing the complacency of some nonviolators of traditional codes:

If throughout your life you abstain from murder, theft, fornication, perjury, blasphemy, and disrespect toward your parents, your church, and your king, you are conventionally held to deserve moral admiration even if you have never done a single kind or generous or useful action. This very inadequate notion of virtue is an outcome of tabu morality, and has done untold harm.[38]

Jesus' moral decision making replaces negative harmlessness with affirmative action. He emphasized three simple foundational principles from which creative expressions should flow. Also stressed was prioritization: "'Love the Lord your God with all your heart, and with all your soul, and with all your mind.' This is the foremost commandment. The second in importance is like it, 'Love your neighbor as you love yourself.' All the law and the prophets depend on these two commandments" (Matt. 22:37–40). Thirdly, there is this principle: "Treat others as you would have others treat you; for this is the law and the prophets" (Matt. 7:12). Jesus gleaned the principles from the Torah scrolls and from the teachings of earlier Jewish sages.

This summary statement displays what Jesus meant when he said: "Do not suppose that I have come to abolish the law and the prophets; I have come not to abolish them but to complete them" (Matt. 5:17). Thomas Manson, the acclaimed scholar of Christian origins, comments on the way in which Jesus presents Jewish ethics at its best:

> His originality lies in the way in which he goes to the heart of the prophetic religion, and sets free a spirit which was in danger of being stifled by rabbinic fundamentalism on the one hand, and, on the other, by the very natural resentment and hatred of the gentile, engendered by centuries of foreign oppression. . . . It was in this context that Jesus gave to Judaism, and to the world, this unqualified and uncompromising statement of the true Israelite ideal.[39]

.10.

Conclusion

The Gospels attempt to respond to the foundational inquiry that Jesus posed: "Who do you say that I am?" (Mark 8:29). As a world-class teacher, he preferred to stimulate reflection rather than declare truths. Jesus' question continues to perplex the pious and the impious, the wise and the otherwise. Was he God or was he a blasphemer? According to the Gospels, he did not claim to be either, but he expressed his identity in an intriguing variety of ways.

Shakespeare reminds us that on the stage of life "one man in his time plays many parts."[1] Multiple roles are usually assigned to the more talented; some are acted out successively, and some simultaneously. Thus, David was a shepherd, musician, warrior, king, judge, and adulterer; Jesus was a carpenter, rabbi, therapist, prophet, sage, and servant-messiah. Some of his roles in life's drama mesh without friction, but others cannot be easily integrated. A rabbi might find it impossible to accept that the voice of God could be counter to the laws of Moses, while a prophet or sage might be open to sources of inspiration apart from the Torah. For example, Deuteronomy was one of Rabbi Jesus' favorite scrolls, but it states some things that cannot be reconciled with his life and teachings. There Moses, as God's spokesman, alleges that abounding prosperity is certain for the religious faithful, while disease, famine, and enemy conquest will crush the unfaithful (Deut. 28). Yet Jesus, like sagacious Job, knew from human experiences that the neat scheme was untrue regardless of the authority who asserted it.

Ernst Käsemann has reflected on the incongruities in the roles of the historical Jesus. He finds in the Gospels a bewildering confusion of allegedly trustworthy portraits of Jesus: now he appears as a rabbi, now as a teacher of wisdom, now as a prophet; or again, as the man who thought of himself as the Son of Man or the Suffering Servant, who stood for an apocalyptic or a realized eschatology; or finally, as some sort of a mixture of all these. . . . All of these are defensible, once you are prepared to give credence to the tradition, because they are all actually contained in the tradition.

All the roles for Jesus in the Gospels are not treated on a par by Käsemann. He convincingly argues that Jesus distinguished himself by "knowing and proclaiming the will of God, which in him is combined with the direct and unsophisticated outlook of the teacher of wisdom. . . . He must have regarded himself as the instrument of that living Spirit of God."[2] Käsemann's emphasis on the role of a wisdom prophet provides a needed corrective for the overemphasis on an apocalyptic Jesus that has characterized twentieth-century New Testament scholarship.

Jesus was both a conserver and an innovator. Sharing the basic beliefs of his fellow Jews, he drew from the Torah the two essential guides for living: love God and love neighbor. The prophetic Pharisee and his learners accepted God as creator-ruler and aimed at responding to the best of scriptural revelation. But Jesus transcended his times, going beyond his contemporaries in imagining a new world order that could realistically be accomplished. Not the usual male chauvinist or regional patriot, he was literally "outstanding," in that he was noted more for standing out than for fitting in any of the various established groups. Although Jesus was in some ways like the Pharisees, the apocalypticists, and the prophets, he was clearly distinct from Pharisee Hillel, Judas the Galilean, and John the Baptist—his older contemporaries.

Jesus can best be understood as a fulfillment of the hopes of some of the Israelite prophets. Micah longed for Bethlehem to produce a new David who would integrate true worship with ethical living (Micah 5:2). Rather than lavish Temple offerings, Micah declared, God requires justice, kindness, and humility (6:6–8). Isaiah envisioned a messianic ruler who would inaugurate a new era. On behalf of the Lord, the prophet proclaimed: "Your countless sacrifices, what are they to me? . . . I am disgusted with the smell of the incense you burn. I cannot stand your new moon and Sabbath assemblies." Over against the ceremonialism often equated with religion, the Hebrew prophets held that moral integrity must percolate through any religion acceptable to God. "Seek justice, correct oppression, defend the fatherless, and plead the widow's cause," Isaiah advised (Isa. 1:11, 13, 17). Jesus joined his luminous prophetic predecessors in stressing the ethical requirements of the Israelite covenant and in applying them to the current cultic activity.

Like some of his prophetic predecessors, Jesus was not a shrill denunciator who sanctimoniously took cheap shots at his fellows. Vis-à-vis Judaism, he was sometimes a nettle and sometimes an echo—to use Emerson's description of the dual roles of a true friend. Like Socrates, Jesus was both a pestering gadfly and a gentle midwife as he assisted in individual and social transformation. As with friendships generally, humor had an important place. In his gospel was this fulfillment: "There shall be heard again the sounds of mirth and gladness, the voices of the bridegroom and the bride" (Jer. 33:10–11). Rabbi Jesus, like Mark Twain, used wit as a weapon against sham religion while encouraging acts of compassion.

Lamentably, the Jewish prophets who promoted transcultural ideals rather than immediate national interests were often treated by their contemporaries as dangerous traitors. Thanks to clarifying hindsight, Jeremiah and Jesus have not been remembered primarily as Jews who advocated accommodating foreign invaders. Rather, their prophecies were treasured and eventually canonized because they pledged their ultimate allegiance to the universal God who was establishing a new covenant that would not be centered in external performances. Those antiwar protesters were motivated by love of country and risked great personal loss in their pursuit of peace.

Conscientious objectors over the centuries have often been inspired by some biblical prophets. They tend to be loyal citizens who want to bring the best ideals of their culture to bear on current unjust practices. These internal critics are usually a powerful force for long-range social betterment. Henry Thoreau was acutely aware of the moral contradiction between the slavery-extending Mexican War and the doctrine that "all men are created equal." He protested this hypocrisy with nonviolent acts, accepting imprisonment rather than pay a tax to help finance the war. Thoreau also attempted to shame fellow Americans by showing that they regarded profits from cotton as more important than basic civil rights. He championed the paradox that engaging in selective lawbreaking was an expression of true patriotism. Although Thoreau's stance on social issues had little effect during his lifetime, his essay entitled "Civil Disobedience" has inspired Mohandas Gandhi, Martin Luther King, and many others to combat inhumane policies in a similar manner.

The evils Jesus confronted have continued prominently into the modern era. In the British culture, for example, philosopher and feminist John Stuart Mill found that few of his contemporaries doubted the established religion, on the one hand, or practiced it, on the other hand. He described the double-mindedness of the nineteenth-century industrial era in this trenchant manner:

> The maxims and precepts contained in the New Testament are considered sacred, and accepted as laws, by all professing Christians. Yet it is scarcely too much to say that not one Christian in a thousand guides or tests his individual conduct by reference to those laws. . . . He has thus, on the one hand, a collection of ethical maxims, which he believes to have been vouchsafed to him by infallible wisdom; . . . and on the other, a set of everyday judgments and practices, which go a certain length with some of those maxims, not so great length with others, stand in direct opposition to some. . . . To the first of these standards he gives his homage; to the other his real allegiance. All Christians believe that the blessed are the poor and the humble; . . . that they should love their neighbor as themselves. . . . They believe them, as people believe what they have always heard lauded and never discussed. But in the sense of that living belief which regulates conduct, they believe these doctrines . . . are serviceable to pelt adversaries with.[3]

In twentieth-century America there continues to be a fondness for using gospel principles as a flag under which to sail rather than as a rudder for steering between treacherous moral shoals. Philosopher John Hospers makes this assessment of our contemporary hypocrisy:

> The majority of Americans profess to be Christians and therefore to accept the Christian way of life; yet very few of them practice these rules. . . . Officially these professed Christians believe it is their duty to turn the other cheek, but in daily life they retaliate even for small injuries. . . . Although they are told that it is easier for a camel to pass through the eye of a needle than for a rich man to enter into the kingdom of heaven, their chief goal is to amass as much money and property as possible, not only for their comfort but to satisfy their exhibitionism and to cause envy among their neighbors. . . . They believe that all men are brothers, but they associate only with those who are in an income group as high as their own. They prefer not to associate with people of different racial or religious background and feel uncomfortable in their presence. The Bible tells these so-called Christians that no man can serve both God and Mammon; but during a lifetime spent in trying to outdo their neighbors in serving Mammon, they assume that their Creator will reward them with eternal bliss. . . . While millions starve, these Christians spend more money each year on liquor than on all charitable enterprises combined.[4]

In spite of many prophetic physicians who have operated on hypocrisy, the pandemic virus has not been eradicated; a gap between principle and practice is part of the human predicament. The goodness of getting and consuming is so acceptable in an affluent society that few heed Jesus' warning about the perils of wealth. Likewise, "getting even" is a mode of living more apparent than forgiveness. Some prefer violence to peacefulness, and cheating to honesty. The irreligious are also afflicted, even though they may naively think that insincerity is just a sickness of the religious. Personal integration can be achieved by lowering high principles to low practices, or by raising practices to principles. Jesus advocated the latter and more difficult way of achieving sincerity.

Given the track record for hypocrisy in religion, discerning Christians have emphasized Jesus' pragmatic test of fruitful performance (Matt. 7:16). John Bunyan, whose impact on English-speaking peoples was profound, commented with respect to judgment day: "It will not be said then, 'Did you believe?' but 'Were you doers, or talkers only?'"[5] William Penn likewise emphasized a main thrust of Jesus' teaching: "It shall be said at the last day, not 'Well professed,' but 'Well done, good and faithful servant.'" The focus of that leading American Quaker on orthopraxy (correct action) rather than orthodoxy (correct doctrine) has continued to characterize the Society of Friends. They have pioneered in human rights movements for native Americans, African Americans, and women.

Penn based his gospel insight on Jesus' parable of the last judgment. Nothing is said in the Matthew 25 story about divine acceptance being based on a profession of belief in Jesus. The "good and faithful servant" is one who does something to relieve human suffering. Penn's simple reading of the Gospels is in line with the results of current scholarly study. For example, Hendrikus Boers concludes his book on the historical Jesus with this statement: "The ultimate meaning of being a Christian was not the public confession of Jesus but the affirmation of him by recognizing, as he did, the human dignity of those who did not count from a religious, social, and moral point of view."[6]

The ending of Jesus' great "sermon"—as recorded in both Matthew 5–7 and Luke 6:17–49—stresses the need for putting words into deeds. The concluding parable contrasts wise and imprudent builders. The one who is commended is described in this way: "Everyone who listens to my teaching and acts accordingly is like a sensible person who built on rock. The rain poured, the rivers rose, and the gales blew against the house, but it did not fall because its foundation was on bedrock." The religion that does not collapse is one that is not erected on the presumption of special divine protection. Founded on the divine Rock, it can withstand the turbulence that confronts everyone. In contrast to folk religion that is as long as history and as wide as the globe, Jesus did not think of faith as a guarantee for avoiding the adverse forces of nature or society. Confidence in God is not to be separated from prudential wisdom. Serenity comes to those who erect, before the storm, structures that can endure the stress.

The parable of the builders is followed in both Matthew and Luke with the story of a centurion whom Jesus praises as the epitome of faithfulness. No information is given on the religious background of that officer, who belonged to the army of occupation in Palestine. He may have worshiped Mythra, a deity popular among Roman soldiers. The information supplied on the centurion shows that he did not share the typical Roman anti-Semitism. Indeed, his love of the Jews involved building them a synagogue. His openness also extended to accepting the authority of someone in the land whom the Romans had conquered. From Jesus he humbly sought healing for a servant who was dear to him. The story concludes with this comment: "When Jesus heard this he was flabbergasted and, turning to the crowd following him, he said, 'I tell you, not even in Israel have I found faith like this'" (Luke 7:1–10). Jesus gives evidence here that he has also risen above the common prejudice of his people against the Romans.

That centurion story goes a long way toward correcting the proper Christian meaning of an often misused term. Paul Tillich may have had the centurion in mind when he discussed his famous definition: "Faith is the state of being ultimately concerned."[7] Tillich observed:

> There are few words in the language of religion which cry for as much semantic purging as the word "faith." It is continually being confused with belief in something for which there is no evidence, or in something intrinsically unbelievable, or in absurdities or nonsense. It is extremely difficult to remove these distorting connotations from the genuine meaning of faith.[8]

For Jesus, faith is not so much belief in what one does not know as responding in practical ways to what one does know. Recognizing that works are inseparable from faith, his outlook is well summed up by these words of the apostle Paul: "All that matters is faith working through love" (Gal. 5:6). The apostle goes on to indicate that to fulfill the Christian's obligation, we must "bear one another's burdens" (Gal. 6:2).

The fullness of the faith possessed and taught by Rabbi Jesus may be unattainable. That does not make faith an inadequate guide for living. Even though ancient mariners never came near to the guiding stars, their ships generally arrived at the desired destinations. Apropos are Robert Browning's words: "A man's reach should exceed his grasp, or what's a heaven for?"[9]

Returning to where we began, the paradox of Jesus' idealistic yet practical faith is grasped by Alfred North Whitehead, who has inspired many twentieth-century theologians. The wisdom of Rabbi Jesus is echoed in this superlative definition by Whitehead:

> Religion is the vision of something which stands beyond, behind, and within the passing flux of immediate things; something which is real, and yet waiting to be realized; something which is a remote possibility, and yet the greatest of present facts; something that gives meaning to all that passes, and yet eludes apprehension; something whose possession is the final good, and yet is beyond all reach; something which is the ultimate ideal, and the hopeless quest.[10]

To conclude that the founder of Christianity pointed to ideals that have inspired few significant actions would be a distortion of history. Some of the seeds Jesus planted "fell into good soil and brought forth . . . a hundredfold" (Mark 4:8). The most notable success may have come outside the sanctuary, in the care for the needy. Prior to the coming of Christianity, the sick who lived in the Eastern Mediterranean countries might have been able to find temporary shelters at temples of Asclepius, but not places of extended care. Hospitals began as an outgrowth of Christian remembrance of the life and teachings of Jesus. In one of the earliest accounts of a Christian Sunday service, Justin Martyr tells of offerings taken for "orphans, widows, those who are in need because of sickness or any other cause, those who are in prison, and strangers who are on a journey."[11] After describing infirmaries operated by monks in Byzantine cities, historian Will Durant comments: "The outstanding moral distinction of the church was her extensive provision of charity. The church . . . founded public hospitals on a scale never known before."[12]

Beginning with their Monte Cassino monastery in the sixth century, the Benedictines were noted for their hospitals. They also cultivated medicinal plants in their gardens for the relief of pain. The *Rule of St. Benedict* shows that the motivation for creating hospitals and pharmacies came mainly from one teaching of Jesus:

> The care of the sick is to be placed above and before every other duty, as if indeed Christ were being directly served by waiting upon them. For he said: "I was sick and you cared for me," and "Inasmuch as you render such services to one of the humblest you do it unto me" (Matthew 25:35–40).[13]

The Benedictines discerned that Jesus based his acceptance of followers not on correct doctrine or prayer habits, but on their outreaching concerns. The order of "Hospitalers" ministered to a variety of needy people because Jesus had encouraged a wide extension of social assistance to the homeless, the paupers, and the prisoners, as well as to the ill.

Medieval morality, whether practiced by the Benedictines or other Christians, was focused on the six compassionate acts specified in Jesus' teaching. In accordance with the standard of judgment he announced, efforts were made by the devout to feed the hungry, to give water to the thirsty, to clothe the naked, to visit the imprisoned, to shelter the homeless, and to care for the sick. The administration of medicine was rudimentary in monastic hospitals, but "the patient was given food, warmth and kindness, and religious services which soothed even if they could not cure."[14]

Across most of the past two thousand years, hospitals and hospices have been among the more effective means for conveying personal concern to those most in need.[15] However, history texts have generally neglected the quiet, Red Cross type of work and have focused rather on the bloody, cross-led military crusades. The continual work of many Christians from early times onward in caring for the ill provides some balance to the cruel racism, unjust wars, arrogant colonialism, and financial exploitation in which church members have been much involved. In recognition of the need for attending to those who suffer from infancy onward, there are now about 29,500 Christian-sponsored medical centers in the world, of which 4,600 are hospitals.[16]

Perhaps the most abiding impact of any religion is the way in which it provides community leadership, organization, and funding for attending to the diseased, the indigent, the aged, and all others who have been relegated to the margins of life. Reasonable persons may be skeptical of the "miraculous" healings attributed to Jesus and to other charismatic religious leaders over the centuries, but they are likely to be impressed by the quiet and cheerful works of mercy done by those following Jesus' example of caring and sharing.

The gospel teaches that Jesus can be seen in individuals who express holy, suffering love to others. Thus, it is fitting to end this study by recognizing two outstanding Germans who epitomize in this century much of Jesus' message and mission. Albert Schweitzer, as a young genius, was troubled by a statue in a park near his hometown. Frédéric-Auguste Bartholdi, famous for his Statue of Liberty creation, had sculpted a local admiral, noted for his aid in colonization, with a wistful African suffering beneath him.[17] Schweitzer was also disturbed by Jesus' parable of an anonymous rich man and Lazarus. "Out there in the colonies," Schweitzer wrote, "sits wretched Lazarus," lorded over by the European colonist.[18] He became aware that most in Christendom were indifferent to this exploitation, although some missionaries were publicizing atrocities in Leopold II's so-called Congo Free State.[19] The Belgian king, typical of many Europeans, was like the rich man described by Jesus. While not despising the have-nots, he was consumed with amassing wealth and living luxuriously. In 1905, when the outcry against Leopold was intense, Schweitzer felt impelled to turn aside from a life of acclaim as historian, philosopher, and musician in Europe in order "to try to live in the spirit of Jesus." After studying medicine and acquiring his fourth doctoral degree, he gave himself to humanitarian service in equatorial Africa. For half a century, in a simple jungle hospital, he shared Jesus' aim "to serve rather than to be served" (Mark 10:45).

Dietrich Bonhoeffer is one of the best modern examples of a cross-carrying Christian. As soon as Adolf Hitler came to power, Bonhoeffer denounced idolatrous devotion to a demagogue. The Nazis got the point and cut off his radio broadcast before he finished speaking to his fellow Germans. Bonhoeffer then spoke out against rising anti-Semitism, and helped pastors form a Confessing Church separate from the domination of state-approved clergy. Later he was imprisoned for his courageous efforts to remove the Nazi Führer and bring Hitler's war to an end. Like Paul during his prison years, Bonhoeffer carried on his ministry by expressing buoyant good humor to other prisoners and by writing to Christians outside. His letters provide fresh interpretations of Jesus, "the man for others." In 1944, the last year of his life, Bonhoeffer encouraged his friends to subordinate words to actions. He made his point by emphasizing the contrasting verbs in a teaching of Jesus: "Not every one who *says* to me, 'Lord, Lord,' shall enter the kingdom of heaven, but he who *does* the will of my Father."[20] Bonhoeffer, like Jesus, was martyred in the fourth decade of life. The influence of each illustrates Rabbi Jesus' wise and witty paradox, that it is buried seed that becomes fruitful (John 12:24).

Notes

Chapter 1: Introduction

1. Allison Johnson, ed., *The Wit and Wisdom of Alfred North Whitehead* (Boston: Beacon Press, 1947), v, 26, 64, 68, 80, 86.
2. Cox News Service, Oct. 30, 1989.
3. Albert Paine, *Mark Twain* (New York: Harper, 1912), vol. 1, 84.
4. Henry Smith, *Mark Twain* (Cambridge, Mass.: Harvard University Press, 1962), 43.
5. Edward Wagenknecht, *Mark Twain* (New Haven, Conn.: Yale University Press, 1935), 206.
6. Albert Paine, ed., *Mark Twain's Notebook* (New York: Harper & Brothers, 1935), 128.
7. Paine, *Mark Twain*, vol. 4, 1556.
8. Wagenknecht, *Mark Twain*, 130.
9. Gordon Allport, *Personality* (New York: Henry Holt, 1937), 226.
10. Nevin Vos, *For God's Sake Laugh!* (Richmond: John Knox Press, 1967), 66.
11. *New York Herald*, Dec. 28, 1870; Charles Neider, ed., *The Outrageous Mark Twain* (New York: Doubleday, 1987), 119–123.
12. Albert Schweitzer, *The Quest of the Historical Jesus* (New York: Macmillan Co., 1910), 403.
13. Rudolf Bultmann, *Jesus and the Word* (New York: Charles Scribner's Sons, 1958), 8.
14. Bultmann, *Jesus and the Word*, 58.
15. Jaroslav Pelikan, *Jesus Through the Centuries* (New Haven, Conn.: Yale University Press, 1985), 11, 20.
16. John Bright, *The Kingdom of God* (Nashville: Abingdon Press, 1953), 196–197.
17. William Phipps, *Paul Against Supernaturalism* (New York: Philosophical Library, 1987).
18. Letter to John Adams, Oct. 12, 1813. Dickinson Adams, ed.,

Jefferson's Extracts from the Gospels (Princeton, N.J.: Princeton University Press, 1982), 352.

19. Letter to William Short, Oct. 31, 1819. In ibid., 388.

Chapter 2: The Prophetic Pharisee

1. Julius Wellhausen, *Einleitung in die ersten drei Evangelien* (Berlin: Reimer, 1905), 113.

2. John Holmes, *The Sensible Man's View of Religion* (New York: Harper & Brothers, 1933), 17.

3. Markus Barth, *Jesus the Jew* (Atlanta: John Knox Press, 1978), 11.

4. Leonard Swidler, *Yeshua* (Kansas City, Mo.: Sheed & Ward, 1988), 2.

5. E. P. Sanders, *Jesus and Judaism* (Philadelphia: Fortress Press, 1985), 19, 335.

6. James Charlesworth, ed., *Jesus' Jewishness* (New York: Crossroad, 1991), 180; Marcus Borg, "A Temperate Case for a Non-Eschatological Jesus," *Society of Biblical Literature: Seminar Papers* (Atlanta: Scholars Press, 1986), 521–535.

7. C. H. Talbert, ed., *Reimarus: Fragments* (Philadelphia: Fortress Press, 1970), 144–153; Joel Carmichael, *The Death of Jesus* (New York: Macmillan & Co., 1962); S. G. F. Brandon, *Jesus and the Zealots* (New York: Charles Scribner's Sons, 1967). Contra: Oscar Cullmann, *Jesus and the Revolutionaries* (New York: Harper & Row, 1970); Ernst Bammel and C. F. D. Moule, eds., *Jesus and the Politics of His Day* (New York: Cambridge University Press, 1984).

8. See, e.g., Edmund Wilson, *The Scrolls from the Dead Sea* (New York: Oxford University Press, 1955), 97; Charles Potter, *The Lost Years of Jesus* (New York: Fawcett, 1958), 13; Upton Ewing, *The Essene Christ* (New York: Philosophical Library, 1961). Contra: Jean Carmignac, *Christ and the Teacher of Righteousness* (Baltimore: Helicon, 1962); Howard Kee, *What Can We Know About Jesus?* (New York: Cambridge University Press, 1990), 17–19.

9. Geza Vermes, *Jesus the Jew* (London: William Collins Sons & Co., 1973), 223.

10. William Phipps, *Paul Against Supernaturalism* (New York: Philosophical Library, 1987), 138–139.

11. R. Travers Herford, *The Pharisees* (Boston: Beacon Press, 1962), 206.

12. *Aboth* 2:2; 4:5.

13. *Yoma* 35b.

14. Abraham Geiger, *Judaism and Its History* (New York, 1865), 214–220; George Berlin, *Defending the Faith: Nineteenth-Century*

American Jewish Writings on Christianity and Jesus (Albany, N.Y.: State University of New York, 1989), 49.

15. Joseph Klausner, *Jesus of Nazareth* (New York: Macmillan Co., 1925), 319.
16. Martin Buber, *Two Types of Faith* (New York: Harper & Row, 1961), 137; cf. 79, 92, 159, 160.
17. Ellis Rivkin, *A Hidden Revolution* (Nashville: Abingdon Press, 1978), 275.
18. Harvey Falk, *Jesus the Pharisee* (Ramsey, N.J.: Paulist Press, 1985), 112.
19. *Journal of Ecumenical Studies*, vol. 19, no. 1 (Winter 1982), 110.
20. See, e.g., Charles Guignebert, *The Jewish World in the Time of Jesus* (New York: E. P. Dutton & Co., 1939) 165; James Parkes, *Judaism and Christianity* (Chicago: University of Chicago Press, 1948), 41; Andrew Greeley, *New York Times Magazine* (Dec. 23, 1973), 28; John Pawlikowski, *Christ in the Light of the Christian-Jewish Dialogue* (Ramsey, N.J.: Paulist Press, 1982), 92; Bernard Lee, *The Galilean Jewishness of Jesus* (Mahwah, N.J.: Paulist Press, 1988), 118, 145; John Meier, "Reflections on Jesus-of-History Research Today," in *Jesus' Jewishness*, ed. James Charlesworth (New York: Crossroad, 1991), 98.
21. Common Era. I support the current trend toward separating year designations from a tacit confession of faith. "In the year of our Lord" (*anno Domini*) may be appropriate for Christians, but it hinders communication with people who have other theology, or no theology. It is a tribute to the impact of Jesus that the non-Christian majority of the global population are generally willing to regard his coming as the watershed of history.
22. Josephus, *Antiquities* 17, 42–45, 151.
23. Josephus, *Antiquities* 13, 298.
24. George F. Moore, *Judaism in the First Centuries of the Christian Era* (Cambridge, Mass.: Harvard University Press, 1927–30), vol. 1, 282–287.
25. *Aboth* 2:5.
26. Josephus, *Antiquities* 18, 18; *The Jewish War* 2, 163.
27. Josephus, *Antiquities* 18, 13.
28. *Aboth* 3:16.
29. *Psalms of Solomon* 9:4.
30. Joachim Schupphaus, *Die Psalmen Salomos* (Leiden: E. J. Brill, 1977), 132; but see James Charlesworth, ed., *The Old Testament Pseudepigrapha* (Garden City, N.Y.: Doubleday & Co., 1985), vol. 2, 642.
31. *Shemoneh Esreh* 11.
32. *Berakoth* 12a; cf. Moore, *Judaism*, vol. 2, 373.

33. *Shabbath* 153a.
34. Josephus, *Antiquities* 18, 14–16.
35. *Aboth* 4:16.
36. *Psalms of Solomon* 3:12; 13:11.
37. Matt. 22:30–32; Acts 23:8; Rivkin, *A Hidden Revolution*, 247.
38. Josephus, *Antiquities* 13, 295; 20, 199.
39. Klausner, *Jesus of Nazareth*, 220–221.
40. *Aboth* 2:5.
41. Josephus, *Antiquities* 18, 2–10 and 23; Rivkin, *A Hidden Revolution*, 71.
42. Josephus, *War* 2, 254.
43. *Aboth* 1:12.
44. *Aboth* 2:7.
45. *Yoma* 39b; cf. Jacob Neusner, *First Century Judaism in Crisis* (Nashville: Abingdon Press, 1975), 135–147.
46. Josephus, *Antiquities* 18, 12; 13, 298.
47. *Aboth* 2:7.
48. Nahum Glatzer, *Hillel the Elder* (New York: Bloch Publishing Co., 1956), 44.
49. *Aboth* 5:10.
50. *Aboth* 1:14.
51. *Erubin* 54a.
52. *Sukkah* 4 and 5.
53. Cf. William Phipps, *Was Jesus Married?* (New York: Harper & Row, 1970), 120–123.
54. Rudolf Bultmann, *Jesus and the Word* (New York: Charles Scribner's Sons, 1968), 101.
55. *Psalms of Solomon* 4:5, 20, 22.
56. Charlesworth, ed., *The Old Testament Pseudepigrapha*, vol. 1, 921; David Flusser, *Jesus* (New York: Herder & Herder, 1969), 47.
57. *Testament of Moses* 7:9–10.
58. *Sotah* 3:4.
59. Jerusalem *Sotah* 19a.
60. *Sotah* 22b; Jerusalem *Berakoth* 14b.
61. Cf. Buber, *Two Types of Faith*, 61–62.
62. Cf. Klausner, *Jesus of Nazareth*, 22–31.
63. "The Pharisees," *Interpreter's Dictionary of the Bible*, ed. George Buttrick (Nashville: Abingdon Press, 1962).
64. Alfred Edersheim, *The Life and Times of Jesus the Messiah* (1900 ed.; reprint, Grand Rapids: Wm. B. Eerdmans Publishing Co., 1972), vol. 2, 15.
65. Josephus, *War* 1, 110.
66. Matt. 22:34–40; Mark 12:28–34; Luke 10:25–28; cf. Israel Abrahams, *Studies in Pharisaism and the Gospels* (New York: Ktav Publishing House, 1967), 18–29.

67. Maurice Goguel, *Jesus and the Origins of Christianity* (New York: Harper & Brothers, 1960), vol. 2, 344.
68. *Tosephta Berakoth* 7, 18.
69. Sirach 25:24; 42:13–14.
70. *Aboth* 2:7.
71. Josephus, *Life* 10; *Against Apion* 200.
72. *Mekilta Exodus* 21, 7 and 20; cf. Ex. 21:7.
73. *Aboth* 1:5; *Berakoth* 3:3.
74. Josephus, *Against Apion* 2, 103.
75. *Niddah* 7:1.
76. *Mikwaoth* 8:5.
77. Nahmanides on Lev. 12:4; quoted in Blu Greenberg, *On Women and Judaism* (Philadelphia: Jewish Publication Society, 1981), 115.
78. *Erubin* 100b.
79. *Shabbath* 110a.
80. *Sotah* 1:5–6.
81. *Sotah* 3:4.
82. Claude Montefiore, *The Synoptic Gospels* (New York: Ktav Publishing House, 1968), vol. 1, 389.
83. Marcus Borg, *Jesus: A New Vision* (San Francisco: Harper & Row, 1987), 133–135.
84. Mark 10:7; cf. William Phipps, *Genesis and Gender* (New York: Praeger Publishers, 1989), 74–76.
85. *Niddah* 4:1.
86. William Phipps, "The Menstrual Taboo in the Judeo-Christian," *Journal of Religion and Health*, vol. 19 (1980), 301–302.
87. Moore, *Judaism*, vol. 2, 385–386.
88. Norman Perrin, *Rediscovering the Teaching of Jesus* (New York: Harper & Row, 1967), 94.
89. *Toharoth* 7:6; *Abodah Zarah* 2:1.
90. Howard Kee, *The New Testament in Context* (Englewood Cliffs, N.J.: Prentice-Hall, 1984), 203.
91. *Psalms of Solomon* 17.
92. *Aboth* 1:5.
93. Jacob Neusner, *From Politics to Piety: The Emergence of Pharisaic Judaism* (Englewood Cliffs, N.J: Prentice-Hall, 1973), 80.
94. *Leviticus Rabbah* 9, 3.
95. *Aboth* 2:6; *Tosephta Shabbath* 1, 15; cf. *Berakoth* 43b.
96. 1 Maccabees 9:27; cf. Moore, *Judaism*, vol. 1, 421–422.
97. Montefiore, *The Synoptic Gospels*, vol. 1, cxx.
98. 1 Maccabees 14:41; Sirach 48:10; *Manual of Discipline* (Qumran) 9:11.
99. *Sanhedrin* 99a.
100. Robert M. Grant, *A Short History of the Interpretation of the Bible* (New York: Macmillan & Co., 1963) 19–20.

101. Moore, *Judaism,* vol. 1, 300–306.
102. *Berakoth* 3:4.
103. *Shabbath* 22:6; *Yoma* 8:6.
104. *Aboth* 3:5; *Berakoth* 2:2.
105. *Aboth* 5:15.

Chapter 3: Interpreting Scripture

1. Although Mary's little lamb is not likely to be encountered in schools, a more troublesome animal is frequently there. By way of warning biblical literature instructors, here is my doggerel, entitled "Alas!":

> A goat who went to class
> Was told, "All flesh is grass."
> With literalism crass,
> He bit the teacher's ass.

2. *Shabbath* 7:2; 15:1–2.
3. George F. Moore, *Judaism in the First Centuries of the Christian Era* (Cambridge, Mass.: Harvard University Press, 1927–30), vol. 1, 269–270.
4. Rudolf Bultmann, *Theology of the New Testament* (New York: Charles Scribner's Sons, 1955), vol. 1, 16.
5. C. Milo Connick, *Jesus: The Man, the Mission, and the Message* (Englewood Cliffs, N.J.: Prentice-Hall, 1963), 241.
6. Thomas Manson, *The Sayings of Jesus* (London: SCM Press, 1949), 135.
7. Qur'an 5:116; 4:171.
8. James Talmage, *Jesus the Christ* (Salt Lake City: Deseret Book Co., 1958), 81; Orson Pratt, *The Seer,* Oct. 1853, 158.
9. Gen. 6:5; *Berakoth* 9:5; Moore, *Judaism,* vol. 1, 478–493.
10. Sirach 21:27.
11. Nonbiblical sources give nonsupernatural causes for these deaths; see Herodotus, *History* 2, 141; Josephus, *Antiquities* 19, 350.
12. Josephus, *Antiquities* 15, 411–412.
13. Artur Weiser, *The Psalms* (Philadelphia: Westminster Press, 1962), 609.
14. *Time,* Feb. 25, 1991, 36–46.
15. Manson, *The Sayings of Jesus,* 45.
16. Reinhold Niebuhr, *Beyond Tragedy* (New York: Charles Scribner's Sons, 1937), 97.

17. William Shakespeare, *The Merchant of Venice* 1, 3, 99–102; 3, 2, 77–80.
18. Moore, *Judaism*, vol. 1, 404.
19. *Berakoth* 1:1; 2:1.
20. Max Joseph, "Phylacteries," *The Universal Jewish Encyclopedia* (New York: Ktav Publishing House, 1969).
21. Archibald Kennedy, "Phylacteries," *A Dictionary of the Bible* (New York: Charles Scribner's Sons, 1900).
22. Foakes Jackson and Kirsopp Lake, eds., *The Beginnings of Christianity* (London: Macmillan & Co., 1933), vol. 4, 243.
23. C. K. Barrett, *The New Testament Background: Selected Documents* (New York: Harper & Row, 1961), 32.
24. "Charms and Amulets (Jewish)," *Encyclopaedia of Religion and Ethics* (New York: Charles Scribner's Sons, 1928).
25. Plutarch, *Moralia* 377–378.
26. James Moulton and George Milligan, *The Vocabulary of the Greek Testament* (London: Hodder & Stoughton, 1930), 678.
27. *Letter of Aristeas* 159.
28. Josephus, *Antiquities* 4, 213.
29. "Tefillin," *Encyclopaedia Judaica* (Jerusalem: Keter, 1972).
30. *Menahoth* 43b.
31. *Menahoth* 3:7; 4:1.
32. *Shebiith* 3:11; *Berakoth* 3:3.
33. *Shabbath* 6:2.
34. Moore, *Judaism*, vol. 2, 192.
35. Julian, *Against the Galileans* 194d.
36. E. A. Wallis Budge, *Amulets and Talismans* (New York: University Books, 1961), 348.
37. *Christian Century*, Oct. 16, 1991, 951.
38. *Gittin* 9:10.
39. *Ketuboth* 7:6.
40. *Yebamoth* 14:1.
41. Sirach 25:26.
42. Philo, *On the Special Laws* 3, 30, 35.
43. Josephus, *Life* 414–415, 426–427; cf. *Antiquities* 4, 253.
44. *Gittin* 9:10.
45. Josephus, *Antiquities* 18, 136.
46. See Richard Friedman, *Who Wrote the Bible?* (San Francisco: Harper & Row, 1987), 86; Harold Bloom, *The Book of J* (New York: Grove Weidenfeld, 1990), 9–10, 34.
47. John Riches, *The World of Jesus* (New York: Cambridge University Press, 1990), 113–114.
48. William Shakespeare, Sonnet 116.
49. Moore, *Judaism*, vol. 2, 125, 152.

50. *Genesis Rabbah* 68, 4; Israel Abrahams, "Marriages Are Made in Heaven," *Jewish Quarterly Review*, vol. 2 (1890), 173.
51. One such effort at fresh exegesis is found in William Phipps, *Genesis and Gender* (New York: Praeger Publishers, 1989).
52. "Equity—?" *The Complete Poetical Works of James Whitcomb Riley* (Garden City, N.Y.: Garden City Publishing Co., 1941), 654.
53. *Tobit* 3:8.
54. Josephus, *Antiquities* 18, 16.
55. *Apocalypse of Baruch* 50:2.
56. J. Hamilton-Patterson and C. Andrews, *Mummies* (New York: Viking Press, 1979), 65.
57. *Sanhedrin* 92b; *Shabbath* 30b.
58. *Berakoth* 17a.
59. Colleen McDannell and Bernhard Lang, *Heaven: A History* (New Haven, Conn.: Yale University Press, 1988), 27.
60. Evelyn and Frank Stagg, *Woman in the World of Jesus* (Philadelphia: Westminster Press, 1978), 139.
61. Susanne Heine, *Women and Early Christianity* (Minneapolis: Augsburg Publishing House, 1988), 62–64.
62. Geddes Macgregor, *Philosophical Issues in Religious Thought* (Boston: Houghton Mifflin Co., 1973), 306.
63. Sidney Callahan, *Beyond Birth Control* (New York: Sheed & Ward, 1968), 6.
64. Carl Sagan, *Cosmos* (New York: Random House, 1980), 40.
65. For an expansion of this exposition, see William Phipps, "Jesus on Marriage and the Afterlife," *Christian Century*, vol. 102 (1985), 327–328.

Chapter 4: Jesus as Teacher

1. E.g., Günther Bornkamm, *Jesus of Nazareth* (New York: Harper & Brothers, 1960), 96; W. D. Davies, *Christian Origins and Judaism* (Philadelphia: Westminster Press, 1962), 20.
2. Jaroslav Pelikan, *Jesus Through the Centuries* (New Haven, Conn.: Yale University Press, 1985), 18.
3. George F. Moore, *Judaism in the First Centuries of the Christian Era* (Cambridge, Mass.: Harvard University Press, 1927–30), vol. 3, 15.
4. Philo, *On the Life of Moses* 2, 216.
5. Luella Cole, *A History of Education* (New York: Holt, Rinehart & Winston, 1950), 65.
6. William Barclay, *Jesus as They Saw Him* (New York: Harper & Row, 1962).

7. Plato, *Phaedrus* 247; *Republic* 518.
8. *The Encyclopedia of Religion* (New York: Macmillan Publishing Co., 1987); *Encyclopaedia Judaica* (Jerusalem: Keter, 1972).
9. Keith Crim, ed., *Abingdon Dictionary of Living Religions* (Nashville: Abingdon Press, 1981).
10. Thomas Manson, *The Sayings of Jesus* (London: SCM Press, 1949), 11.
11. Gilbert Highet, *The Art of Teaching* (New York: Vintage Books, 1950) 11–25, 168–170.
12. Highet, *The Art of Teaching*, 175.
13. Albert Schweitzer, *Out of My Life and Thought* (New York: Henry Holt, 1933), 103.
14. Viktor Frankl, "Psychiatry and Man's Quest for Meaning," *Journal of Religion and Health*, vol. 1 (1962), 100; *Man's Search for Meaning* (New York: Pocket Books, 1963), 157–177.
15. Walter Brueggemann, *In Man We Trust* (Richmond: John Knox Press, 1972), 121.
16. *Berakoth* 4:3.
17. Aristotle, *Rhetoric* 1404a, 16–19; *"Hypokrinomai," Theological Dictionary of the New Testament*, ed. Gerhard Friedrich (Grand Rapids: Wm. B. Eerdmans Publishing Co., 1972).
18. Fyodor Dostoevsky, *The Brothers Karamazov* 6, 3.
19. Richard Crashaw, "Steps to the Temple" (1648).
20. E. P. Sanders, *Jesus and Judaism* (Philadelphia: Fortress Press, 1985), 338–339.
21. Cf. Moore, *Judaism*, vol. 2, 273–275.
22. *Aboth* 2:5.
23. *Erubin* 13b; *Berakoth* 28b.
24. Gilbert Highet, *The Anatomy of Satire* (Princeton, N.J.: Princeton University Press, 1962), 72.
25. C. S. Lewis, *The Screwtape Letters* (New York: Macmillan Co., 1961), ix.
26. Neal Fisher, *The Parables of Jesus* (New York: Crossroad, 1990), 25.
27. Dudley Zuver, *Salvation by Laughter* (New York: Harper & Brothers, 1933), 21.
28. George Santayana, *Soliloquies in England* (New York: Charles Scribner's Sons, 1924), 98–99.
29. Charles Kingsley, "A Farewell" (1856).
30. *Gospel of Thomas* 47.
31. Washington Irving, *New Yorker*, Nov. 12, 1836.
32. Edward Wagenknecht, *Mark Twain* (New Haven, Conn.: Yale University Press, 1935), 130.

Chapter 5: Wry Humor

1. Sarah Cohen, ed., *Jewish Wry* (Bloomington, Ind.: Indiana University Press, 1987).
2. Lucian, *Philosophers for Sale* 26.
3. Ernest Harms, "The Development of Humor," *Journal of Abnormal and Social Psychology*, vol. 38 (1943), 356.
4. Conrad Hyers, *And God Created Laughter* (Atlanta: John Knox Press, 1987), 17.
5. Aristotle, *Nicomachean Ethics* 1128.
6. William Hazlitt, *Lectures on the English Comic Writers* (London: J. M. Dent & Sons, 1910), 5.
7. Reinhold Niebuhr, *Discerning the Signs of the Times* (London: SCM Press, 1946), 106.
8. Gordon Allport, *Personality* (New York: Henry Holt, 1937), 223–224.
9. Homer, *Iliad* 1, 599.
10. Calvin, *Institutes* 3, 19, 9.
11. The Shorter Catechism, *Book of Confessions* 7.001, Part I, *The Constitution of the Presbyterian Church (U.S.A.).*
12. Robert Corrigan, ed., *Comedy, Meaning and Form* (San Francisco: Chandler, 1965), 17.
13. Dudley Zuver, *Salvation by Laughter* (New York: Harper & Brothers, 1933), 186.
14. Conrad Hyers, ed., *Holy Laughter* (New York: Seabury Press, 1969), 216.
15. Definition of Chalcedon, 451 C.E.
16. Charles Baudelaire, *Oeuvres Complètes* (Paris: Editions du Seuil, 1968), 371.
17. John Morreall, *Taking Laughter Seriously* (Albany, N.Y.: State University of New York, 1983), 126.
18. Origen, *Sermons of Numbers* 23, 2.
19. Kenneth Foreman, *Romans, 1 and 2 Corinthians* (Richmond: John Knox Press, 1961), 37.
20. Confession of 1967, *Book of Confessions* 9.08, Part I, *The Constitution of the Presbyterian Church (U.S.A.).*
21. Philo, *On Rewards and Punishments* 31–35.
22. "Paronomasia in the Old Testament" was submitted in 1894 to Johns Hopkins University by I. M. Casanowicz. This has been supplemented by "Paronomasia and Kindred Phenomena in the New Testament," which was submitted in 1920 to the University of Chicago by E. Russell.
23. Josephus, *Against Apion* 1, 202–204.
24. Victor Hugo, *Les Misérables* (Paris: Garnier Frères, 1963), vol. 1, 171.

25. Terrot Glover, *The Jesus of History* (New York: Harper, 1917), 48.
26. Josephus, *Antiquities* 13, 297.
27. *Aboth* 1:1.
28. *Aboth* 2:1.
29. *Maaseroth* 4:5; *Demai* 2:1; *Shebiith* 9:1.
30. Winston Davis, "Wealth," *The Encyclopedia of Religion* (New York: Macmillan Publishing Co., 1987).
31. *Baba Metzia* 38b.
32. John Calvin, *Commentary on a Harmony of the Evangelists* (Grand Rapids: Wm. B. Eerdmans Publishing Co., 1949), vol. 2, 401.
33. William Barclay, *The Gospel of Luke* (Philadelphia: Westminster Press, 1956), 238.
34. G. E. Post, "Camel," *A Dictionary of the Bible* (Edinburgh: T. & T. Clark, 1898).
35. Walter Rauschenbusch, *Christianity and the Social Crisis* (New York: Macmillan & Co., 1911), 77–78.
36. Edward Gibbon, *The Decline and Fall of the Roman Empire* (1776–88) 15, 4.
37. Eusebius, *Church History* 6, 8; William Phipps, *Recovering Biblical Sensuousness* (Philadelphia: Westminster Press, 1975), 50–51.
38. Bruce Metzger, *The New Testament: Its Background, Growth, and Content* (Nashville: Abingdon Press, 1965), 137.
39. Thomas Manson, *The Sayings of Jesus* (London: SCM Press, 1949), 51.
40. Norman Perrin, *Rediscovering the Teaching of Jesus* (New York: Harper & Row, 1967), 147.
41. Epictetus, *Discourses* 4, 1.
42. A photograph of Bleifeld's sculpture is in *Life,* June 28, 1963, 106.
43. Elton Trueblood, *The Humor of Christ* (New York: Harper & Row, 1964), 9.
44. Norman Cousins, *Anatomy of an Illness* (New York: W. W. Norton & Co., 1979), 83–87; *Head First* (New York: E. P. Dutton, 1989), 125–140, 313.
45. Horace, *Satires* 1, 1, 24.
46. Justin Miller, "Prophecy in the Fast Lane: A Psychological Typology of Jewish Wit," *Criterion,* Autumn 1989, 15.
47. Kenneth Latourette, *A History of Christianity* (London: Eyre & Spottiswoode, 1954), 46.
48. Jakob Jonsson, *Humour and Irony in the New Testament* (Reykjavik: Bokautgafa Menningarsjods, 1965), 223–242, 258–275.
49. James M. Robinson, ed., *The Nag Hammadi Library* (New York: Harper & Row, 1977), 208.
50. William Phipps, "Did Ancient Indian Celibacy Influence Christianity?" *Studies in Religion,* vol. 4 (1974), 45–50.

51. Basil, *Ascetic Works*, The Long Rules, 17.
52. John Chrysostom, *Sermons of Matthew* 6, 8–9.
53. John Chrysostom, *Sermons on the Statues* 20, 23.
54. Ambrose, *On Offices* 1, 20, 85.
55. Jerome, *Letters* 130, 13.
56. Jerome, *Sermons* 16.
57. Epictetus, *Manual* 33.
58. Diogenes Laertius, *Lives of Eminent Philosophers* 3, 26.
59. Plato, *Republic* 389.
60. Theodoret, *Church History* 3, 20.
61. Algernon Swinburne, "Hymn to Proserpine" (1866).
62. Edgar Goodspeed, *Modern Apocrypha* (Boston: Beacon Press, 1956), 88–89.
63. *The Rule of St. Benedict* 7.
64. Hyers, *Holy Laughter*, 227.
65. Ignatius Loyola, *Spiritual Exercises* 80.
66. *Luthers Werke* (Weimar, 1883–), vol. 46, 598.
67. Merton P. Strommen et al., *A Study of Generations* (Minneapolis: Augsburg Publishing House, 1972), 367.
68. Herbert Asbury, *A Methodist Saint* (New York: Alfred A. Knopf, 1927), 265.
69. Nikos Kazantzakis, *England* (New York: Simon & Schuster, 1965), 134.
70. George Bernard Shaw, *Works* (London: Wise, 1931), vol. 23, viii.
71. Friedrich Nietzsche, *Thus Spake Zarathustra*, 1, 21; 4, 13, 20.
72. Francis Thompson, *Works* (New York: AMS Press, 1913), vol. 3, 113.
73. See, e.g., Marvin Ross, *The Life of Christ in Masterpieces of Art* (New York: Harper & Brothers, 1957); Joseph Jobe, *Ecce Homo* (New York: Harper & Row, 1962).
74. *Time*, August 15, 1988.
75. Marion Wheeler, *His Face* (New York: Chameleon Books, 1988).
76. Isa. 53:2–3; Clement of Alexandria, *The Instructor* 3, 1; Origen, *Contra Celsus* 6, 75.
77. Zuver, *Salvation by Laughter*, 5.
78. Cal Samra, *The Joyful Christ* (San Francisco: Harper & Row, 1986), 171–192.
79. James Dickey and Marvin Hayes, *God's Images* (New York: Seabury Press, 1978), plate 49.
80. William Barclay, *The Mind of Jesus* (New York: Harper & Row, 1961), 94.
81. Henri Cormier, *The Humor of Jesus* (Staten Island, N.Y.: Alba House, 1977), 10–12.
82. Nevin Vos, *For God's Sake Laugh!* (Richmond: John Knox Press, 1967), 49.

83. Harvey Cox, *The Feast of Fools* (Cambridge, Mass.: Harvard University Press, 1969), 140–142.
84. Peter Berger, *The Precarious Vision* (New York: Doubleday & Co., 1961), 213–214.
85. Carl Sandburg, *Abraham Lincoln* (New York: Charles Scribner's Sons, 1946), vol. 5, 308–309.
86. Plato, *Symposium* 223.

Chapter 6: In Light of Philosophers

1. Karl Marx, *Die Philosophie des Epikurus.*
2. Plato, *Apology* 23.
3. Plato, *Phaedo* 118; Xenophon, *Memorabilia* 4, 8, 11.
4. Plato, *Apology* 23.
5. Xenophon, *Memorabilia* 1, 2, 5.
6. Plato, *Phaedrus* 279.
7. Edith Hamilton, *Witness to the Truth* (New York: W. W. Norton & Co., 1957), 33.
8. Plato, *Republic* 514–518; Isa. 42:1–4; 49:6; Matt. 12:19–21.
9. E.g., Plato, *Meno* 82–86; Xenophon, *Memorabilia* 4, 6, 1–11.
10. Plato, *Euthyphro* 3–4.
11. Plato, *Apology* 30.
12. Plato, *Crito* 49.
13. Plato, *Apology* 41.
14. Plato, *Symposium* 220–221.
15. Plato, *Republic* 470.
16. Plato, *Republic* 375.
17. Roland Bainton, *Christian Attitudes Toward War and Peace* (Nashville: Abingdon Press, 1960), 66–68.
18. Plato, *Phaedo* 67.
19. Plato, *Apology* 29.
20. Plato, *Crito* 54.
21. Xenophon, *Memorabilia* 4, 8, 2.
22. Francis Cornford, *Before and After Socrates* (Cambridge: Cambridge University Press, 1960).
23. Arnold Toynbee, *An Historian's Approach to Religion* (New York: Oxford University Press, 1956), 64.
24. Cicero, *Tuscan Disputations* 5, 4, 10.
25. J. S. Mill, *On Liberty* 2.
26. Justin, *Apology* 1, 16; *Dialogue with Trypho* 8.
27. Letter to Joseph Priestley, April 9, 1803. Dickinson Adams, ed., *Jefferson's Extracts from the Gospels* (Princeton, N.J.: Princeton University Press, 1983), 327–328.

28. Vincent McCarthy, *Quest for a Philosophical Jesus* (Macon, Ga.: Mercer University Press, 1986), 82.
29. Vernon Robbins, *Jesus the Teacher* (Philadelphia: Fortress Press, 1984), 143–146.
30. Karl Jaspers, *Nietzsche and Christianity* (New York: Henry Regnery, 1961), vii.
31. Robert Solomon, ed., *Nietzsche* (Garden City, N.Y.: Doubleday & Co., Anchor Books, 1973), 153.
32. Nietzsche, *Ecce Homo*, "Why I Write Such Excellent Books" 2; "Why I Am So Wise" 7.
33. John Bernstein, *Nietzsche's Moral Philosophy* (Cranbury, N.J.: Fairleigh Dickinson University Press, 1987), 19.
34. Nietzsche, *Beyond Good and Evil* 195.
35. Nietzsche, *The Anti-Christ* 26.
36. Nietzsche, *The Anti-Christ* 25; *Joyful Wisdom* 138; *Twilight of Idols*, "The Four Great Errors" 7.
37. *The Anti-Christ* 26.
38. *The Anti-Christ* 27.
39. *The Anti-Christ* 32.
40. *The Anti-Christ* 29.
41. Nietzsche, *The Will to Power* 161.
42. *The Anti-Christ* 34.
43. *The Anti-Christ* 33.
44. *The Anti-Christ* 41.
45. *The Anti-Christ* 33.
46. *The Anti-Christ* 35.
47. *The Will to Power* 162.
48. *The Anti-Christ* 40.
49. *The Anti-Christ* 32.
50. *The Will to Power* 164.
51. *The Anti-Christ* 37.
52. *The Anti-Christ* 40–41.
53. Nietzsche, *Dawn* 68.
54. *The Anti-Christ* 42.
55. *The Anti-Christ* 51.
56. *The Anti-Christ* 45 and 47.
57. *Twilight of Idols*, "What I Owe to the Ancients" 4.
58. *Twilight of Idols*, "Morality as Anti-Nature" 1.
59. *The Anti-Christ* 46.
60. *Ecce Homo*, "Why I Write Such Excellent Books" 5.
61. *The Will to Power* 205.
62. *Twilight of Idols*, "The 'Improvers' of Mankind" 4.
63. *The Will to Power* 215.
64. *The Will to Power* 184.

65. *The Anti-Christ* 43.
66. *The Anti-Christ* 39.
67. *The Anti-Christ* 28–29.
68. *The Anti-Christ* 24.
69. *The Will to Power* 169.
70. *The Anti-Christ* 36.
71. *The Anti-Christ* 42.
72. Nietzsche, *Thus Spake Zarathustra* 3, 12, 26.
73. *The Anti-Christ* 39.
74. *The Will to Power* 983.
75. *The Anti-Christ* 40.
76. *The Anti-Christ* 46.
77. Walter Kaufmann, *The Portable Nietzsche* (New York: Viking Press, 1968), 30.
78. Bertrand Russell, *History of Western Philosophy* (London: Allen & Unwin, 1946), 602, 800.
79. Bertrand Russell, *Why I Am Not a Christian* (New York: Simon & Schuster, 1957), 16.
80. See Thomas Manson, *The Sayings of Jesus* (London: SCM Press, 1949), 182; Norman Perrin, *Rediscovering the Teaching of Jesus* (New York: Harper & Row, 1967), 201–202; Marcus Borg, *Jesus: A New Vision* (San Francisco: Harper & Row, 1987), 14, 20.
81. Russell, *Why I Am Not a Christian*, 17–18.
82. Mark Twain, *Letters from the Earth* (Greenwich, Conn.: Fawcett, 1962), 47.
83. Plato, *Phaedo* 114.
84. Plato, *Republic* 615.
85. Homer, *The Odyssey* 11, 593–600; Plato, *Apology* 41; *Cratylus* 403.
86. John Greenleaf Whittier, "Maud Muller" (1856), stanza 53.
87. Jean-Paul Sartre, *No Exit and Three Other Plays* (New York: Vintage Books, 1955), 17, 47.
88. *Aboth* 5:22.
89. Albert Nolan, *Jesus Before Christianity* (Maryknoll, N.Y.: Orbis Books, 1978), 89.
90. Russell, *Why I Am Not a Christian*, 54.
91. Bertrand Russell, *Common Sense and Nuclear Warfare* (New York: Simon & Schuster, 1959), 13–28; cf. Jer. 18:7–10.
92. Bertrand Russell, *Education and the Social Order* (London: Allen & Unwin, 1932), 115.
93. Plato, *Timaeus* 71–72; 1 Cor. 14:2–25.
94. Luther Weigle, *Jesus and the Educational Method* (Nashville: Abingdon-Cokesbury Press, 1939), 18.
95. *Anguttara-Nikaya*; John Waters, *The Essence of Buddhism* (New York: Thomas Y. Crowell Co., 1964), 147–148.

96. Russell, *History of Western Philosophy*, 772.
97. *The Autobiography of Bertrand Russell 1872–1914* (Boston: Little, Brown & Co., 1967), 3.
98. Russell, *Why I Am Not a Christian*, 56.
99. Bertrand Russell, *The Impact of Science on Society* (New York: Simon & Schuster, 1953), 92.
100. George Santayana, *The Life of Reason* (New York: Charles Scribner's Sons, 1953), 179.

Chapter 7: Supernatural and Other Signs

1. Martin Noth, *Exodus* (Philadelphia: Westminster Press, 1962), 74; Walter Harrelson, *Interpreting the Old Testament* (New York: Henry Holt, 1964), 82.
2. Robert Pfeiffer, *Religion in the Old Testament* (New York: Harper & Row, 1961), 46–48; David Tiede, *The Charismatic Figure as Miracle Worker* (Missoula, Mont.: Scholars Press, 1972), 317–324.
3. Gerd Theissen, *The Miracle Stories of the Early Christian Tradition* (Philadelphia: Fortress Press, 1983), 17.
4. *Baba Mezia* 59b; *Berakoth* 9:1.
5. Diogenes Laertius, *Lives of the Philosophers* 8, 59, and 67.
6. Justin, *Apology* 1, 22.
7. Philostratus, *Apollonius of Tyana* 3, 38–39; 4, 45; 8, 30.
8. Tacitus, *History* 4, 81; Suetonius, *Vespasian* 7.
9. C. Milo Connick, *Jesus: the Man, the Mission, and the Message* (Englewood Cliffs, N.J.: Prentice-Hall, 1963), 281.
10. E. R. Dodds, *Pagan and Christian in an Age of Anxiety* (New York: W. W. Norton & Co., 1965), 125.
11. Lucian, *The Passing of Peregrinus* 13; *The Liar* 13.
12. *Dhammapada* 18, 254.
13. "Miracle," "Buddha," *Encyclopaedia Britannica* (Chicago: 1974).
14. Qur'an 6, 110; 10, 221; 13, 30; 21, 5–6; 29, 49.
15. "Miracles," Thomas Hughes, *A Dictionary of Islam* (London: Allen, 1885).
16. Winthrop Hudson, *Religion in America* (New York: Charles Scribner's Sons, 1965), 265.
17. Bertrand Russell, "What Is an Agnostic?" *Religions in America*, ed. Leo Rosten (New York: Simon & Schuster, 1963), 203.
18. William Phipps, *Paul Against Supernaturalism* (New York: Philosophical Library, 1987).
19. Dennis Duling, *Jesus Christ Through History* (New York: Harcourt Brace Jovanovich, 1979), 58; J. Christiaan Beker, *Paul the Apostle* (Philadelphia: Fortress Press, 1980), 300.

20. Theissen, *The Miracle Stories of the Early Christian Tradition*, 274.
21. Hannah Tillich, *From Place to Place* (New York: Stein & Day, 1976), 216.
22. Ernst and Marie-Luise Keller, *Miracles in Dispute* (Philadelphia: Fortress Press, 1969), 231.
23. Günther Bornkamm, *Jesus of Nazareth* (New York: Harper & Brothers, 1960), 133.
24. Fyodor Dostoevsky, *The Brothers Karamazov* 1, 5, 5.
25. Josephus, *War* 2, 118.
26. Josephus, *Antiquities* 17, 272, and 295; "Judah the Galilean," *Encyclopaedia Judaica* (Jerusalem: Keter, 1972).
27. Josephus, *Antiquities* 20, 102; Joseph Klausner, *Jesus of Nazareth* (New York: Macmillan Co., 1925), 205.
28. Shirley Case, *Jesus* (Chicago: University of Chicago Press, 1927), 208–209.
29. John Riches, *Jesus and the Transformation of Judaism* (New York: Seabury Press, 1982), 99–100, 188.
30. Josephus, *War* 2, 172–174.
31. Qumran scroll, *War of the Sons of Light and the Sons of Darkness* 12: 8–10.
32. E. P. Sanders, *Jesus and Judaism* (Philadelphia: Fortress Press, 1985), 235.
33. Thomas Manson, *The Sayings of Jesus* (London: SCM Press, 1949), 160.
34. Sherman Johnson, *Jesus in His Homeland* (New York: Charles Scribner's Sons, 1957), 109.
35. *Sukkah* 4:5.
36. Marcus Borg, *Jesus: A New Vision* (San Francisco: Harper & Row, 1987), 174.
37. Luthers Werke (Weimar, 1883–), vol. 7, 586.
38. Shusaku Endo, *A Life of Jesus* (New York: Paulist Press, 1978), 173.

Chapter 8: Fulfillment for Everyone

1. Georgia Harkness, *Sources of Western Morality* (New York: Charles Scribner's Sons, 1954), 238.
2. Adolf Harnack, *What Is Christianity?* (New York: Harper & Brothers, 1957), 67.
3. Quoted in George Buttrick, ed., *Interpreter's Bible* (Nashville: Abingdon Press, 1955), vol. 11, 447; cf. Adolf Hitler, *My New Order* (New York: Reynal & Hitchcock, 1941), 199.
4. Albert Nolan, *Jesus Before Christianity* (Maryknoll, N.Y.: Orbis

Notes

Books, 1978), 54; Marcus Borg, *Jesus: A New Vision* (San Francisco: Harper & Row, 1987), 105, 119–120.

. *Aboth* 2:1.

6. Robert Carkhuff, et al., *The Skills of Teaching* (Amherst, Mass.: Human Resources Development Press, 1973), 152.
7. William Dean Howells, *My Mark Twain* (New York: Harper, 1910), 5.
8. Helen Dukas, ed., *Albert Einstein, the Human Side* (Princeton, N.J.: Princeton University Press, 1981), 82.
9. Reinhold Niebuhr, *Beyond Tragedy* (New York: Charles Scribner's Sons, 1937), 146–147.
10. William Blake, "Auguries of Innocence."
11. Richard Taylor, *With Heart and Mind* (New York: St. Martin's Press, 1973), 78.
12. Tennessee Williams, *The Rose Tattoo*, Introduction.
13. Terrot Glover, *The Conflicts of Religion in the Early Roman Empire*, (Boston: Beacon Press, 1960), 122.
14. *Tao Te Ching* 49.
15. Robert Coles, *The Spiritual Life of Children* (Boston: Houghton Mifflin Co., 1990).
16. Sigmund Freud, *The Future of an Illusion: New Introductory Lectures on Psycho-Analysis*, Lecture 35.
17. Eugene Kamenka, ed., *The Portable Karl Marx* (New York: Penguin Books, 1983), 51.
18. *Aboth* 1:5; *Jerusalem Sotah* 19a; cf. *Sotah* 3:4.
19. John 20:17–18; Rom. 16:7. This latter verse should be translated: "Greet those outstanding apostles, Andronicus and Junia. . . ."
20. Quoted in Alice Tyler, *Freedom's Ferment* (Minneapolis: University of Minnesota Press, 1944), 431.
21. *Jubilees* 20:4; 33:20.
22. Mary Daly, *The Church and the Second Sex* (New York: Harper & Row, 1968), 37.
23. Dorothy Sayers, *Are Women Human?* (Grand Rapids: Wm. B. Eerdmans Publishing Co., 1971), 47.
24. Charles Carlston, "Proverbs, Maxims, and the Historical Jesus," *Journal of Biblical Literature*, vol. 99 (1980), 96–97.
25. Eaton Barrett, "Woman," part 1.
26. Shakespeare, *Henry VIII* 3, 2, 428; *Macbeth* 4, 3, 230.
27. Sirach 6:22–31.
28. Aristotle, *Politics* 1, 254b–260a.
29. Elisabeth Moltmann-Wendel and Jürgen Moltmann, *Humanity of God* (New York: Pilgrim Press, 1983), 38.
30. Rosemary Ruether, "The Sexuality of Jesus," *Christianity and Crisis*, May 29, 1978, 136.

40

31. *Sukkah* 4:5.
32. Louis Finkelstein, *The Pharisees* (Philadelphia: Jewish Publishing Society, 1938), 102–103.
33. William Phipps, *Recovering Biblical Sensuousness* (Philadelphia: Westminster Press, 1975), 25.
34. *Acts of John* 94–97.
35. Edward Andrews, *The Gift to Be Simple* (New York: Augustin Publishers, 1940), 136.
36. Aristotle, *Nicomachean Ethics* 1124b.
37. Joseph Haroutunian, *God with Us* (Philadelphia: Westminster Press, 1965), 207–212.
38. Rosemary Ruether, *Mary—The Feminine Face of the Church* (Philadelphia: Westminster Press, 1977), 40–41.
39. Nikos Kazantzakis, *The Last Temptation of Christ* (New York: Simon & Schuster, 1960), 2, 3 (hereafter cited as *LTC*).
40. *LTC*, 146.
41. *LTC*, 150.
42. *LTC*, 42.
43. *LTC*, 26.
44. *LTC*, 81.
45. *LTC*, 66–67.
46. *LTC*, 82.
47. *LTC*, 87–94.
48. *LTC*, 99.
49. *LTC*, 176.
50. *LTC*, 257.
51. *LTC*, 329.
52. *LTC*, 3.
53. *LTC*, 449–450.
54. *LTC*, 496.
55. Quoted in Helen Kazantzakis, *Nikos Kazantzakis* (New York: Simon & Schuster, 1968), 505.
56. "Pope Warns on Lust in Marriage," *New York Times*, Oct. 10, 1980, 3; Jerome, *Against Jovinian* 1, 49.
57. Shakespeare, Sonnet 129.
58. Frederick Grant, *An Introduction to New Testament Thought* (Nashville: Abingdon-Cokesbury Press, 1950), 321.
59. Martin Luther, *Commentary on the Sermon on the Mount* (Philadelphia: Fortress Press, 1892), 158–160.
60. David Mace, *Whom God Hath Joined* (Philadelphia: Westminster Press, 1953), 30–31.
61. *Kiddushin* 4:13.
62. *Yebamoth* 6:6.
63. *Gospel of Philip* 59 and 63.

64. William Phipps, *Was Jesus Married?* (New York: Harper & Row, 1970; reissued, Lanham, Md.: University Press of America, 1986).
65. Cf. William Phipps, *The Sexuality of Jesus* (New York: Harper & Row, 1973), 79–85.
66. *LTC* 27.
67. Augustine, *Against Julian* 5, 8, 15; cf. William Phipps, *Was Jesus Married?* 174.
68. H. T. Lehman, ed., *Luther's Works* (Philadelphia: Fortress Press, 1957), vol. 54, 154; cf. Phipps, *Was Jesus Married?* 12–13.
69. Elisabeth Moltmann-Wendel, *The Women Around Jesus* (London: SCM Press, 1982), 88.
70. Richard Langsdale, *The Sixth Jar* (New York: Vantage Press, 1973), 115, 141.
71. William Shakespeare, *Romeo and Juliet* 2, 2, 133–135.
72. *U. S. Catholic*, Oct. 1985, 12.
73. For a listing, along with their academic institutions, see Robert Funk, *The Parables of Jesus* (Sonoma, Cal.: Polebridge Press, 1988), 95–97.
74. Cox News Service, Oct. 30, 1989. Robert Funk has informed me that the quotation is accurate.

Chapter 9: The Central Theme

1. E.g., Thomas Hobbes, *Leviathan* 1, 14; J. S. Mill, *Utilitarianism* 2; Charles Darwin, *Descent of Man* 4; Mark Twain, "Concerning the Jews," *Harper's Magazine*, Sept. 1899, 535.
2. William Barclay, *The Gospel of Matthew* (Philadelphia: Westminster Press, 1975), vol. 1, 273; Bruce Metzger, *The New Testament: Its Background, Growth, and Content* (Nashville: Abingdon Press, 1965), 160.
3. *Tobit* 4:15.
4. Robert Hume, *The World's Living Religions* (New York: Charles Scribner's Sons, 1959), 276–278.
5. *American Atheist*, July 1989, 36.
6. Immanuel Kant, *The Fundamental Principles of the Metaphysic of Morals* 2.
7. Joseph Klausner, *Jesus of Nazareth* (New York: Macmillan Co., 1925), 92.
8. Paul Tillich, *The New Being* (New York: Charles Scribner's Sons, 1955), 30–32.
9. Joachim Jeremias, *The Sermon on the Mount* (Philadelphia: Fortress Press, 1963), 17; Helmut Koester, *Ancient Christian Gospels* (Philadelphia: Trinity Press, 1990), 133–134.

10. David Kin, ed., *Dictionary of American Maxims* (New York: Philosophical Library, 1955), 210.
11. *Manual of Discipline* 9, 10.
12. *Damascus Document* 15, 15–17.
13. Walt Whitman, "You Felons on Trial in Courts."
14. *Didache* 1:5–6; 11:3–7.
15. Leo Tolstoy, *What I Believe* (1882), chs. 1–3.
16. Max Weber, *Politics as a Vocation* (Philadelphia: Fortress Press, 1965), 45–46.
17. Richard Horsley, *Jesus and the Spiral of Violence* (San Francisco: Harper & Row, 1987), 326.
18. John Meir, *The Vision of Matthew* (New York: Crossroad, 1991), 134.
19. Sirach 28:2–3.
20. Ernest Saunders, *Jesus in the Gospels* (Englewood Cliffs, N.J.: Prentice-Hall, 1967), 147.
21. Edwin Markham, "Outwitted."
22. David Flusser, *Jesus* (New York: Herder & Herder, 1969), 70.
23. Victor Furnish, *The Love Command in the New Testament* (Nashville: Abingdon Press, 1972), 66.
24. Mark Twain, *The Tragedy of Pudd'nhead Wilson* (New York: Penguin Books, 1964), 39.
25. *Taanith* 24b; *Yoma* 53b; Targum on Eccl. 11:3.
26. John Calvin, *Institutes of the Christian Religion* 1, 16, 5.
27. William Shakespeare, *Hamlet* 5, 2, 232.
28. Eleanor Prosser, *Hamlet and Revenge* (Stanford: University Press, 1971), 232.
29. Ursula Niebuhr, ed., *Justice and Mercy* (New York: Harper & Row, 1974), 14–22.
30. Aristotle, *Physics* 198b, 17–23.
31. Sigmund Freud, *New Introductory Lectures on Psychoanalysis* (New York: W. W. Norton & Co., 1964), 146.
32. George Santayana, *The Life of Reason* (New York: Charles Scribner's Sons, 1953), 198–200.
33. *Tosefta Sanhedrin* 8:4.
34. "*Awen*," *Theological Dictionary of the Old Testament,* ed. W. Botterweck and H. Ringgren (Grand Rapids: Wm. B. Eerdmans Publishing Co., 1974).
35. John Dewey, *Theory of the Moral Life* (New York: Holt, Rinehart & Winston, 1960), 114–115.
36. *Didache* 1. 2–3.
37. *Shabbath* 31a.
38. Bertrand Russell, *Human Society in Ethics and Politics* (London: Allen & Unwin, 1954), 40.

39. Thomas Manson, *The Sayings of Jesus* (London: SCM Press, 1949), 50–51.

Chapter 10: Conclusion

1. Shakespeare, *As You Like It* 2, 7, 142.
2. Ernst Käsemann, *Essays on New Testament Themes* (London: SCM Press, 1964), 35, 42.
3. J. S. Mill, *On Liberty*, 2.
4. John Hospers, *Human Conduct* (New York: Harcourt, Brace & World, 1961), 11.
5. John Bunyan, *The Pilgrim's Progress* (1678) 1, 12.
6. Hendrikus Boers, *Who Was Jesus?* (San Francisco: Harper & Row, 1989), 131.
7. Paul Tillich, *Dynamics of Faith* (New York: Harper & Brothers, 1958), 1.
8. Paul Tillich, *Systematic Theology* (Chicago: University of Chicago Press, 1963), vol. 3, 130.
9. Robert Browning, "Andrea del Sarto."
10. Allison Johnson, ed., *The Wit and Wisdom of Alfred North Whitehead* (Boston: Beacon Press, 1947), 75.
11. Justin, *Apology* 1, 67.
12. Will Durant, *The Age of Faith* (New York: Simon & Schuster, 1950), 1002.
13. *Rule of St. Benedict* 36.
14. Samuel and Vera Leff, *From Witchcraft to World Health* (New York: Macmillan & Co., 1957), 89.
15. William Phipps, "The History of Hospices/Hospitals," *Death Studies*, Spring 1988, 91–99.
16. David Barrett, *World Christian Encyclopedia* (Oxford: Oxford University Press, 1982), 944.
17. George Seaver, *Albert Schweitzer: The Man and His Mind* (New York: Harper & Brothers, 1955), 53–54.
18. Albert Schweitzer, *On the Edge of the Primeval Forest* (London: A. & C. Black, 1928), 1.
19. William Phipps, *The Sheppards and Lapsley* (Louisville, Ky.: PCUSA Global Missions, 1991), 19–20, 92–97, 109–110.
20. Dietrich Bonhoeffer, *Letters and Papers from Prison* (New York: Macmillan Publishing Co., 1972), 298; Matt. 7:21, Bonhoeffer's emphasis.

Index of Scripture References

Index of Names

Abraham, 24, 52, 55, 75, 86, 140, 169
Akiba, 13, 47
Allport, Gordon, 3, 82
Aristotle, 81 106, 132, 173, 178, 203

Barclay, William, 59, 90, 102, 189
Bonhoeffer, Dietrich, 222
Borg, Marcus, 20, 155
Bornkamm, Günther, 146, 230
Brueggemann, Walter, 68
Bultmann, Rudolf, 4, 16, 33

Caesar, 11, 57, 66, 100, 123, 148, 151–152, 171, 174
Calvin, John, 82, 90, 201
Charlesworth, James, 9
Coles, Robert, 165
Confucius, 65, 106, 165, 189
Connick, Milo, 33, 141
Cox, Harvey, 103

David, 5, 8, 62, 95, 111, 153, 172, 212–213
Dostoevsky, Fyodor, 70, 146

Einstein, Albert, 8, 162
Elijah, 6, 25, 68, 122, 138–139, 143, 146, 201
Elisha, 25, 122, 138–140, 146, 200–201

Epictetus, 93, 99
Essenes, 9, 12, 18

Flusser, David, 60, 199, 226
Freud, Sigmund, 8, 37, 165, 203

Gamaliel, 10, 14, 69
Geiger, Abraham, 10, 44
Glover, Terrot, 88, 164

Herod, 11–12, 14, 18, 40, 47, 62–63, 137, 150, 196, 203
Highet, Gilbert, 60–61, 65, 73
Hillel, 5, 11–12, 14–15, 18, 23, 27, 29, 47–48, 73, 106, 185, 209, 213
Hitler, Adolf, 8, 159, 222
Horsley, Richard, 196
Hosea, 28, 49, 146, 182
Hyers, Conrad, 81, 83, 100

Isaiah, 21–22, 24, 28, 32, 35, 63, 76, 87, 102, 136, 146, 154, 161, 173, 213–216

Jefferson, Thomas, 7, 50, 115–116
Jeremiah, 26, 35, 106, 130, 146, 155–156, 172, 214
Jerome, 99, 183–184
Job, 39–40, 203, 212

251

Index of Subjects